Paolo Sarpi

Between Renaissance and Enlightenment

The Bodleian Library portrait of Sarpi

Paolo Sarpi

Between Renaissance and Enlightenment

DAVID WOOTTON

Assistant professor in history
Dalhousie University, Canada

CAMBRIDGE UNIVERSITY PRESS

Cambridge
London   New York   New Rochelle
Melbourne   Sydney

Published by the Press Syndicate of the University of Cambridge
The Pitt Building, Trumpington Street, Cambridge CB2 1RP
32 East 57th Street, New York, NY 10022, USA
296 Beaconsfield Parade, Middle Park, Melbourne 3206, Australia

First published 1983

Printed in Great Britain by the University Press, Cambridge

Library of Congress catalogue card number: 82–17691

British Library cataloguing in publication data
Wootton, David
Paolo Sarpi: between Renaissance and Enlightenment.
1. Sarpi, Paolo   2. Theology, Doctrinal
I. Title
230'.092'4   BR350.S3

ISBN 0 521 23146 9

Contents

Chapter 1: The *Pensieri filosofici*

Chapter 2: Sarpi and the Venetian Interdict

Chapter 3: Sarpi's place in Europe

Contents

Chapter 4: The man and his masks

Illustrations

Acknowledgments

Dermot Fenlon first suggested that I read Paolo Sarpi, and Lord Dacre of Glanton, then Professor Trevor-Roper, supervised my research in its early stages. Amongst those who have read parts of this book in draft I am particularly indebted to Peter Burke, Nicholas Davidson, John Dunn, Brian Pullan and James Tully.

I cannot acknowledge here all the friends, colleagues and students who have discussed Sarpi with me and have made valuable suggestions, but I would like, by way of exception, to acknowledge my debt to Nicolai Rubinstein. There are two personal obligations of which I am particularly aware: the first is to Joseph Hunt, who first taught me history; the second, in order of time at least, is to Gay Weber, without whose companionship and advice this book would never have been completed.

My research has been assisted by grants from the Gladys Krieble Delmas Foundation and the Twenty-Seven Foundation. The text and notes of this book were patiently typed (and retyped) by Cathy Duggan.

Sarpi's portrait is reproduced by kind permission of the Bodleian Library. The other illustrations are reproduced by permission of the British Library.

London, July 1982

Introduction

The contemplative atheist is rare: a Diagoras, a Dion, a Lucian perhaps, and some
others; and yet they seem to be more than they are; for that all that impugn a
received religion or superstition are by the orthodox part branded with the name
of atheists. But the great atheists indeed are hypocrites; which are ever handling
holy things, but without feeling; so as they must needs be cauterized in the end.
(F. Bacon, 'Of Atheism', *Essays* (definitive edition, London, 1625))

The most important of *congenital* obligations is that which concerns the duty of
all men toward God, the final arbiter of this universe; by it we are obligated to
venerate Him and to acknowledge His dominion and laws. Whoever wholly denies
this obligation brings upon his own head the stigma of atheism. And this takes
place whenever anyone denies either that God himself exists, or else that He takes
an interest in human affairs. For these two statements as regards moral effect are
equal, and by each of them all religion is destroyed and reduced to a bit of
mummery, wherewith to curb the unlicensed mob. (S. Pufendorf, *de Iure Naturae
et Gentium Libri Octo* (Amsterdam, 1688), bk III, ch. 4, p. 259)

...atheists, who deny either the existence of God or his divine providence, and
to whom those persons who deny the immortality of the soul are closely related.
For the only justice these last know is that which is based on advantage, measured
by their own judgement. With them you may also class those whose manner of
life is an open profession of villainy, such as pirates, thieves, murderers, pimps,
courtesans, and others of their kind who take a pleasure in perjury. (*ibid.*, ch. 6,
p. 281)

Paolo Sarpi (1552–1623) is best known for his *History of the Council of Trent*
(1619), which has always been recognised as one of the greatest historical works
of its day. Indeed it is more than that, for Sarpi's unremitting consistency in
portraying the history of the Catholic Church in terms of purely worldly, secular
concerns not only made him a continuing source of inspiration for those who
were opposed to clerical interference in secular affairs, to religious persecution,
and to doctrinal intolerance, but it also opened the way to a purely secular vision
of history and of society, so that it has entitled him to be considered one of
the most important precursors of Gibbon and of the Enlightenment.[1] As an
historian alone Sarpi would be worthy of fame, but the writing of history was
only one small part of the activities. Historians of science remember him for
his association with Acquapendente and the Paduan school of anatomy: his

1

biographer and amanuensis Fulgenzio Micanzio claims for him, amongst other things, the original discovery of the valves in the veins, although, knowing nothing of the circulation of the blood, Sarpi concluded that they were there to stop the blood from pooling in the feet and legs.[2] Nor were his interests confined to anatomy. Gilbert, the discoverer of magnetism, regarded Sarpi as a great mathematician, while he was a friend of Galileo's, and one of the first to look through his telescope.[3] But science played a less important part in Sarpi's life as he grew older.[4] He found his real vocation in 1606, when he became a legal adviser to the Venetian Republic. Thanks to this position he was able to work in closest collaboration with Venice's leading politicians, seeking to fortify the Republic in her struggle against the Counter-Reformation papacy and the Habsburgs, and winning European fame (and a place in histories of political thought alongside William Barclay and James I) for his public defence of the rights of secular sovereigns.[5]

As historian, scientist and political philosopher, Sarpi's place in history is assured. But this book is as much about Sarpi's private thoughts, the views recorded in his *Pensieri*, as it is about his public activities, and in order to understand these *Pensieri* it looks at Sarpi's contemporaries as much as at Sarpi himself.[6] My purpose in concentrating on Sarpi's private thoughts is not just to throw new light on his public actions, for Sarpi's *Pensieri* throw new light on the intellectual and political life of his age, as well as on his own personal biography. They do this simply because they were revolutionary, and they pose the exciting question of how it became possible to think such things. For Sarpi, I believe, was hostile not merely to the Counter-Reformation papacy, but to Christianity itself. More than this, it seems likely that he was unique in his day in holding that the existing social order could be sustained without the support of religious belief. Sarpi's political objective – an unrealisable and unavowable one – was the foundation of a secular society. If he held such opinions then commonly held views regarding the intellectual life of his day need to be revised, as do the assumptions most of us hold regarding the reasons for the decline of religious faith over the last few centuries.

Sarpi's true beliefs and real historical importance become apparent, I believe, through the study of his *Pensieri*, his private notebooks, and particularly the *Pensieri* which deal with religion. When I first read these notes I found them so strange, so direct an attack on beliefs which I had felt sure all intellectuals of Sarpi's day regarded as unquestionable, that my first reaction was to conclude that they were an eighteenth-century forgery. Once I had realised that the authenticity of the *Pensieri* was indubitable, I set myself the task of trying to make sense of them, of trying to understand under what circumstances these ideas would have carried conviction.[7] In carrying out this undertaking I have concentrated on three questions: what were the intellectual traditions which crucially influenced Sarpi in reaching the conclusions spelled out in the *Pensieri* on religion? What were the political and social circumstances in which these conclusions seemed realistic? And what significance do Sarpi's views as expressed in the *Pensieri* have for our understanding of his activities in later years, especially of his unremitting struggle against Spain and the papacy, and of his intentions in writing his magnum opus, the *History of the Council of Trent*?

In answering these questions I have sought to provide an interpretation of Sarpi's beliefs and his actions. But my account of Sarpi is also intended to serve as a case study which will serve to illustrate a range of problems which lie at the heart of any account of the place of religion in early modern intellectual life.

In the first place I hope that my analysis of Sarpi's *Pensieri* will suggest that people in the sixteenth century found it easier not to believe in God than has been claimed, for example, by Lucien Febvre, whose *La religion de Rabelais: le problème de l'incroyance au seizième siècle* (1942) argued that the sixteenth century was 'un siècle qui veut croire', a century in which the very concepts and assumptions necessary for a systematic unbelief were lacking. We will see Sarpi in the *Pensieri* finding and forging all the arguments an atheist might need, and I hope my study of Sarpi may encourage a new approach to the question of the nature and limits of intellectual unbelief in the period between the Reformation and the Enlightenment to complement the studies of popular unbelief undertaken by Carlo Ginzburg and Christopher Hill.[8]

In studying Sarpi's *Pensieri* I have concentrated upon one theme in particular, that of the possibility of a society of atheists. This is in the first place because this was one of the most original of Sarpi's arguments: a similar claim was not to be made in print until Pierre Bayle's *Pensées diverses sur la comète* of 1682. But it is also because I believe that the conviction that belief in God alone made social life possible represented the most powerful obstacle to the progress of unbelief in the early modern period.[9] Historians like Febvre have tended to see progress in man's understanding of nature as the essential precondition for the emergence of a rational unbelief. But Aristotelianism had long been recognised as providing an account of nature which left no scope for revelation, miracles or a life after death. What was lacking in the early modern period was not a secular theory of nature but a secular theory of society such as the Enlightenment was to find in Bayle, Mandeville and Hume.

Sarpi's belief that religion was not the most important social bond meant that he, unlike Naudé and the *libertins érudits* studies by René Pintard, could allow his unbelief to become a guide to practice. Like other unbelievers of his day Sarpi had to confine knowledge of his unbelief to a small circle of personal intimates, but unlike most of them Sarpi sought to employ his public avowal of faith not merely as a passive defence against prosecution but also as a shield behind which he could advance the cause of irreligion. Sarpi, on my account, was a hypocrite. What was remarkable about him, however, was not his hypocrisy – for this was an age which contemporaries believed to be riddled with deceit – but the creative use to which he put it.

Sarpi represents a fascinating problem in the history of ideas. To determine what his beliefs were and to establish the relationship between them and his actions has been the first objective of this study. But Sarpi is also, I believe, a key figure in three histories which have yet to be written, three histories which are intimately interconnected: the history of unbelief, the history of the secularisation of social and political theory, and the history of intellectual deception. In each of these histories he deserves to take his place alongside Hobbes and Bayle. I have tried to suggest in this study that the idea that atheists are not necessarily anti-social provides the crucial link between Sarpi's private beliefs and his public actions. I hope later in a more general study to argue that this same idea lies at the heart of the seventeenth-century transition from a religious to a secular viewpoint. But a consideration of such general issues is beyond the scope of the present study. My purpose here is to analyse Sarpi's relationship to the world of which he was aware: the world of Venice, of scholastic philosophy, of Catholicism and Calvinism. My hope is to reconstruct the drama within which he saw himself as acting a part during his years of public activity, and to discover the intellectual convictions which led him on to the political stage. Only when a place has been found for Sarpi amongst the arguments and the events of his own day can the historian hope to establish his proper place in the history of ideas.

Before I proceed, however, I would like to pause and establish a clear terminology with which to discuss Sarpi's beliefs. Care is necessary here, both because words in the early modern period did not always mean what they mean now, but also because in order to bring out the common assumptions of men in the past it is sometimes necessary to adopt a terminology which is more exact than the one they themselves employed, and this involves giving ordinary words a precise and technical meaning. My purpose is not to devise a novel vocabulary, but to find a way of giving clear expression to the views of Sarpi and his contemporaries. Throughout this book I use the word *atheist* to mean someone who believes not only that there is no God, but also that belief in God is irrational. An *unbeliever* is someone who finds himself unable to believe in God, although he may well feel that reason is on the side of belief. A *fideist* is someone who holds that it is impossible to prove that his own theological beliefs are the true ones, but who has nevertheless decided to set reason aside and to trust himself to faith.

These distinctions, however, are insufficient for our purposes. One can believe in a divine creator but not believe in any divine revelation. We may call this *deism. Deists* are *irreligious* in that they do not believe that any particular religion has been divinely ordained. Deists however fall into two categories: some believe that God is just God, and that he will therefore punish the bad and reward the good, either in this life or the next. Such deists believe in a divine *providence*. By this I mean not just that they believe that the universe is divinely ordered, but that they hold that an essential part of this order is God's law for the punishment of evil and the reward of good: in this book I nearly always use *providence* in this limited and technical sense. Other deists do not believe in divine punishment, believing either that God is merciful, or that there is no life after this in which the injustices of this life will be righted. In the sixteenth century such people were called '*atheists*', and when I employ the term in inverted commas I mean to refer to people who would have been called 'atheists' by their contemporaries because they denied the existence of a divine providence, whether or not they believed in God. Such a usage may seem confusing, but it is almost impossible to avoid it when giving expression to the views of contemporaries. Recognising this problem J. C. A. Gaskin has invented the term *moral atheist* for one 'who denies the existence of any God having moral attributes', and who consequently, whether he believes in the existence of a God or not, is in the same position as an atheist as far as arguments about morality are concerned. This coinage seems to me a useful one, and I will use the term *moral atheist* to refer to people contemporaries would have bluntly termed 'atheists'. *Moral atheists* are thus, for our purposes, people who do not believe in a providential God; they may act morally, or they may not.[10]

Three other terms need to be defined at the outset. In my view Sarpi was a *secular* social theorist who believed in the possibility of a *secular society*. That is to say that his theories about society do not presume society or social institutions to be divinely instituted, and that he believes that society could survive even if people did not believe that anti-social behaviour would meet with divine punishment, even if people were 'atheists' who denied the existence of a providential God. To have a theory of a secular society it is necessary to believe that moral atheists are not inherently more anti-social than other people. For convenience sake I refer to this belief as a belief in the *sociability* of 'atheists', by which I do not mean a belief in their good-fellowship and warm-heartedness, but in their ability to live together in society, to obey their sovereign and the law.

Sarpi was also, I believe, a proponent of *absolutism*. By this I do not mean that he believed in the unchecked rule of one person. Theorists of absolutism like Bodin (at least on occasion) and Filmer argued that the only legitimate form of government was monarchy, on the grounds that no corporate body could properly be said to have a will of its own. But Hobbes, although he preferred monarchy, was quite willing to approve government by an assembly as long as that assembly exercised absolute powers. Sarpi was an absolutist in this broader sense. He believed that the ruler, be he a single individual or a corporate entity, must not be overruled by any other authority in this world.

Absolutism as a political philosophy, however, is often associated with absolutism as a social order: what Marxists call feudal-absolutism. In my view it is important to recognise, if one is to understand how Sarpi came to be deeply influenced by French political philosophy, that the Venetian nobility and the French *noblesse de robe* had much in common. In the course of the sixteenth century many Venetian nobles had given up trade to become landowners.[11] But many of the poorer ones had become increasingly dependent on the income they obtained from offices in the state administration.[12] Thus in Venice, as in France, a large section of the nobility made its living from office-holding, that is to say from the proceeds of taxation. In Venice the members of the senate and in France the members of the Parlement had a common interest in extending the power of the state if that would serve to improve their income from office-holding. Behind the rhetoric of absolutism there lay therefore the social reality of *absolutist society*. This may be defined as a social order where a substantial part of the income of the ruling class comes from state expenditure, the rest coming largely from rent extracted from the peasantry. Income from state expenditure may, as in the Prussia of the Great Elector, supplement income from rent, or it may, as in the France of Richelieu, support a distinct fraction of the ruling class, a fraction whose interests do not always coincide with those of the landed nobility.[13]

From one point of view Venice in the early seventeenth century can be portrayed as the last surviving independent republic of Renaissance Italy, surrounded by the princely courts of the new absolutist states – the ecclesiastical lands, ruled by the pope; the duchy of Milan, ruled by a governor-general appointed by the king of Spain; Tuscany, ruled by the Medici.[14] But from another point of view one may note that the social elite was a landed aristocracy in Venice as elsewhere, and that patronage was as important to the Venetian nobility as to the nobilities of other states, even if it was dispensed through the votes of the senate, rather than by a prince and his favourite.[15] In the sixteenth century Gasparo Contarini and Paolo Paruta had been concerned to stress the peculiarity of Venetian institutions in order to praise Venice's republican traditions.[16] In the seventeenth century Sarpi was concerned to emphasise that Venice was a state like other states. Meanwhile his more conservative contemporaries complained that young nobles were abandoning the distinctive somber dress of their forefathers and were beginning to dress in courtier's clothes, to ride horses and to wear swords, in short to behave like nobles everywhere.[17] Thus, if we are to understand Sarpi's relationship to his political milieu it will be necessary to reconsider the significance of Venetian republicanism. I would suggest that the Venetian nobility were, in our period, an aristocracy who happened to exercise power through republican institutions. They were no more attached to liberty or social harmony than the other aristocracies of western Europe.

Finally, a word about theories, beliefs and motivations. Sarpi's *Pensieri* provide a record of his thoughts. He may not have believed all the thoughts he recorded. He may have believed them and at the same time believed other things quite incompatible with them: Evans-Pritchard in his famous study of the Azande successfully demonstrated that it is possible to believe simultaneously many quite incompatible doctrines, and we are all capable of more mundane forms of inconsistency.[18] Darwin, for example, continued to think in terms of a divine architect long after he had demonstrated the inadequacy of arguments from design.[19] Finally, Sarpi may have accepted the arguments of the *Pensieri* and not believed other things he wrote elsewhere. In order to facilitate choosing between these three possibilities I have as far as possible kept distinct the different types of statement Sarpi made in different contexts: when writing for himself, on behalf of the Venetian government, to Protestant friends, as an historian addressing an anonymous audience. I hope to show that Sarpi's actions can be shown to be explicable in terms of the views he expressed when writing for himself, and that there is no other explanation which makes coherent sense of Sarpi's behaviour. The possibility of incoherence, however, can never be finally eliminated.

If this was primarily a biography of Sarpi, my account of Sarpi's beliefs and motives would be the core of the book. But it is not. The core of this book is Sarpi's thoughts. What is astonishing is that he was able to think what he did. Perhaps he did not always believe what he wrote in the *Pensieri*, or always act in the light of it. If so, then he may not have been as great a man as I have taken him to be, but the importance of the *Pensieri* is scarcely diminished. It was long thought that Copernicus never believed that the earth went round the sun; even had this been the case he would still have made the belief a reasonable one.[20] So, an account of Sarpi's beliefs and motivations must be speculative. What need not be speculative is an account of his words, his arguments, his thoughts. This book is thus in the first place an interpretation of a set of texts, and only in the second place a study of Paolo Sarpi.

Sarpi's life: a brief survey

Sarpi was appointed state theologian to the Venetian Republic on 28 March 1606, two days after the election of Leonardo Donà as doge, and a month before Venice fell under papal Interdict.[1] He was already fifty-three years old, and might have been thought to have accomplished all he was going to. After an early introduction to nominalist philosophy at the hands of a friend of his family, a Servite friar, Sarpi had entered his mentor's order at the age of fourteen. His father was a bankrupt and evil-tempered merchant of Friulian background. His mother came from a respectable Venetian family which belonged to the 'citizen' class which monopolised posts in the Venetian state administration. But Sarpi's future seemed to lie in a quite different direction from that of his forebears. His talents as a philosopher, theologian and canon lawyer were quickly recognised, and he was soon teaching in Mantua where he formed a friendship with Camillo Olivo, who had been secretary to one of the legates at the Council of Trent, and had been imprisoned by the Inquisition. He aroused in Sarpi an interest in the secret history of the Council, but he was dangerous company, and soon Sarpi was himself having to rebut charges laid against him before the Inquisition: it was said that he had denied that the doctrine of the Trinity could be deduced from the first chapter of Genesis.

At the age of twenty-two Sarpi was recruited by Carlo Borromeo, the greatest of Counter-Reformation bishops, to form part of his reforming team in the archdiocese of Milan. But Sarpi can have had little in common with this saint, whose achievements included the invention of the confession-box, and whose preoccupations extended to attempts to make men and women worship in separate churches.[2] Soon Sarpi was back in Venice, where his career prospered. At the age of twenty-six he was prior of the Venetian province of his order, in which capacity he participated at the great chapter-general of 1579 at which the prior-general, Giacomo Tavanti, launched a movement of internal reform. Sarpi there established for himself a leading position within the reforming party, being nominated as one of those entrusted with the task of revising the order's regulations. In private, though, he was, as we shall see, probably already an agnostic.

By the age of thirty-five Sarpi had been elected to the second highest post in the order. But as he had risen in the order, so he had developed interests outside it. He had become a friend of Arnaud Du Ferrier, twice French ambassador to Venice, who had represented the king of France during the last stages of the Council of Trent, and who was in secret a convert to Calvinism.[3] Du Ferrier, moreover, was an acquaintance of Montaigne's, the greatest of the neo-stoics,[4] a friend of Michel de l'Hôpital, political leader of the *politiques* until his death in 1573, and a jurist whose qualities had been praised by Jean Bodin himself. During these years too Sarpi had developed an interest in medicine, and carried out an extensive programme of dissection.

Unfortunately for Sarpi, his own rise to high office coincided with the return to power of the conservative faction in his order. Sarpi, however, now resident in Rome, made a favourable impression in the highest quarters, and struck up a friendship with Robert Bellarmine, whose *Controversies* would have been placed upon the Index but for the timely death of Pope Sixtus V, so lukewarm were they in their defence of papal authority.[5] Sarpi, indeed, was forming a network of contacts among the surviving reformers in Rome. But these men were representatives of a defeated cause, and when after three years Sarpi left Rome it was with relief. One friend, Gabriele Dardano, wrote and advised him that it would be good for his career to stay on. Sarpi replied in cipher: 'E che volete ch'io speri a Roma, ove li soli ruffiani, cerreti et altri ministri di piacere e di guadagni hanno ventura?' ('Would you want me to waste away in Rome, where only ruffians, charlatans, and other devotees of pleasure and profit flourish?')[6] He had turned his back upon an ecclesiastical career.

Back in Venice, he was, as we will see, to occupy himself with rereading Pomponazzi's *de Immortalitate Animae*, and with writing the first of his meditations on religion. The break with Rome was not just a turning point in his career, but also it seems in his intellectual life, giving his existing irreligious tendencies new scope for development. Where his intellectual life in Rome had been confined to Catholic reforming circles, in Venice Sarpi moved in a cosmopolitan world. At the house of Andrea and Nicolò Morosini, for example, people met to hold discussions about philosophical and theological subjects, discussions which often turned to talk about current events, especially in France. At a shop owned by a Dutchman, the *Nave d'oro*, Sarpi was able to meet foreigners living in Venice, and others passing through on business. And either at one of these places, or at the house of the Nis family, Sarpi met with others from a wide range of backgrounds to discuss forbidden subjects, such as the teachings of Machiavelli and Pomponazzi. Meanwhile Sarpi successfully defended himself against accusations brought before the Inquisition by his former friend Dardano, who accused him of having contact with Jews and of denying that the Holy Spirit assists Christians. During this period he seems to have kept his activities within his order to a minimum, though the election of a reforming prior-general, Angelo Montorsoli, in 1597 led to a passing involvement in the execution of a new programme of reforms.

The death of Montorsoli, and the election of Dardano to his office in 1601, seems to have been the decisive event which led Sarpi to seek a bishopric, an ambition which Dardano himself was instrumental in thwarting. Sarpi at this time seems to have desired to give his life over to academic study, and perhaps the studies he had in mind were those in the history of religion which first bore fruit in the *Pensieri sulla religione*. From this period too may date the *Pensieri medico-morali*, with their emphasis on the need for dissimulation, for the rebuff he had received in his attempts to obtain a bishopric provided ample evidence that he had allowed his views to be too widely known.

The *Pensieri* on the *tora*, the first of Sarpi's meditations on religion, marked the end of Sarpi's commitment to an ecclesiastical career and his break with Rome. The *Pensieri sulla religione* almost certainly stand at the beginning of his political career. By 1603 he was beginning to encourage nobles of his acquaintance to pursue anti-papal policies and to establish himself as the man best equipped to advise the Republic in the theological problems posed by Church–state conflicts.

By 1605 Sarpi's intellectual formation was probably largely complete, and he had no remaining intellectual obstacles to overcome. Yet we owe the survival of his *Pensieri* only to the importance which was to be attached to the preservation of his papers as a result of the long years of service to the Republic which were to come. Even the accusations of irreligion made against him in 1601 have only come down to us in a detailed form because they were repeated against the state theologian of 1606. Had Sarpi died in 1605 he would have been deserving of no more than a footnote in some learned tome: a reforming prior with scientific interests, a minor paradox. His appointment as state theologian, however, was swiftly to give him an international reputation and to earn him a place in history. His defences of Venice against the papacy were the most widely read and admired of the numerous pamphlets produced to justify the conduct of the two antagonists during the year from April 1606 to April 1607, when Venice was under papal Interdict.[7] Some thought, indeed, that the Interdict crisis would herald a new era of Reformation, comparable to that launched by Luther's attack on indulgences.[8] Although these expectations were disappointed, Venice's stand provoked a new outburst of Gallican and eirenicist propaganda in France and aroused widespread sympathy in England.[9]

After the sad compromise of the Interdict settlement, Sarpi set out unhesitatingly to exploit his new prominence and to take advantage of the Venetian state's obligation to protect him, her authorised champion, against the Inquisition. In October 1607, Sarpi survived a murderous assault by men who took refuge in Rome and were eventually granted a pension by the viceroy of Naples. He had probably already completed his *History of the Interdict*, which was intended for Auguste de Thou, who planned to base a section of his famous *History of His Own Times*, then in progress, upon it. Unfortunately, it proved difficult – or perhaps impolitic – to smuggle the manuscript to Paris, and the work remained unpublished until after Sarpi's death. Soon Sarpi had finished a *History of Benefices*, an attack on clerical wealth which was likewise unpublished until after his death, and was immersed in his *History of the Council of Trent*, a work completed in 1616 and published pseudonymously in England in 1619. Two years before Sarpi had published an addition and supplement to Minuccio Minucci's *History of the Uskoks*, an officially authorised defence of Venetian policy in the war she was currently waging with Austria, a war which had its origins in the protection given by Austria to the Uskok pirates who preyed on Venetian shipping.

Alongside the composition of these volumes, Sarpi continued to be actively employed as an adviser on theological, jurisdictional and political questions to the Venetian Republic. At the same time, too, he was engaged in a vast network of correspondence with Protestants like Dudley Carleton, English ambassador first to Venice and then to Holland, with prominent Gallicans like Jacques Gillot and Jacques Leschassier, and with eirenicists like François Hotman. The great theme of this correspondence was the need for Venice to enter into an anti-papal alliance with France and the Protestant powers, an alliance which would finally destroy the power of Rome. Sarpi's ambition was to see Protestant troops in Italy, an ambition which was realised by 1619, when Venice entered into a military alliance with Holland, although war with the papacy did not result. Moreover, in his attempts to foment anti-papal policies abroad Sarpi was not playing a merely academic game, for he was working in collaboration with a group of Venetian nobles, led by Nicolò Contarini, who shared his desire for a network of Protestant alliances, and who aspired to control the Republic's foreign policy.[10]

The Interdict was thus the great turning point in Sarpi's life. It made of him an intellectual and a politician of European stature. It is on the basis of his activities after his appointment as state theologian that the two great contrasting views of Sarpi's life – Sarpi the Catholic reformer and Sarpi the Protestant – have been founded. Yet Sarpi was already a reformer, already an associate of heretics, and already an infidel at the time of his appointment.

APOLOGIA

PER LE OPPOSITIONI

FATTE

Dall' Illustrissimo, & Reuerendiss.^{MO}

Signor Cardinale Bellarminio

ALLI TRATTATI, ET RISOLVTIONI

di Gio. Gersone sopra la validità delle Scommuniche.

DEL PADRE MAESTRO PAVLO

da Vinetia dell'Ordine de' Serui.

NON EST

REGNVM MEVM DE HOC MVNDO.

Ioan. cap.18.

In VENETIA, Appresso Roberto Meietti. 1606.

ConLicentia de' Superiori.

I

The *Pensieri filosofici*

Je sçay bien, que mon labeur sera deplaisant à trois manières de gens: premièrement aux heretiques formez et de profession, secondement, à ceux qui en sont de cueur et du ventre, et non de ceremonie: et tiercement aux politiques, qui n'ont autre Dieu que le repos, et qui ne se soucieroyent pas beaucoup de Dieu ny de son Paradis, qui le servist ny qui l'offençast, pourveu qu'il luy pleust leur accorder une perpetuelle residence en ce monde: desquels le plus beau mot est, VIVONS, VIVONS; ne se souvenans pas, que vivans en ce monde hors la crainte de Dieu ils sont infiniment plus morts, que le plus vieil trespassé, dont les os purroyent estre à sainct Innocent.

> (A. Sorbin, preface to *Conciles de Tholose, Beziers, et Narbonne...contre les Albigeois*, Paris, 1569)

(I know that my undertaking will displease three sorts of people: firstly those who are heretics by conviction; secondly those who are fellow-travellers, even if they are not members of heretical Churches; and thirdly the *politiques*, who worship no other God but their own convenience, and who would give little thought to God, or to Paradise, nor to the question of what constitutes service of God and what constitutes heresy, provided they could be guaranteed a perpetual residence in this world. Their favourite phrase is 'Let us live! Let us live!', but they forget that if they live in this world untouched by the fear of God they are far more truly dead than the oldest cadaver, whose bones could be those of a saint.)

Combien y a il aujourd'huy d'atheistes, c'est à dire, d'hommes sans Dieu, qui sont ne Iuifz, ne Turcz, ne heritiques, ne catholiques, ne chrestiens? qui n'ont ne foy, ne loy, mais qui se moquent de toutes les religions, coustumes, ordonnances, et ceremonies du monde, et qui vivent comme epicuriens, sans attente d'autre vie que de cest cy...

> (Gabriel du Preau, *Des faus prophètes séducteurs et hypocrites, qui viennent à nous en habit de brebis: , mais au dedans son loups ravissans*, Paris, 1563)

(These days there are so many atheists, that is to say, men without God, who are neither Jews, nor Turks, nor heretics, nor Catholics, nor Christians. They have no faith and recognise no law, having no respect for any religion, or for any of the laws, rules and conventions of this world. They live like Epicureans, without expectation of any life after this one...)

Il fine dell'uomo, come d'ogn'altro animato, e vivere.

> (Paolo Sarpi, *Pensieri sulla religione*)

(The end of man, as of every other living creature, is to live.)

The *Pensieri filosofici* and scholastic philosophy

We come now to the texts whose meaning for our understanding of Sarpi and his times this book seeks to clarify: Sarpi's *Pensieri*, and in particular his *Pensieri sulla religione*. In particular, for there are three sets of *Pensieri* of importance to us, but each is of importance primarily in so far as it helps us to understand Sarpi's views on religion. The largest group of Sarpi's *Pensieri* are the *Pensieri filosofici e scientifici*, which have survived only in two eighteenth-century copies, the original having been destroyed by fire later in the same century.[1] Of these *Pensieri* many are concerned with problems in physics, mathematics and geometry. Those few concerned with religion are, however, of crucial importance. Important, too, is the fact that the best copy of these *Pensieri* has in the margin a set of dates. Although these are not necessarily authentic transcriptions from the original, there must be a strong presumption in their favour, and they provide valuable assistance in dating the development of Sarpi's thought. The second group of *Pensieri* are the *Pensieri medico-morali*, which outline principles which should enable the wise man to control his own psychological health. Although these, too, are known to survive only in an eighteenth-century copy, it seems probable that a copy by one of Sarpi's amanuenses still existed in the nineteenth century. The third group are the *Pensieri sulla religione* themselves, which survive in a copy by one of Sarpi's amanuenses, with autograph corrections by Sarpi himself, and are bound up with a collection of documents by or belonging to Sarpi, but varying very widely in date.[2] The dating of both of these two last groups of *Pensieri* presents a problem to which in due course I will suggest a solution.

The first partial edition of the *Pensieri filosofici* dates from 1910. The other two sets of *Pensieri* were not published until 1969. This, and their lapidary, often obscure, style is sufficient to explain the small part they have played in accounts of Sarpi's thought. Sarpi's first biographer took the trouble to describe that part of the *Pensieri sulla religione* which is compatible with orthodoxy;[3] Acton, who knew the Venetian archives well, believed the *Pensieri* were the key to Sarpi; and the need for a complete edition of the *Pensieri filosofici* and for the first editions of the others has provoked recent interest. But it may safely be said that there exists no serious account of the importance of the *Pensieri* in the intellectual life of Sarpi or of Europe. It is this, in so far as they concern religion, which it is the central objective of this book to provide.

Before looking at those amongst the *Pensieri filosofici* which deal specifically with religion we need to briefly consider the philosophical position expressed in the earliest of the *Pensieri*, for these will provide us with valuable evidence regarding the development and evolution of Sarpi's attitude to religion.

The earliest of Sarpi's philosophical *Pensieri* are concerned with problems of knowledge and the nature of existence, and appear to date from 1578, three years after Sarpi had returned from Milan to Venice, and when his climb to high office in his order was just beginning.[4] From around 1585, the year in which Sarpi was elected procurator-general and moved to Rome, problems of psychology and moral philosophy become increasingly common. It was three years later, around the time when Sarpi left Rome in disgust, that he wrote those of the *Pensieri filosofici* which deal explicitly with religion, and with which we will be particularly concerned. There is thus a rough correlation between changes in Sarpi's philosophical preoccupations and changes in his way of life and career, and we may suspect, even though we cannot prove, a causal connection. Changes in Sarpi's preoccupations, however, are not evidence for changes in his views: there is no sign that Sarpi's views on knowledge and existence changed after 1585, indeed it seems clear that they did not.

From the beginning, Sarpi appears in the *Pensieri* as a materialist.[5] His materialism expresses itself in four distinct areas. In the first place Sarpi holds that all knowledge is derived from sensation: the intellect has no material to work with apart from that obtained through the senses. In the second place Sarpi insists that existence is a purely material phenomenon. Things are what they are because they have the appropriate size and shape, are made of matter of the right density, and so forth. Sarpi rejected outright any Aristotelian doctrine of 'essences' informing matter. A thing's form or essence is a set of purely material characteristics. Sarpi was not an atomist, in that he believed that matter could be changed: it was not made up of unalterable unitary atoms, but could be compressed, expanded and so on. But he was a materialist, in that he rejected any form of idealism in philosophy.[6] In consequence of his materialism Sarpi was a determinist. He believed that there is no such thing as an unnatural event, that nothing comes of nothing, that nothing is arbitrary. The chain of causation linking one event to another is, Sarpi insists, an unbreakable one, and, in this sense, all events are predetermined.[7] Finally, Sarpi held that there were no rational grounds which compelled belief in a God, in a Being outside the world of material reality and natural causation.

Sarpi's materialism was thus associated with the rejection of all philosophical arguments for the existence of God, including those acceptable to the most strict of Aristotelians. In order to get a sense of the originality of Sarpi's position as it emerges in the early *Pensieri*, it is worth comparing it with that of Cesare Cremonini, a near contemporary of his who taught philosophy at Padua from 1591 to 1631: Padua was the university attended by those Venetians who wanted to acquire an advanced education, and Sarpi himself obtained a doctorate of theology there in 1578.

Cremonini was a faithful interpreter of Aristotle who is now perhaps best known because he rejected an opportunity to look through Galileo's telescope: physics for him was a matter for philosophical deduction, not experimental enquiry. Nevertheless, Cremonini fell foul of the Inquisition because he insisted on publishing books in which he expounded Aristotle without refuting him on Christian grounds. In particular, he taught that the *primum mobile*, the heavens, from which all movement was derived, was eternal and not created; that the soul of the individual human being was a purely material aspect of the body; and that God was incapable of intervening in nature: he might be the final cause of all things, but he could not be the architect of a providential scheme for man's salvation.[8]

Cremonini was reluctant to stress that philosophy must give way to theology and reason to faith. Consequently, he was popularly believed to be an 'atheist'. It was said, although probably falsely, that he had composed as his own epitaph *hic iacet totus Cremoninus*, thus denying the immortality of the soul.[9] Gabriel Naudé, the French sceptic and *esprit fort* is said to have spent three months in Cremonini's company, and to have described him as follows:

Cremonini was a great man, with a lively mind which knew no inhibitions. He was free of illusions and stupid prejudices, and he knew the truth perfectly well, although in Italy no one dared spell it out. All the professors in that country, and especially those in Padua, are freethinkers...Cremonini skilfully kept his private opinions to himself, being in Italy: *nihil habebat pietatis et tamen pius haberi volebat*. One of his maxims was: think what you like, but say what is expected of you (*intus ut libet, forus ut moris est*).[10]

As an Aristotelian, Cremonini was convinced that there were rational arguments for belief in a God, but not in life after death or divine providence. The arguments he would have adduced in favour of moral atheism would have been readily available to almost any seventeenth-century intellectual. But Sarpi's philosophy was quite different in character: it pointed in the direction of an authentic atheism, or at the least agnosticism. This is particularly evident in Sarpi's discussion of infinity and of causation.

Sarpi distinguishes between four different kinds of infinity: of smallness, of potential, of magnitude, and of perfection.[11] The first is demonstrated by the existence of incommensurables; the second Sarpi holds to be established by experience. The third and fourth, however, bear on the question of God's existence. As far as Sarpi is concerned the universe must be infinite in size, unless one posits an external agent who has delimited it. The idea of a God is thus necessary not as the creator of matter, but for the creation of a finite universe. It is evident though that Sarpi had no reason to believe the universe to be finite.[12] Finally, as for the idea of some infinitely perfect entity, i.e. God, Sarpi dismisses it as being self-contradictory.

Sarpi thus refuses to admit that the idea of infinity implies the existence of an infinite God. The same conviction emerges in his treatment of causation.[13] Sarpi distinguishes between what he terms eternal causes – natural laws which are always at work in nature – and temporal causes – particular events which are the cause of subsequent events. Particular events are the result of an infinite chain of preceding contingent events, while those events which exemplify general laws are also the result of eternal causes which themselves have no prior cause.[14]

As far as Sarpi is concerned everything has a natural cause. Bodin had written: 'Natural things do not happen by chance, at random or in blind sequence, but proceed uniformly according to the same laws, so that given the cause the effect follows, unless they are kept from doing so by the divine will in all things, or human will in some or by the power of demons in many.'[15] For Sarpi there are no exceptions. On the one hand there is the 'blind sequence' of events, the one giving rise to the other, which others had termed 'fate'. On the other there are the immutable laws of nature which keep the universe in being. All events are to be explained in terms of either or both of these.[16]

The sequence of contingent events is infinite, but the eternal causes are finite in number. In making this distinction Sarpi may well have been influenced by Ockham's treatment of arguments for the existence of God based on the notion of infinity. Ockham had denied that one could prove the existence of God by arguing for the necessity of a *first* cause: there was nothing intrinsically wrong with the idea of an infinite temporal series of causes. There was something wrong, though, in Ockham's view, with the idea of an infinite number of 'causes of conservation'. John Smith might have an infinite number of forebears, but he must owe his present existence to a finite number of causes of conservation, otherwise one would have to admit the existence of an infinite universe. There must therefore be one or more supreme causes of conservation which conserve without being conserved. Ockham's whole argument thus rested on the assumption that an infinite universe, in the sense of an infinite number of co-existing entities, was inconceivable.[17] Ockham was satisfied that he had a rational proof of the existence of a God or Gods, although it was hardly a strong one, and evidently did not convince Sarpi, who saw both that an infinite universe was not inconceivable, and that one could have an infinite number of co-existing entities but yet only a finite and comprehensible number of natural laws.[18] What did convince Sarpi however were Ockham's attacks on other attempts to prove the existence of God.

And indeed there is much of Ockham in the *Pensieri filosofici*.[19] Ockham had held that all knowledge is based upon sensation, and that no essences exist aside from sensation, thus laying the foundations for a consistent materialism. But Ockham had held that God was capable of *anything*, that he was not bound by reason, morality or the laws of nature. Sarpi thus seems to have combined an Ockhamist critique of Aristotelian accounts of essences and of the different infinities with an Aristotelian conception of natural necessity. In doing so he abandoned the teleological schema of Aristotle, which was derived from the Aristotelian conception of essences and which involved belief in a perfect Being, the final cause of all things, in order to develop a novel, scientific theory of natural causation.

Sarpi's synthesis of nominalism and determinism meant that he had developed the first modern philosophy of nature, one which in no way presumed the existence of God. It is not surprising then that he dismisses the idea of God as irrational. He argues that we believe things have a supernatural origin when we do not understand their cause. This is especially true of being itself, whose origin we all attribute to an infinite cause, God, although this provides no real explanation. 'To attribute an effect to a spirit, because we do not know what caused it, is merely to seem to give an explanation, for it amounts to no more than saying: there is a cause capable of having this effect' (no. 417). Consequently only material realities are comprehensible.[20]

Sarpi had thus developed a philosophy which was compatible with atheism. Even so, there is no need to feel sure that he was an atheist, as opposed to an agnostic. We will shortly see that there is reason to think that he was not a fideist, and therefore that he was no sort of Christian. What makes it unlikely that he was an atheist is that he continues to talk of God: God as right reason, as destiny, as the epitome of non-discursive, instinctive knowledge, as exemplifying right behaviour without effort of will.[21] 'God' thus makes an appearance in these earlier *Pensieri*, although not in the later *Pensieri filosofici* where Sarpi discusses religion. It is evident, though, that Sarpi could have dispensed with the concept of God had he chosen to: he is using the term merely to dramatise and enliven philosophical arguments.

Having rejected all rational arguments for God's existence, Sarpi is free to give belief in God a purely psychological explanation: it originates in human ignorance and in man's desire for things that are contrary to nature, and even things that are impossible. To compensate for their own sense of frustration men invent an omnipotent God, capable of doing what they are unable to do. Their unwillingness to confine their desires to what is naturally useful is the root of all human misery. True felicity on the other hand lies in the realisation of the Pyrrhonist ideal of indifference: the ability to be unperturbed by external events and the blows of fortune, restricting one's desires within the circle of natural necessity.[22]

It was with thoughts of this kind that Sarpi occupied himself whilst in Rome. Should we be surprised? Lucien Febvre himself might not have been, for he argued that the men of the sixteenth century were unable to develop an irreligious philosophy of nature partly because they were unable to conceptualise an infinite universe: the main obstacle being their humanism, which prevented them from appreciating and developing scholastic discussions of infinity.[23] Sarpi, though, had had a scholastic, not a humanist, education, and it is not surprising therefore that he was able to make use of a tradition of argument whose existence Febvre himself drew attention to.

Sarpi's early *Pensieri filosofici* are thus of considerable importance in the history of philosophy. Their originality has not been fully recognised, however, partly because it has been assumed that Sarpi, like so many of contemporaries, must have believed that reason should be subordinated to faith. Amerio, who was the first scholar to study the *Pensieri* seriously, and who demonstrated that Sarpi was a materialist and a determinist, believed that Sarpi had indeed explicitly insisted on the superiority of faith to reason.[24] But Amerio had been misled by his own expectations: what Sarpi argues is precisely, and uniquely, the opposite. It is this which makes it all but certain that he was no fideist. He wrote that 'true philosophy is not medicine but food for the soul. It is religion which is a medicine. Applicable here is the saying [of Hippocrates] "the more you feed a sick body [food suitable for the healthy] the more harm you do".' We will return to this *Pensiero*, no. 380, and to the others associated with it, later, but it is evident that Sarpi is arguing that the healthy man needs food not medicine, just as the sick man needs medicine not food. Philosophy is therefore superior to faith, but only suitable for those who are strong enough to cope with it.

Convinced of Sarpi's fideism, Amerio thought he had evidence that Sarpi believed that the soul, although naturally material and mortal, could survive after death if God chose to intervene, setting aside the laws of nature. Sarpi's argument however is quite different:

Unreasonable creatures seek only those pleasures which are natural and necessary, and so would a perfect man, although the mediocre man wants also those pleasures which are natural but unnecessary, and the evil man, not satisfied with them, wants pleasures which are contrary to nature. Our ability to enjoy a variety of pleasures can thus lead to vice...and all useless appetites [*vani appetiti*] result from it. There is nothing useless however, indeed it is an indication of the excellence of mankind, in the desire for immortality, the concern for one's grave and one's reputation after death, and the love of children who grow up beneath us or remain after us. (No. 255)

Amerio takes Sarpi to be saying that there is nothing hopeless about the desire for immortality, even though in the *Arte di ben pensare*, another early work, Sarpi lists the idea of the immortality of the soul amongst a number of 'false hypotheses'. What Sarpi is actually saying is that the desire to be remembered after one's death is socially useful, and is thus in accord with nature.[25]

The Sarpi who turned his back on Rome in 1558 was thus a materialist, a determinist, a man who saw no reason to believe that God existed, and who believed that belief in God was the consequence of man's morbid inability to be content and to cultivate the virtue of indifference. Sarpi's views were novel ones, but at the same time they were mere thoughts which could not be embodied in actions. Despite his philosophy, Sarpi had continued to present the appearance of an orthodox churchman, to practise that hypocrisy later advocated by Cremonini and by Sarpi himself in his *Pensieri medico-morali*. And indeed his philosophy was useless to him. It did not open the way to scientific discoveries, although it must have convinced him of the truth of Copernicanism;

nor, if religion was indeed a valuable medicine for the soul, did it provide any justification for an attack upon the institutions and doctrines of the Church. Believing what he did while in Rome, Sarpi might as well, for all practical purposes, have been a believer. This was soon, however, to cease to be the case.

The *Pensieri filosofici* and Pomponazzi's *de Immortalitate Animae*

The *Pensieri filosofici* which deal with religion were apparently all written between 1588 and 1591. The first three of them, nos. 380, 403 and 404, argue that both the state and religion are inventions employed to mitigate defects in man's character: they are medicinal. The healthy man would need neither state nor religion, but take them away from the unhealthy man and you do him harm, just as you harm a sick man if you feed him food suitable for a healthy man (Sarpi here quotes Hippocrates). The healthy food for which religion is a medicinal substitute is philosophy. Philosophy is a good in its own right, but religion is valuable only if it is adapted to the ills which it is intended to cure, which it rarely is. Best of all, though, would be to be able to do without it altogether.

The next one, no. 405, carries the argument a stage further. The state is necessary to make social life possible. Society, the state and religion have all existed as long as men have done, although religion has of course changed greatly through history and differs from state to state. But, Sarpi wants to claim, since it is the state which is primarily created to make social life possible, religion must be regarded as no more than an institution which gives support to the sovereign authority. Consequently, the Church must be under the control of the state.

Pensiero no. 406 develops the historical theme first announced in no. 405. Societies, states and religions all change and decay. Sarpi is interested in two factors which encourage continuity in religion and the state. The Church is protected by a powerful interest group whose fortunes are tied up with hers – Sarpi is thinking of the clergy, and this, as we shall see, is to be the theme of his *History of Benefices*. The state, on the other hand, survives unchanged because it is invigorated by its reaction to the threat to it posed by the Church – Sarpi is talking of the Christian Church, which has managed, because it exists as an independent interest group, to free itself from the domination that the state ought to exercise over it. The state, Sarpi tells us, has survived because of its opposition to the Church; before it came under attack from the Church it was decaying, but afterwards it grew strong. This looks very like a reference to concrete historical developments, and I find it hard to believe that Sarpi is not thinking of Venice (his word for state is *la republica* which would facilitate such a transition from the general to the particular). Venice saw herself as coming under increasing attack from the Church with the progress of the Counter-Reformation. A few years before, in 1582, the anti-clerical faction, with which Sarpi was associated, had begun to establish its ascendancy, and as he wrote they were seeking to pursue bolder and more adventurous policies.[26]

Before we proceed further we must pause to identify Sarpi's main source for his treatment of religion as a 'medicine'. To do so we need to start with Averroes, who had treated religious truth as a species of rhetoric or myth. Embodied in doctrines – *leges* in translations of Averroes – its function was to ensure good behaviour, to keep those who were incapable of apprehending philosophical truths within socially acceptable bounds.[27] Averroes' view of religion, which treated it as fallacious – for only philosophy could be true – but socially useful, was espoused by Bruno, who believed in the existence of an authentic natural religion, but insisted on the need for doctrinal religions teaching untruths, regarding for example the existence of free-will, in order to persuade the *rozzi populi* to obey their rules.[28] But before Bruno Averroes' views had been favourably expounded by Pomponazzi, who seems indeed to have been the only scholastic to have emphasised this side of Averroes' teaching, a fact which tends to support the idea that his own religious convictions may have been open to question.[29]

Sarpi might possibly have read Bruno; he would assuredly have read Averroes.[30] Pomponazzi, as we shall see, he had also read, and there he would have found Averroes cited chapter and verse. Sarpi's awareness of this Averroist tradition of argument helps to explain, I think, not just his view of religion as socially useful but historically relative, but also a more specific, and at first sight mysterious, feature of the *Pensieri filosofici*. Apart from his first reference to religion, in no. 380, Sarpi consistently uses, where I have spoken of 'religion' or 'the Church', the word *Tora*. In context, this has been interpreted as meaning 'the complex of religious norms accepted within any human society', and the word itself is clearly the word 'Torah', the Hebrew word for the Mosaic law.[31] But why use this word, with such specific meaning, for such a general idea? One explanation might of course be that Sarpi wanted to avoid making a directly incriminating statement, but probably more important, I think, is the desire to overcome an ambiguity in Averroes' treatment of religion, for which he employs the word 'law'. Obviously in this context one wants to distinguish between laws of supposedly divine and laws of avowedly secular origin. Once recognise the need for this, and the word 'Torah' would instantly come to mind, since the word *lex* was often used in ecclesiastical Latin to refer specifically to the Mosaic law. *Tora* is thus a natural gloss on *lex* when the word is used in a religious context.

We may, as I have done, translate the word as 'religion' or 'the Church', but Sarpi, like Averroes, is interested in a specific aspect of religion: its ability to modify social behaviour through offering the hope of reward and the fear of punishment, through presenting itself as a *law*.[32] It is not the whole complex of religious norms with which he is concerned; rather it is with religion as a set of beliefs about God's providence, and the Church as a set of institutions sustaining those beliefs. Sarpi employs the word *tora* not because he wants to look at religion in its outward manifestations – its ceremonial, its ritualistic, its sociological aspects – but because he wants to look at it as a system of law modifying man's relationship to himself and his behaviour towards others.[33] Judaism was often regarded as a peculiarly worldly and unspiritual religion;[34] but Sarpi is not interested in the 'Judaical' aspect of religion, in the Mosaic law as a set of religious observances, a complex of religious norms. He is interested in the Torah's *medicinal* role as a check on anti-social behaviour, a role which it can only fulfill because men, for the most part, not only practise their religion, but also believe in it.

It is Averroes, or rather perhaps more immediately Pomponazzi's account of Averroes' views, which is the source of Sarpi's treatment of religion as medicine. In his book *On the Immortality of the Soul* (1516), Pomponazzi defends his claim that the soul is mortal against the argument that the immortality of the soul is affirmed by all religions (all *leges*) and so represent the common conviction of mankind by pointing out that, since they disagree with each other on fundamental questions, most religions, and most people, must have a false conception of God and of man. Even so, he recognises that there is general agreement on this question. Such general agreement, however, does not demonstrate the truth of the doctrine in question: 'For you should know that the fact is that, as Plato and Aristotle put it, the statesman is the doctor [*medicus*] of the soul, and his main concern is to render men virtuous rather than wise.' Pomponazzi then develops this metaphor by distinguishing between four types of men: those who do good for its own sake; those who do good to be thought well of; those who do good for the sake of material reward; and those who do good for fear of hellfire:

The great majority of mankind, when they act well, do so more out of fear of eternal damnation than out of hope of eternal bliss, for punishments are more familiar to us than an eternal happiness of that sort. In order to make this myth of eternal damnation beneficial to all men, whatever category they may fall into, the legislator, seeing how inclined men are to do evil, lays it down that the human soul is immortal, for he is concerned with the common good, his commitment is to utility, not to truth, and his objective is to make men act virtuously. The doctor too misrepresents many things in the course of his treatments of the sick...And if men were healthy or at one with themselves [*compos mentis*]...such fictions would not be necessary.[35]

So far then Sarpi's treatment of religion – his use of the term *tora*, and his account of religion as a medicine, not a food – represents no more than a commentary upon Pomponazzi. Suddenly, though, in nos. 413, 414 and 423, Sarpi's argument breaks entirely new ground. It is not true, he writes, that the *tora* sustains the state, and that otherwise it would collapse. And Sarpi sets out to argue against Pomponazzi, to mount an argument which would have delighted Bayle. Timid men, he says, can be restrained from doing evil by less awful threats than that of hellfire. Bold men cannot be restrained even by that. In this respect the *tora* makes little difference. Of course we think that fear of hell restrains us, just as we think that we do some things simply to advance our reputations, although we would in fact do them anyway. The fact is that men who cease to believe in hell continue to act as morally as before. There is no difference, Sarpi claims, in the behaviour of two men with the same character, one of whom believes in hell and the other does not. Religion merely supplements the other social pressures which come to bear upon us, but it does not have a crucial or preponderant influence.

In these few lines Sarpi propounds an argument which no other moral atheist had dared advance: that men who had no belief in divine providence, no religion, would be capable of forming a civilised society. This is not an argument Sarpi has got from Pomponazzi, for it involves denying the existence of Pomponazzi's fourth and largest category of men, a category whose existence was universally recognised. Even so, it is an argument which presupposes Pomponazzi's claim that religion is merely a tool in the hands of politicians, for Sarpi's argument is that politicians have available other and adequate tools.

Sarpi had thus demonstrated that it might be permissible to attack providential religion, for the fear of hell was not necessary to sustain social stability. He was also evidently convinced that there was a conflict of interest between Church and state, a conflict which might make it necessary for the state to dispense with the support given it by providential religion. Now indeed he was in possession not merely of an agnostic philosophy, but of a theory of society which was capable of legitimating an attitude to doctrinal religion which his contemporaries would have regarded as subversive of all social order. What he was to go on to develop in the *Pensieri sulla religione* were two arguments which would serve to give direction and coherence to any attack upon the institutions and doctrines of the Church: an account of the relative merits of different religions, from deism to paganism, and an account of why Christianity was particularly threatening to the state. Already, in his account of how the Church is protected by a powerful interest group whose fortunes are tied up with hers, Sarpi was beginning to develop an approach to Church history which was to characterise all his later work: here the Church appears to represent a set of interests in direct conflict with those of society, rather than an institution which, no matter how corrupt it may be, serves to preserve social stability and respect for authority. The *Pensieri* on religion thus laid the foundations for the *History of the Council of Trent*, for an attack upon the papacy which is unhampered by the recognition of a need to defend the true Christian faith, or to identify an authoritative Church.

The *Pensieri sulla religione* and Charron's *De la sagesse*

We have seen that Sarpi's *Pensieri filosofici* contain, as a result of his meditations upon Pomponazzi, an argument for the possibility of a society of moral atheists. It is doubtful, though, whether Sarpi would have been able to conceive of the existence of a society of atheists in the strict sense, for he seems to have considered belief in a God of some sort as being almost impossible to eradicate.

The first project Sarpi sets himself in the *Pensieri sulla religione* is that of providing an account of how men come to believe in the existence of God. Fear of the unknown, desire for things which they cannot obtain, and natural processes which they cannot explain all combine to convince men that there exist immaterial beings who need to be placated. Moreover, just as the gods are imagined more powerful than men because men are frustrated by their own incapacities, so they are believed to be more perfect because men lament their own imperfections. Thus men move slowly from a belief in numerous gods to belief in a single perfect Deity. But since this idea continues to be rooted in men's perception of their own strengths and weaknesses it is of necessity bedevilled by internal contradictions. God is no more than a distorted reflection of man, and Sarpi seizes on exactly the same inconsistencies in the idea of God which were later to be emphasised by the anonymous author of the *Quatrains du déiste*: God does not have human emotions, yet He feels compassion; He has nothing to gain from men, yet He takes an interest in them; He is unchanging and incorruptible, yet He is swayed by prayers and presents.[36]

Just as God is a reflection of man, so man's worship of God is a reflection of human social relations: God is treated as a guest, a patron, a judge, a benefactor and so forth. Moreover, religion cannot remain a purely private affair. It is communicated, if imperfectly, from one man to another, and because of its importance in human affairs it is inevitably brought under the control of the state. The state's first task is to adapt religion so that it meets the needs of both the common people and the intelligentsia. This is done by employing creeds and mysteries which can be understood and interpreted in different ways by different groups within society. The people have then to be persuaded to accept the resulting religion, and miracles are often faked for this purpose. Such an established religion can have beneficial psychological and social effects, but also harmful ones; in this respect it is like any other medicine.[37]

This first section of the *Pensieri sulla religione* betrays two influences. First of all we find in it the continuing influence of Pomponazzi, reflected in the discussion of religion as a medicine, and in the claim that the fabricating of miracles is legitimate, 'for everyone believes that lying is justified when it is employed medicinally, and thinks themselves justified in persuading someone to believe what is useful and true by using false arguments'.[38] But secondly we find in this section clear evidence of Sarpi's dependence upon an unexpected source: Charron's *De la sagesse* (1601). Sarpi's phrase, in the context of his account of the state's efforts to teach religion to the people, that 'Men learn that they are Jews or Turks before they know that they are men' is an echo of Charron, and an echo rather of the first, uncensored edition of *De la sagesse* than of the revised edition of 1604. Charron of course had learnt this conceit from Montaigne, but Montaigne had written 'We are Christians for the same reason that we are Perigordians or Germans', while Charron wrote, 'We are circumcised or baptised Jews, Mahommedans, Christians, before we know we are men.'[39] Similarly, Sarpi writes of 'the fantastic fact that there is no chimera nor unworthy object that has not been deified and has not been worshipped in some place or other', while Charron had written that 'It is...a fearful thing that there are and have been so many different religions, and even more fearful is the strangeness of some of them, which have demanded belief in such fantastic doctrines that it is astonishing that human reason can have been so brutalised or so inebriated as to believe such fabrications: for it seems that there is nothing in this world, worthy or unworthy, which has not been deified somewhere, and has not found somewhere to be worshipped.'[40]

The first important thing to note about the identification of *De la sagesse* as a source for the *Pensieri sulla religione* is that it provides a *terminus post quem*. They must date from well after the discission of Pomponazzi's views in the *Pensieri filosofici*. We will see later that there is evidence that Sarpi had been acquainted with *de Immortalitate Animae* for many years before he began to consider the view of religion there suggested. We can thus feel confident that the discussion of religion in the *Pensieri filosofici* results from a new interest on Sarpi's part in the social role of religion, while we can suggest that Sarpi had acquired a copy of Charron because he knew it had a reputation as an irreligious book, for when he read Charron his views were already largely formed. It is not possible, unfortunately, to propose a definite date by which the *Pensieri sulla religione* must have been written. I agree with Gaetano and Luisa Cozzi, though, in thinking that they betray a detached, academic approach which suggests that they were written before Sarpi became fully involved in politics and public activity, that is before 1606.[41]

We now have some idea of the sort of document we are dealing with. In part at least the *Pensieri sulla religione* are a critical reflection upon Charron's account of religion, in the same way that the *Pensieri filosofici* contain a critical reflection upon Pomponazzi's. But, unless he has other sources I have been unable to identify, Sarpi is willing to go beyond the limits of a mere commentary. His account of the psychological origins of religion, for example, is clearly to be placed in a tradition of stoical and sceptical discussion of religion, for Pomponazzi and Charron were both much influenced by stoicism, and Charron by scepticism. But it seems to have no direct precursor.[42]

If we now continue to follow the argument of the *Pensieri sulla religione*, we find Sarpi turning to a new subject, that of the comparative analysis of religions. The best religions, he tells us, combine an elevated conception of God, for this gives man greatest cause for hope, with an emphasis on human weakness, for this encourages men to restrain their passions. They demand of men a form of worship and way of life that is socially useful and does not harm the interests of individuals, and they present a doctrine which is comparatively convincing and can be expounded to both the learned and the unlettered. They either deny personal responsibility for sin or emphasise only those sins which are dangerous to society, laying down forms of repentance which are useful to society or the sinner. In short, good religions make men feel at peace with themselves and encourage them to be generous and humane. Bad religions, naturally enough, have the opposite characteristics: an ignoble conception of God, an undue faith in man, and a belief in sin as pervasive and of God as unforgiving and unjust. They make men fearful, even desperate, anxious and selfish.[43]

This argument involves a slight contradiction with the account of religion which Sarpi has derived from Pomponazzi. For where Sarpi had previously treated the merits of a religion as being relative to the society in which it is accepted, he now suggests that certain types of religion are everywhere psychologically beneficial, others everywhere psychologically harmful. And this is because Sarpi has not distanced himself sufficiently from his sources, for he is here simply providing a commentary upon Charron's distinction between true piety and superstition. According to Charron true piety is based upon a noble conception of God and a humbling conception of man and makes men feel at peace, as well as encouraging generosity and openness. Superstition on the other hand frightens men and insults God, presenting him as jealous and exigent.[44]

Like Charron, Sarpi goes on to give an account of the best form of piety. An important difference, though, is that Charron is concerned to assess different religious views which can exist within an at least nominal Christianity, while Sarpi's purpose seems to be to discuss different religions. What is the best form of private religious conviction according to Charron becomes with Sarpi the best form of religion. This would recognise that God, because he is infinite, is beyond human understanding. It would combine belief in his existence with unwillingness to specify his nature or characteristics. It would hold that God approves all worship that men direct towards him, of whatever form, but discourage people from believing that there is anything to hope or fear from God. It would recognise that religion itself is natural, not supernatural, in its origins and is to be used instrumentally to the benefit of man.[45]

It would be easy to show how Sarpi's short account of the best religion conforms to Charron's much longer account of the best form of piety and of the correct attitude for the wise man to adopt to the religious views of others.[46] But what is interesting is the way in which Sarpi has drawn out the implications of Charron's argument. Charron was writing for publication, and had to be careful how he expressed himself. Sarpi has read *De la sagesse* with a view to drawing out its irreligious implications, not to reconciling it with Christianity. Charron, for example, never suggests that there may be no such thing as personal guilt at all. He never claims that men have nothing to hope or fear from God. It is true that, following the Christian stoic Guillaume Du Vair, he says we should always pray *fiat voluntas tua*, and never seek for anything contrary to God's providence, but it is a long step beyond this to imply that God may be relatively indifferent to human affairs. In short, Sarpi has read Charron as the author of the *Quatrains du déiste* would have done, as a man who does not believe in hell. Similarly, Charron says that the point of religion is to render honour to God and to benefit man, but he does not say that it is to be used instrumentally.[47] He says that all religions claim to be based on supernatural revelation, although all are, in fact, sustained by human means, but he does not say, even if he implies, that the only true religion is the one that recognises that it has no supernatural foundation but is based solely on man's inability to satisfy his desire to explain his world.[48]

Where in many respects Sarpi's account seems to be simply making explicit the implications of what Charron says, in one respect it appears to be crucially different. Sarpi's failure to distinguish between a discussion of different forms of piety and a discussion of different forms of religion reflects a hostility to doctrinal religion which is not to be found in Charron. Charron carefully distinguishes between the inward and outward worship of God. Inward worship should be directed towards an impersonal divine being, a God who is 'le dernier effort de nostre imagination vers la perfection' (a God who 'represents our best efforts to conceive of perfection').[49] Outward worship, on the other hand, is more for the benefit of man than of God, being designed to unite and moralise society. This outward religion need not be based upon any private conviction. If one wishes not to be irreligious, he writes, one must not judge for oneself in matters of religion: 'one must be simple, obedient and easy-going if one is to be inclined to accept religion, believing according to the laws and respecting their authority, submitting one's private judgment and allowing oneself to be led and controlled by the state'.[50] Natural piety is thus to be accompanied by religious observance. Sarpi, however, seems far from happy with this un-questioning acceptance of doctrinal religion. He appears to be able to imagine the establishment of a religion which is tolerant of the beliefs of others and of the practices and opinions of its own members, of a purely natural religion. He certainly has no desire to emphasise, as Charron does, the need for an official, supernatural religion which goes beyond, and even contrary to, the principles of true piety. And this can only be because he is not convinced, as Charron is, that outward conformity to a doctrinal religion is socially and politically necessary.

Charron's insistence on the need for an established and doctrinaire religion is entirely compatible with his secular account of religion and of morality. It should already be apparent from the aspects of his thought seized on by Sarpi that Charron presents religion as a human invention employed for socially and psychologically useful purposes. But Sarpi's account throws in doubt his own faith in God in a way that Charron's does not. It is not just that Sarpi gives a much more extensive account than Charron does of the irrational foundations of religious belief. All Charron's arguments can be read as advocating an inward deism and an outward religious conformity. That Charron believes one ought to believe in God, whether his existence can be proved or not, there seems no doubt, for he maintains that belief is psychologically fertile while disbelief is sterile, that belief elevates the mind, presenting it with an idea of perfection, and ennobles the spirit, presenting it with an idea of divine beneficence. Charron is a fideist once it comes to belief in God, even if he is no more than a sceptical conservative when it comes to belief in Christianity.

But Sarpi's account of belief is different. For Charron belief is natural, while atheism is pathological.[51] For Sarpi on the other hand belief itself has pathological origins. We have seen that he sees fear, desire and ignorance as being the origins of belief in God. These, he explains, are the vices of *l'ingegno non ben temperato*, the mind which is not at one with itself.[52] At the very end of the *Pensieri sulla religione*, and on a separate page, Sarpi outlines the characteristics of *l'ingegno di buon temperatura*, the wise man.[53] The first, the most important of these characteristics, is that he recognises that his efforts at obtaining knowledge always come up against the infinite, and, knowing this is beyond his grasp, he stops and comes to no final decision on any matter, deciding to live according to the day-to-day appearance of things and, in public, support those beliefs which are commonly held.[54]

Sarpi's wise man is thus not a deist, but an agnostic. In this respect even the best of religions, the religion which Charron portrays as being the outcome of natural reason, is portrayed by Sarpi as having its origins in man's psychological inadequacies. Even a deism which makes no appeal to revelation is no more than another, milder form of medicine, although one of importance for the individual psyche rather than for the state. True health and true wisdom on the other hand lie in the indifference and detachment of the agnostic, although only a few exceptional individuals will ever be capable of this. Thus Charron's position is similar to that advocated in the *Quatrains du déiste*: one should combine a private deism with the public confession of Catholicism. Sarpi's esoteric doctrine, however, is agnosticism, while deism he believes to be suitable as an exoteric doctrine, since society is quite capable of sustaining itself without providence and revelation.

The *Pensieri sulla religione* and the defects of Christianity

Sarpi's comparative study of religion continues where Charron's leaves off. Charron outlines the difference between superstition and piety, and suggests that natural religion is different from, and superior to, both. Sarpi at first follows this scheme, but then he embarks upon an account of concrete historical religions quite unlike anything to be found in Charron, although much influenced by Charron's assessment of religion in terms of the relative status given to God and to man.[55] First of all he describes the religions of the gentiles, then that of the Jews.[56] Finally, he comes to the Christian religion, remarking first of all upon some of its central doctrines. Unlike Judaism, it presents itself as a religion for men of all nations. Its message is that all men share in Adam's sin and that no man is capable of virtue, but that men's sins may be redeemed through faith in Christ.[57] This account of Christianity may seem tinged with Protestantism, but Sarpi's purpose is not to recall Christianity to its true principles, but rather to provide an historical reconstruction of the beliefs of the early Church, and to account for the changes in those beliefs over time.[58]

Sarpi identifies two main agents of change.[59] The first is the conversion of the gentiles. Originally there was no Christian creed. The gentiles, however, invented a whole series of articles of faith, all of them placing a strain upon belief, and each leading to the formation of religious factions and sects. Along with the growth of sectarian conflict, of course, went the growth of 'atheism', that is to say an unwillingness to commit oneself to any particular set of religious doctrines. This conflict between Christian theology and the original simplicity of the Christian message has presented continuing and insuperable problems for the Christian Church.

The other great turning point in the history of Christianity, in Sarpi's view, is the conversion of Constantine and the establishment of Christianity as a state religion. In its origins Christianity was profoundly anti-social. It held men to be incapable of virtue, regarded worldly affairs as an encumberance, and believed that the Second Coming was at hand. It was, in short, 'contraria al viver civile' (socially subversive).[60] In order to become a state religion it had, of necessity, to be transformed. Men had to be taught that they were capable of acting, and required to act, virtuously, and salvation had to be made dependent on works as well as faith. Even so, no satisfactory ethical theory could be developed, because morality and piety were confused. Moreover, although men were encouraged to act virtuously, they were still discouraged from committing themselves fully to political and social life. The Church had established itself as independent of the state, the clergy claiming as great an authority over the secular ruler as over the rest of the faithful. The result was that where the Jewish religious community had been identified with the state of Israel, Christians were taught to recognise two conflicting communities, the

Heavenly and the earthly cities, and Christianity committed itself to the defence of values which conflicted with the political and economic needs of society. The world, Sarpi says, has been exhausted by the resulting contradictions.

Sarpi's presentation of the history of Christianity in uncompromisingly secular terms is, I believe, completely original. He does not insist that the early Church was different in kind from the Church of later years in order to restore the values of primitive Christianity, for these were anti-social and were founded on a misapprehension, that of the imminence of the Second Coming. Rather his purpose is to explain the peculiar unsuitability of Christianity as a state religion.

Nothing would have shocked someone like Charron more than to see Christianity portrayed in such terms, for, he had devoted two-thirds of a work entitled *Les trois vérités* (1593) to demonstrating that, granted one must have a religion, Christianity is the best of all religions, and Catholicism the best form of Christianity.[61] However Charron's arguments for Christianity concentrated on its psychological, not its social or intellectual benefits, and Charron thus effectively side-stepped current accounts of the demerits of Christianity. Both Machiavelli and Bruno, for example, had attacked Christianity, the one claiming it was incompatible with military valour, the other that it encouraged stupidity and ignorance.[62] However, the implication of their arguments was that Christianity should be reformed or replaced by a more socially useful or more philosophical religion. I know of only two discussions of the demerits of Christianity which argue that the state must establish an appropriate set of values without relying upon the support of any religion. There is no reason to suppose that Sarpi was aware of either of them, but they are of great assistance for our understanding of Sarpi. The crucial respect in which their arguments differ from Sarpi's helps to confirm my claims for the originality of Sarpi's secular conception of the state. But equally important are the similarities between their arguments and Sarpi's , which help us to identify the intellectual tradition which, aside from scholastic philosophy, stoicism and scepticism, was of the greatest importance for Sarpi.

The two discussions of the unsuitability of Christianity as a social and political ideology which I wish to consider are, unfortunately, both anonymous. One was published in 1591 and entitled *De la vraye et legitime constitution de l'estat*; the other was published in 1599 and entitled *De la concorde de l'estat par l'observation des edicts de pacification*.[63] These two little books have so much in common that it is difficult to resist the view that they were written by the same man. If not, they spring from the same preoccupations and testify to the same principles. There are important differences between them, but these are readily explicable in terms of the different circumstances under which they were written. The work of 1591 was published soon after the death of Henri III and the announcement of Henri IV's claim to the throne. The work of 1599 was

published six years after Henri's conversion to Catholicism, and a year after
the promulgation of the Edict of Nantes. The one looks forward to a new
political and religious order in abstract and general terms, while the other seeks
to defend a new but still insecure political and religious settlement in concrete
terms, while not denying the radical aspirations of the earlier work. Despite the
differences in their treatment of political and religious questions, the two works
are strikingly similar in the structure and formulation of their arguments.

Both works take as their premise an understanding of the state as something
other than the king's estate or the king's person.[64] The earlier text, however,
presents what one might term a philosophical account of state power, the later
text a sociological one. In the text of 1591 the state is presented as an abstraction,
as the monopoly of force, of political power. The defining characteristic of the
state is the ability to punish and to instill fear. But the state is embodied in
the person of the ruler. The ruler stands in the place of God; obedience to him
is a preparation for obedience to the Ruler of Rulers. Rebellion is equivalent
to idolatry. Rulers, moreover, are held to be in a direct relationship to God,
and have no need of a religion or a Church to mediate between them and Him.
For the text of 1599, on the other hand, the state is embodied in the magistrate.
The book is written as an appeal to the *noblesse de robe*. If they will rally round
the edicts of toleration and enforce them, they will be able to impose peace on
the nation. The princes of the blood and the higher nobility will continue to
plot, but deprived of popular support they will be forced to devote themselves
to court intrigues rather than civil war. The government of Henri IV is thus
now in process of becoming a sociological reality, a bureaucratic authority.

Both works are concerned to argue the need for religious toleration, and they
employ the same arguments to make their point. In the first place they argue
that the ideal of unity is itself a misleading one, so that religious differences
need not be subversive of all order. In the text of 1591 the impossibility of
achieving unity is expressed in terms of the impossibility of persuading a
collection of clocks to chime simultaneously.[65] In the later text it is argued that
if unity within one nation were possible, then it would be right to demand
political and religious unity throughout the world, and, indeed, the abolition
of all magistracies, for why should not all men think and act as one, pursuing
the same ends in the same way?[66] But just as this is clearly impossible, so too
is complete unity in politics. All that is needed is a basic agreement on certain
central political issues, and differences over religion need not threaten this
agreement.

In the second place, they both argue that religion and politics cannot, in any
case, be brought into close correspondence, so that the state must at all times
stand on its own, independent of religious support. It must have the strength
to do this if it is to survive religious disunity, but it needs to have this strength
even where there is religious unity, for the values of social life and Christianity

inevitably conflict, and the state must be capable of ensuring respect for its own principles and values. Both give as an example the conflict between Christian and secular views of justice. The Church promises that those who repent their sins will not be punished, while the state must punish even those who regret their evil deeds. The text of 1591 gives as a further example the fact that magnificence is a virtue in politics, but a sin if viewed from a religious standpoint, while that of 1599 argues that the true Christian always seeks to withdraw from the affairs of this world, becoming a monk or a hermit.[67]

In the third place, both present Catholicism and Protestantism as false religions, implying that unity on the basis of the victory of either one would be unacceptable. In the text of 1591 Catholicism is attacked as superstitious, while Protestantism is held to be at fault for its presumption in claiming to understand God's decrees.[68] In the text of 1599 both religions are defended in that neither is intrinsically subversive, but both are attacked for having allowed themselves to fall under the control of clerical factions who are seeking to dominate the nation. The author, who is nominally a Catholic, like his king, is particularly hostile to the Counter-Reformation, which has proved itself subversive of all social order and introduced 'une religion de Scythes, de Barbares, et de quelques Anthrophages', and correspondingly keen to defend the liberties of the Gallican Church.[69]

Finally, both texts regard toleration as but the prelude to a transformation of religious attitudes. Political divisions have politicised religion. Take them away, and people will recognise the points on which Catholics and Protestants agree, and a new understanding of Christianity and of Christian unity will result. According to the text of 1599 toleration will restore that liberty of conscience which is the only possible foundation for faith. With the establishment of political order the different sects will compete to excell in virtue, but this will quickly lead them to recognise the importance of the doctrines they hold in common.[70] The earlier text also puts forward an eirenicist position, but in doing so it foreshadows some of the arguments of Charron, and arouses similar suspicions as to the nature of its author's religious convictions. According to it, liberty is the greatest good one can wish for, and the precondition for happiness. Only where there is liberty of conscience can one hope to discover the true faith, for he who seeks the true religion must free himself of idolatry and vanity, but free himself too of the anxieties instilled by those who want always to sit in judgment on the beliefs of others. The aim of true religion is not to instill fear but to give peace, and we can only make our peace with God, who is infinite and incomprehensible, if we make it first with our neighbour, who is known to us.[71] Where the later text thus seeks to reduce Christianity to the creed, the earlier one seems to advocate a natural religion.

The fundamental claim that both texts make, however, has yet to be considered. It is that doctrinal religion depends for its existence on the state, which punishes heresy, while the state itself is not dependent upon religion. As the text of 1591 puts it, to claim that the state is dependent upon the Church is to encourage a Machiavellian cynicism in the magistrate, who may well conclude that he should invent a politic religion to suit his purposes. In fact Christianity cannot be defended for its political utility, and can only be justified as a means to salvation.[72] At this point we might expect that this outright rejection of the political role of doctrinal religion would require the author or authors of the two texts to claim that the state can survive independently of belief in divine providence. This, however, is certainly not the intention of the author of the text of 1599. He insists that any religion will serve the state as well as any other, because all teach that God punishes evil and rewards good. It is belief in a providential deity which is essential for the social order, not belief in a particular set of religious doctrines. And this belief is common to all men and precedes the states imposition of a particular creed.[73]

The earlier text is less explicit on this point. Its author's insistence on the state's dependence on compulsion as opposed to the Church's dependence on persuasion might seem to cast in doubt the ability of faith to decisively influence behaviour. And his conviction that true religion gives peace of mind might seem to suggest doubts as to the existence of hell. He even goes so far as to say that there exist well-ordered states without any religion.[74] But in fact, I think, he simply takes for granted the arguments of the later text. He refers gratuitously to hell and the devil, which suggests he believes in them.[75] And, most importantly, he insists that before the state establishes an official set of religious ceremonies, all men already have a sense of natural piety.[76] He seems to see this natural piety as the guarantor of political order, and it seems reasonable to conclude that it is ceremonies and creeds, not belief in divine justice, which the state establishes and which depend upon it for their continued existence. A further argument in favour of this interpretation is the confidence with which Charron and the author of the text of 1599 both insist that no one has questioned the necessity of belief in providence for the maintenance of political order, for had contemporaries believed the text of 1591 to deny the necessity of belief in providence it would surely have provoked sufficient scandal to bring it to the attention of a wide audience.[77]

If either or both of the texts of 1591 and 1599 is the work of a deist, then his deism was like that of Bodin and Lord Herbert of Cherbury, and did not involve the denial of divine providence that we find in the *Quatrains*. The commitment to toleration expressed by the texts of 1591 and 1599 is based on a confidence in the social value of natural piety and natural religion which no one familiar with the stoic arguments against divine justice – arguments implicit in Du Vair, Lipsius and Charron, and explicit in the *Quatrains* and Pomponazzi – could share.[78]

Once the argument that natural religion did not guarantee the existence of divine punishment had been widely expressed, the importance of doctrinal, revealed religion became unquestionable. This not only encouraged sceptics to leap to the defence of orthodoxy, as Charron, Bruno and Campanella, the Italian long resident in the Inquisition's dungeons who is best known for his account of a Utopian society of sun-worshippers, the *Civitas Solis* (1623), were willing on occasion to do.[79] It also undermined any eirenicist programme, for all of them threatened to call in question the two sources of authority which alone seemed capable of sustaining a doctrinal creed, the Bible, literally interpreted, on the one hand, and the papacy on the other. The defeat of the eirenicist hopes expressed not only by these two texts but by most of those who advocated toleration in sixteenth-century France was made inevitable by Henri IV's fear of the subversive capacities of doctrinaire Catholics and Protestants. But it owed something too to the impact of stoicism and libertinism, both of which insisted on the need for irrational, unquestionable doctrines if belief in providence was to be sustained.

De la vraye et legitime constitution de l'estat and *De la concorde de l'estat* are *politique* texts in that they insist that the establishment of political order must take priority over the defence of the true faith, and that the state is capable of surviving even if its subjects are not united in one Church. They are Gallican in so far as they look to the establishment of a state religion which will keep clerical power within check, and *De la concorde de l'estat* makes an explicit appeal to the traditional liberties of the Gallican Church. They are, moreover, eirenicist in so far as they wish to set aside the doctrinal differences between Catholics and Protestants and rebuild Christian unity. Indeed there is a natural affiliation between these three positions, which may be said, by and large, to hang together.

Even so, this unity on a wide range of issues must not blind us to important disagreements and differences within the camp of those willing to defend the authority of the state and defy that of the clergy. Because the French *politique* tradition is the predominant influence apparent in the works Sarpi wrote for publication, affecting both his defence of Venetian policies at the time of the Interdict and his presentation of the history of the Council of Trent, it is as important for us to pay attention to the differences within the *politique* movement as it is for us to recognise the points of agreement which united it, for otherwise we cannot hope to identify the aspects of *politique* thought to which Sarpi responded, nor the ways in which Sarpi sought to make an original contribution to the tradition of *politique* argument. It is worth noting at this point, therefore, the wide range of opinions on the state, on the Gallican Church, and on the reunification of Christianity which could exist within the *politique* movement. On the state, there were important differences between those who, like Bodin, were concerned to attack the traditional idea of a mixed constitution and assert an untrammelled royal absolutism, and those on the other hand, like de Thou, who were committed to the institution of the Parlement as the final authority on the nation's laws.[80] Within Gallicanism, there was a great gulf between someone like Charles Dumoulin, a Protestant who defended the liberties of the Gallican Church against the threat posed by the decrees of the Council of Trent because he believed that Protestantism, Gallicanism and absolutism were well adapted to each other, and someone like Richer, who during Louis XIII's minority developed the conciliar tradition within Gallicanism to advocate a democratic conception of the Church which would have threatened the king's control of ecclesiastical preferment.[81] Finally, within eirenicism, there was a world of difference between someone like Casaubon, who wished to restore the doctrines of the early Church, someone like Hotman, like Casaubon a correspondent of Sarpi's, who was willing to whittle Christianity down to a minimum set of beliefs, and those few who, like the author of *De la vraye et legitime constitution de l'estat*, may even have wished to undermine Christian belief itself.[82]

Such a survey may serve to bring home the fact that the difficult question about Sarpi is not whether he was a *politique*, but what sort of *politique* he was. We will see later how *politique*, Gallican and eirenicist arguments were put to use in his work, but at this point it is worth noting that our study of Sarpi's *Pensieri* gives us grounds for suspecting that what would most have attracted Sarpi to *politique* views is that denial, at least in practice, of God's providence which the enemies of the *politiques* falsely claimed was typical of the *politiques* as a whole. One contemporary protested against the *politiques* because they only worship idleness, and care little about God and his Paradise, about who obeys God and who offends against Him, for their only desire is that God should grant them a perpetual residence in this world. Their motto is *Let us Live, Let us Live*, forgetting that if they live in this world without fearing God, they are far more dead than the oldest cadaver, the bones of which may belong to a saint.[83] It is precisely the attitude attacked here which is characteristic of Sarpi's approach to religion: the first words of the *Pensieri sulla religione* are 'The end of man, as of every other living creature, is to live.'[84]

The *Pensieri medico-morali*: philosophy and propaganda

It has been said of Sarpi that his originality lies not in the views he defends, but in the verve with which he defends them.[85] It is certainly true that what Sarpi wrote with the intention of publishing he always intended to reflect the views of a broad spectrum of anti-papal opinion. As a result he made it impossible for his readers to draw any conclusions about his private views. Even Naudé, who like all the *libertins érudits* had a great admiration for Sarpi, felt unable to conclude more than that he was probably an Epicurean, or at the least a Lutheran![86] Even so, in his letters and occasionally in the works he wrote for publication, we come across viewpoints which are idiosyncratic and original.

The central thesis of this book is that Sarpi was irreligious and willing to contemplate the establishment of a society of moral atheists. We have now looked at the most important, though not all, the evidence for this view. Much of the rest of this book will be concerned to elucidate the relationship between Sarpi's private views and his public activities, and to suggest that this relationship was more intimate than might at first be thought, that Sarpi was not just a propagandist for *politique* and anti-papal views, but that, tentatively and cautiously, he was trying to prepare his readers to accept secular and irreligious ideas. In order to make this claim convincing, we must first look at the rules Sarpi laid down for conducting an argument with someone who does not share your assumptions.

In order to understand Sarpi's attitude to polemical argument, our starting point must be Sarpi's emphasis on the limitations of human reason. The *Pensieri filosofici* include notes on the relativity of human conceptions of beauty, of morality, and of knowledge.[87] The *Pensieri sulla religione* end with a few notes attacking the Aristotelian and Christian concepts of natural law: if moral principles are learnt through habituation, as Aristotle argues, then men's understanding of natural law cannot be governed by reason, nor indeed can it be shown to be reasonable; do unto others as you would wish them to do unto you is contrary to nature, for it takes no account of the need for self-preservation; moreover people's wishes are so varied as to provide no consistent standard of behaviour; the only law of nature is that the strong always rule over the weak; the only sensible principle is to consider everything in terms of its implications for yourself.

This scepticism regarding human reason is apparent in Sarpi's attitude to study. He maintains that one can never hope to find anything in books that one does not already know: books exercise the mind, but do not teach.[88] Study itself should only be pursued for the pleasure it gives, for knowledge is never more useful than ignorance. Socrates' most admirable characteristic was his ability to play at marbles with young children.[89] In short, one should always be suspicious of the supposedly rational and prefer the avowedly useful or pleasurable, for there is always an objection to be made to any argument, and your own views may change tomorrow. For this reason you should respect other people's views, no matter how foolish they seem, for one day you may share them. Meanwhile, all you can do is accept your own opinions for what they are, and live according to them: 'la peste dell'uomo e l'opinione della scienza' ('the source of men's miseries is the illusion of knowledge').[90]

It would be possible to elaborate on this sceptical side to Sarpi's thought at length, but to do so would be to distort Sarpi's views. For despite Sarpi's contempt for human reason, he believed it to be capable, if rightly employed, of reaching certain sound conclusions. The best summary of his position is perhaps *Pensiero* no. 146:

There are four methods of philosophising: the first employs reason alone; the second sense perception alone; the third employs reason first and then the senses; the fourth begins with sense perception and uses reason to build upon it. The first method is worst, because it gives the results one wants to begin with. The third is bad, because often what is is misrepresented as one would like it to be, instead of one's desires being checked against the facts. The second is sound, but poor, for it teaches you little, and gives knowledge of beings rather than causes. The fourth is the best that in this poor life we can hope to have.

Sarpi is then, in the first place, an empiricist. But his commitment to sense perception goes further than mere empiricism. We have seen that he believes that there are certain philosophical truths which conflict with religious belief: these are the truths which are food to the healthy intellect. True philosophy leads one to a rigorous materialism, a recognition that there is no reality aside from the world of sensory experience.

Granted that the healthy mind, understanding the limits of human reason and free of misleading hopes and fears, can reach philosophical truth, how can it persuade others to accept this truth? Sarpi gives his answer to this question in the *Pensieri medico-morali*, an account of how to make the mind healthy, which were probably written at around the same time as the *Pensieri sulla religione*.[91] The starting point for Sarpi's treatment of this problem is the belief that merely to present the truth straightforwardly will do no good. Just as healthy food is harmful for the sick body, so it is for the sick mind.[92] Consequently, it is often best to leave well enough alone, especially if one is dealing with beliefs which are held to be socially necessary (like religion).[93] However, if the false belief has damaging consequences one must resort to constructive falsehood – we have already seen that Sarpi believed that in such matters the end justifies the means. Sarpi recognises two techniques which need to be combined in this process of re-education. First the sick man's conviction must be undermined by attacks on the principles which underlie them and some of the particular conclusions which are drawn from them. The purpose of this is to render the mind receptive to new ideas. Second, the false beliefs which are being attacked must be counterbalanced by an opposing, equally false, set of beliefs. Just as in medicine health comes from the balance of contrasting humours, so intellectual health can be reached by balancing contrasting opinions.[94] Thus sound arguments against the fallacious standpoint are combined with false arguments in favour of a contrasting standpoint.[95] In this way the individual's attachment to falsehood is broken down and he is prepared for a knowledge of the truth.

Sarpi is thus equipped with a theory of propaganda, but he remains unhappy about any attempt to improve other people's opinions which leaves one open to attack for not sharing in common prejudices. The best advice is to express popular views in public, whilst retaining one's philosophical views intact in private. One should 'stare così mascherato con tutti' ('conceal one's true beliefs at all times').[96]

Sarpi's views on the techniques of persuasion thus provide, potentially, a key to the understanding of his propagandistic activities. First of all, they tell us that Sarpi believed one should often espouse beliefs which conflict with those one really holds, if one thinks they will serve to undermine popular prejudices. But secondly, he believed that one should as far as possible express oneself in conformity with popular opinion. In view of Sarpi's own statements it would be unwise, therefore, to adopt a literalist approach to his words and deeds. When, as is often the case, these words and deeds seem to be in conflict with themselves and each other, one should ask whether they may not be intended to act together as different aspects of a mental therapy. If Sarpi's goal is taken to be to undermine superstition and to work towards a secular society, then the different, conflicting aspects of his life fall into place: the attack on papal monarchy represents an attack on established and damaging prejudices; the secret advocacy of Protestantism represents an attempt to counterbalance one falsehood with another; and the public defence of secular jurisdiction and *politique* views is a defence of that aspect of the truth which can be expressed in popularly acceptable terms. To take one example, is Sarpi's often expressed desire to see Protestant troops invade Italy evidence of his commitment to Protestantism?[97] In the light of the *Pensieri* it might rather be taken to reflect his desire to see Catholic power counterbalanced by Protestant power. The religious conflicts in France had led, after all, to the growth of the *politique* movement and, it was generally held, to the spread of moral atheism. Might not religious conflict of this sort be a necessary precondition for the establishment of a secular society?

The modern reader, however, is liable to recoil from such an interpretation. He lives in a society in which great value is placed on self-expression, openness, integrity.[98] He is liable to feel that Sarpi, described in this way, is being portrayed as a hypocrite and double-dealer, even were it psychologically plausible that someone should undertake such a complicated task of systematic misrepresentation. But such a response is an unhistorical one. The recurring theme of much of the literature of the age – of Sarpi's *History of the Council of Trent* or of Boccalini's *Ragguagli di Parnaso* to mention two examples – is that hypocrisy has become a way of life, and that to understand men's behaviour one must penetrate behind appearances and 'unmask' their secret motives and intentions.[99] The interpretation of Sarpi proposed in this book is not one he himself would have found psychologically implausible, nor is Sarpi's behaviour, on my account of it, of a sort he would have found morally objectionable.

Sarpi unmasked

In a study of seventeenth-century Italian libertines, Giorgio Spini has commented on how difficult it is to penetrate behind the masks of men like

Sarpi.[100] I believe that a study of the *Pensieri* exposes the man behind the mask, although this leaves the problem of explaining why he wears the particular mask, or set of masks, he does. It is worth, I think, noting at this point that the case for regarding Sarpi as irreligious is already, on the basis of the evidence we have looked at so far, stronger than that for so regarding Pomponazzi, or Dolet, or Charron, for it is a case founded upon his own explicit statements. Historians often object to an inquisitorial approach to history which seeks to convict authors of holding opinions that they never admitted holding.[101] Pomponazzi, for example, said one ought to believe in the immortality of the soul, despite the philosophical arguments against it. In fact when one takes into account the circumstances under which authors expressed their opinions one can usually form a well-grounded suspicion as to their real views. Suspicion and irrefutable evidence, however, are not the same thing. In Sarpi's case, though, the *Pensieri* do more than provide grounds for suspicion. Their meaning, despite occasional obscurities, is clear, and there is no reason why Sarpi should have misrepresented his views in what are essentially private documents.

In order to argue that the views expressed in the *Pensieri* are not Sarpi's, one would need to adopt one of two strategies. One might dismiss them as a mere *jeu d'esprit*, a commentary upon Pomponazzi and Charron which the author himself was never convinced by; or one might dismiss them as juvenilia, and argue for some later modification in Sarpi's view of religion. But the weakness in both of these strategies is that themes and ideas pioneered in the *Pensieri* recur throughout the later work, so that it is impossible to establish the necessary contrast between the *Pensieri* and Sarpi's publicly expressed views.[102] If one takes the *Pensieri* literally Sarpi's public views can be explained in the light of them. If one takes Sarpi's public views literally it is difficult to see how they can be made to yield a coherent picture of the man, let alone be used to explain his authorship of the *Pensieri*.

Before we abandon our study of the *Pensieri* though, and turn to Sarpi's public activities, there is one final question we need to ask. Is there no evidence, aside from Sarpi's own statements elsewhere, to corroborate the account I have given of the *Pensieri*? Do not contemporaries accuse Sarpi of 'atheism'? Have no historians suspected him of irreligion?

Corroborative testimony of the sort required has long been available. Indeed, Bianchi-Giovini, author of the standard nineteenth-century biography of Sarpi,[103] was aware of the contemporary accusations directed against Sarpi, but he and Sarpi's other nineteenth-century biographers saw nothing in the admittedly cryptic text of the *Pensieri filosofici* to substantiate such accusations. Without the text of the *Pensieri sulla religione* – which, prior to the 1960s, seem to have been read only by Acton – to help define the problem this is perhaps not entirely surprising. Thus, believing the testimony of contemporaries was unsupported by Sarpi's own writings, they felt free to dismiss it as mere malicious slander.[104] When we discover, however, that contemporaries had grounds for believing that Sarpi was sincerely committed to views expressed in the *Pensieri*, it goes a long way towards excluding any interpretation of them as a mere *jeu d'esprit*.

A great deal of the contemporary testimony seems to centre around an episode which occurred in 1601. In that year Sarpi was put forward by the Venetian government as its nominee for a bishopric in Dalmatia. The pope, however, refused to appoint Sarpi, and this was because the nuncio in Venice had reported that he had been warned that Sarpi was 'a man who may believe some things he should not believe, and who may not believe some things he ought to believe' and that he was a member of 'una scoletta piena d'errori', an academy of errors. The nuncio's sources were an enemy of Sarpi's within his own order, Gabriele Dardano, and a leading Jesuit, Achille Gagliardi.[105]

The nuncio does not seem to have specified the questions on which Sarpi's beliefs were suspect. But according to Antonio Possevino, a Jesuit, in a pseudonymous attack on Venice published in 1607, Sarpi had been reported to Clement VIII for belonging to an 'academy', an intellectual association, in which nobles and others participated, where it was generally accepted that the immortality of the soul was to be rejected on philosophical grounds. Indeed Possevino claims that the members of this academy conspired to prevent anyone who did not interpret Aristotle in this sense from being appointed to the University of Padua.[106] According to the anonymous letter dating from shortly after the Interdict, and probably written by Angelo Badoer, a leading anti-clerical noble, who was, it seems, acting in association with Dardano, Sarpi and the members of his academy had also been the moving force behind Venetian resistance to the Interdict.[107] Did this academy actually exist? It is perhaps indicative that a reply defending Venice against Possevino's attacks contested the doge's membership of it, not its existence.[108]

A number of other sources bear witness to the fact that these accusations against Sarpi were widely known and often believed. On 20 March 1606, evidently on news of Sarpi's appointment as state theologian, an agent of the French government wrote to Paris: 'They have chosen an important person, who has a considerable reputation in Italy, although more than a year ago I learnt that there was more of the philosopher and of the libertine in him than of the monk.'[109] In 1613 Bruslart, the French ambassador to Venice, was persuaded that Sarpi was 'a man without religion, without faith, and without conscience who did not believe in the immortality of the soul'.[110] The year after Sarpi's death Peiresc, one of the great literary correspondents of the day, and an admirer of Sarpi's *History of the Council of Trent*, was informed by a correspondent in Rome that Sarpi 'was believed to be a man who believed neither in God nor the devil', neither in heaven nor hell.[111]

An anonymous history of the Interdict written probably around the time of

Sarpi's death accuses Sarpi of having denied the immortality of the soul on Aristotelian grounds.[112] More circumstantial is the account of someone called Nicoletti, who wrote a life of Maffeo Barberini, Urban VIII, who had been nuncio in Paris at the time of the Interdict and who died in 1644. According to Nicoletti the academy had met at the house of a man we know to have been a friend of Sarpi's, Gherard Nis, a Dutch Calvinist merchant. He tells us that Clement VIII had already heard of this academy before Sarpi was proposed for the bishopric in Dalmatia.[113] This would suggest that the accusations were first levelled against Sarpi earlier in 1601, when there seems to have been some suggestion that he might be appointed to another bishopric, one which eventually went to the nuncio's confessor.[114] This would explain why the nuncio saw no need to give a more specific account of the accusations being made against Sarpi when his name was put forward officially later in the year.

Examples could surely be multiplied, but this would not necessarily strengthen the case against Sarpi, as most and perhaps all of the denunciations we have looked at so far probably take their origin from the accusations of Dardano and Gagliardi.[115] It is evident that the central charge made against Sarpi was that he was an Aristotelian who rejected the doctrine of the immortality of the soul. We know from the *Pensieri* that Sarpi was no Aristotelian, for he rejected the whole Aristotelian doctrine of substances. Nevertheless there is good evidence in his own writings that he regarded his philosophical position as being compatible with the defence of Pomponazzi's version of the arguments against the Christian doctrine of immortality.

In an early unpublished work, the *Arte di ben pensare*, Sarpi explicitly includes the idea of the immortality of the soul in a list of false hypotheses.[116] Equally important, though, are Sarpi's grounds for rejecting this hypothesis. *Pensiero* no. 4, which seems to have been written some twenty years before Sarpi was rejected as unsuitable for promotion to a bishopric, reproduces the central argument that Pomponazzi had employed to demonstrate the mortality of the soul, the argument that there is no knowledge without sensation.[117] On the basis of this, Pomponazzi had claimed that, philosophically speaking, the soul must be regarded as strictly mortal, and had attacked the view of Averroes, who had denied that there was any personal immortality, but had taught that all men participated in an immortal reason. For him the rational soul was accidentally mortal, but essentially immortal. It is Pomponazzi's views on immortality, not Averroes', which Sarpi must have defended in his academy, for they are entirely compatible with the materialist position which Sarpi adopts in the *Pensieri*.

The accusation that Sarpi did not believe in the immortality of the soul was, we have established, fairly widely disseminated amongst contemporaries. This accusation of mortalism, however, touches on only one aspect of the *Pensieri*.

Of that part of the *Pensieri* which is of greater interest for our purposes, their treatment of the relationship between politics and religion, the only contemporary echo was the claim that the doctrines of Machiavelli had been discussed in Sarpi's academy.[118] All this goes to suggest, however, that in the years before the Interdict Sarpi was surrounded by a circle of like-minded individuals, all of them anti-clerical, and many of them, we are told, young nobles, and that in their company Sarpi was prepared to give fairly frank expression to his views. And this gives us some grounds for accepting another piece of contemporary evidence which is clearly independent of the accusations of Dardano and Gagliardi and which confirms Sarpi's materialism. In 1636 Campanella assured Peiresc that he had it on good authority that in 1593 both Sarpi and Galileo had been adherents of the system of Democritus.[119] One would give little weight to such testimony, after the lapse of so many years, were it not for the *Pensieri*. As it is, it may tell us nothing useful about Galileo, but it does seem to confirm that the views Sarpi expressed in the *Pensieri* were views he also expressed to some few of his contemporaries.

The most remarkable and detailed of the contemporary attacks upon Sarpi as an atheist is discussed in an appendix. But even leaving aside the testimony of brother Giovanni Francesco Graziani, there is, as we have seen, a considerable amount of contemporary evidence which, taken together, is sufficient to confirm the interpretation I have put upon the *Pensieri*. There would be no need to hesitate in accepting this account, were it not for the vast body of scholarship which has agreed in attributing Christian doctrines to Sarpi. Before this only one historian has, as far as I know, come anywhere close to a correct account of Sarpi's views, and that was Acton, in a brilliant but flawed essay he published in 1867.

Acton's conclusion was that Sarpi 'despised the doctrines which he taught, and scoffed at the mysteries which it was his office to celebrate. Therefore, his writings must have been composed in order to injure, not to improve, the religion he professed to serve...[He was] the most consummate tactician in modern polemics, a sceptic and an absolutist at heart, who sought to encompass his evil ends in Church and State alike by assailing the authority of the Holy See.'[120] Unfortunately Acton commences by arguing from a *Tract on the Venetian Republic*, generally attributed to Sarpi. Sarpi's authorship of this work had already been questioned, although on no very substantial grounds, by Bianchi-Giovini, so it was rash of Acton to put stress upon it. More recently it has been conclusively demonstrated that the work is not by Sarpi.[121] For Acton, however, it was important, because he believed that in it Sarpi had advocated the use of murder for political ends. This made it possible for him to attack those who sought to murder Sarpi, and the Inquisition, which put one of his associates to death, while insisting that Sarpi never defended the principle of freedom. In the history of freedom Acton long planned to write Sarpi would obviously have found no place of honour.

Because Acton's starting point is Sarpi's place in the history of freedom, his most important, his most original evidence is given insufficient prominence:

> Sarpi's own diaries and notebooks, containing the record of his inmost thoughts, and the secret of his religious views, are still preserved. The views are singularly striking and original. But they are not Christian. Sarpi admits neither the divine origin of the Church, nor the divine character of Revelation. Judaism and Christianity, Catholicism and Protestantism, are forms of speculation which he tries to explain by human causes, valuing them not as influences, and studying them as phenomena with less interest than Schelling or Comte – without passion, but without approbation or any degree of assent. These fragments deserve to be admitted in a complete and critical edition of his works...They exhibit his opinions and the nature of his faculties better than his books or letters. They will overturn the image which Venice preserves of him...[122]

Thus for Acton Sarpi was a hypocrite who defended despotism, not the defendant of liberal principles presented by Bianchi-Giovini and others. But what really matters is that this conclusion was based on a reading of, at the least, the *Pensieri sulla religione*, and that Acton was convinced that those *Pensieri* left no room for doubt as to Sarpi's true opinions regarding Christianity.

CONSIDERATIONI
SOPRA LE CENSVRE
Della Santità di Papa Paulo V.

CONTRA
LA SERENISSIMA
REPVBLICA DI VENETIA.
DEL P. M. PAVLO
DA VENETIA
Dell'Ordine de Serui.

Psal. 108.

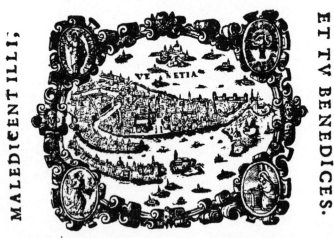

MALEDICENTILLI;

ET TV BENEDICES.

IN VENETIA, M D C V I.
Appresso Roberto Meietti.

CON LICENZA DELLI SVPERIORI.

2

Sarpi and the Venetian Interdict

Il serenissimo prencipe della republica veneziana Andrea Gritti, vedendo nella sua republica in questi tempi moderni alcune novità grandi circa il governo pubblico, fortemente cominciò a temere che fossero veri i prognostichi della vicina morte di quella tanto famosa e tanto antica libertà; e perciochè alcuni giorni sono andò all'oracolo delfico e lo supplicò a fargli grazia di liberamente scuoprirgli il secreto, se la libertà veneziana, la quale egli avea sempre tenuto essere con il mondo immortale, dovea aver fine e quando. Vide a lato al simulacro di Apollo apparir una tavola di corografia, la quale alle città che vi vide dipinte di Bergamo, Padova, Vicenza, Verona e alla stessa città di Venezia conobbe benissimo che era il ritratto dello Stato che i signori veneziani posseggono in terra ferma; ma gran maraviglia gli diede il veder che Venegia, non già nelle lagune dove ella sta posta, ma fosse dipinta in mezzo una verde campagna, di modo che, non potendo creder che quella tavola dipinta da divina mano contenesse in sè tanto errore, grandemente si dolse con il sacerdote del tempio, che l'oracolo l'avesse stimato indegno di una chiara risposta. Rispose il sacerdote al Gritti, che l'oracolo per maggiormente contentarlo, non gli avea data la risposta incerta, ma con la pittura più chiara delle parole, avea risposto che la libertà veneziana allora sarebbe mancata, che la città di Venegia si fosse ridotta in terra ferma.

(T. Boccalini, *Ragguagli di Parnaso*, vol. III, no. 44, abbreviated)

(Andrea Gritti, the former doge of Venice, seeing major innovations in the government of his republic in these modern times, began to greatly fear that the forecasts of the imminent end of Venice's famous and ancient republican constitution were true. So a few days ago he went to the delphic oracle and begged him to kindly tell him whether the Venetian Republic, which he had always believed would last until the end of the world, was going to come to an end, and if so when. Beside the statue of Apollo he saw appear a panorama, which he could easily tell from the cities he saw portrayed in it—Bergamo, Padua, Vicenza, Verona, and even Venice herself—was a representation of the territories which the Venetians govern on the mainland. But he was greatly surprised to see that Venice was depicted, not surrounded by lagoons as she actually is, but rather in the middle of a green countryside. Unable to believe that this picture, drawn by a divine hand, was so completely in error, he complained sharply to the priest of the temple that the oracle had thought him unworthy of a straightforward reply. The priest replied that the oracle, in its desire to please him, was far from having given him an ambiguous response, for, with a picture which spoke more clearly than words, it had replied that the Venetian Republic would come to an end only when Venice herself became part of the mainland.)

Introduction

In the first chapter of this book I have tried to clarify the meaning of Sarpi's *Pensieri* on religion and to establish the intellectual context within which they were written. In this and the next chapter we will be looking at Sarpi's activities as state theologian, historian, member of the republic of letters, Protestant conspirator. We will see who Sarpi's friends were and learn something about his enemies. I hope that it will become evident that Sarpi's activities are explicable in terms of the beliefs and principles outlined in the *Pensieri*, and that no other set of beliefs and principles can explain the full range of those activities. Sarpi, I will suggest, was trying to give practical implementation to the ideas he had expressed in private: his political activities were intended to subvert religious authority in general; his published works were intended to undermine the intellectual foundations of religious argument.

Sarpi's political and intellectual activities do not immediately betray his underlying motives and objectives, and this is so, I would contend, because they were intended not to. The problem lies in establishing what his objectives were, or in demonstrating that he had no consistent objectives. With the *Pensieri* the real difficulty lies not in determining what they mean, but in establishing what importance Sarpi gave to them. So, too, when it comes to Sarpi's public activities, it is much easier to establish what he did than it is to determine what significance his actions had in his own eyes.

In chapter 3 I will be putting forward interpretations of Sarpi's *History of Benefices*, his *History of the Council of Trent* and his dealings with Protestants in terms both of the significance they had for his contemporaries and of the significance they must have had for Sarpi himself. In this chapter I want to examine Sarpi's polemics in defence of Venice during the crisis of the Interdict of 1606–7, and along with them a number of problems which arise from Sarpi's deep involvement in Venetian political life. We will start, then, with an account of the arguments put forward by Sarpi and his leading antagonist, Cardinal Bellarmine. This will lead us on the one hand to a consideration of the Church's role in Venetian society, and on the other to a discussion of Sarpi's place in the Gallican intellectual tradition. At each point we will find that Sarpi's polemics betray a common origin with the *Pensieri*.

Bellarmine can stand as a representative of the Catholic Church's attacks upon the theological principles espoused by Venice and enunciated by Sarpi. Amongst the many anti-Venetian polemicists, however, three set out to demonstrate the political dangers of Venice's policies, and of these three one, Tommaso Campanella, insisted that the inevitable outcome of Venice's policies was the creation of a society of moral atheists. Campanella understood little about Venetian politics, but he had known Sarpi, and his tract – unpublished at the time – is of interest in that it provides a direct link between the themes of the *Pensieri* and the principles adopted by Venice during the Interdict.

The last two sections of this chapter will turn from the polemics of the Interdict to consider the question of the influence of Venetian political life upon Sarpi. We will look first of all at Sarpi's closest associates in Venetian politics, and try and establish whether they shared his values. That they did share them has been assumed by those who have seen Sarpi as the spokesman of a united phalanx within the Venetian patriciate referred to as the *giovani*, the young men. From this perspective, Sarpi's later publications are a mere development of the attitude towards the Church expressed by Sarpi, on behalf of the *giovani*, in 1606. For us, starting not with Sarpi's polemics but with his *Pensieri*, the link presumed to exist between Sarpi's beliefs and those of the Venetian patriciate must remain open to question, for few can have shared the extraordinary views expressed in the *Pensieri*. In any case, as I have sought to show elsewhere, the *giovani*'s unity and their common commitment to a shared set of political values is more a matter of historical myth than of reality.[1] If Sarpi's views were shared by others it was by a few individuals, not by a political group.

In the last section we will start from the obvious fact that Sarpi was for years surrounded by politicians debating political affairs in the characteristically Venetian language of reason of state, and proceed to enquire how far this tradition of discourse, and above all its intellectual formulation in terms of Tacitism, may have influenced Sarpi's historical writing. Between Sarpi's *History of Trent* and his polemics during the Interdict there took place, however, a transformation in Sarpi's viewpoint. In 1606 he believed that the defence of Venice might lead to the realisation of his ideals, and he imagined that Venice's actions could transform the religious map of Europe. The historian of Trent, however, had largely abandoned his hopes of reform in Venice. Consequently, he upheld no positive ideal, and he appealed not for European support for a particular political community, but for a general reassessment of the Catholic Church's history. Had Sarpi continued to place his hopes in Venice it would have been impossible for him to write so negative a work as the *History of Trent* for he would have had a concrete set of institutions and traditions to defend.

The years after the Interdict were thus to make Sarpi something more than a political spokesman, but they were also to make him for the first time aware of himself as what would now be termed an alienated intellectual. A central theme of the *Pensieri* is the gap between the private opinions of the wise man and the popular commonplaces to which he pays lip service. Nevertheless, during the Interdict crisis Sarpi was, by his own testimony, optimistic, for an intimate correspondence seemed to have been established between his own views and the policies of the Venetian ruling elite.[2] Sarpi's optimism was made possible by a fundamental misunderstanding about the nature of Venetian society, a misunderstanding shared by many of his Venetian contemporaries. Once events had betrayed Sarpi's hopes, he could no longer be content with returning to the company of a few intellectuals of similar persuasion. His ambition was to restore that lost moment of collaboration between philosophy and political power, and this ambition distracted him from science and philosophy, isolating him in the process from the intellectual world in which he had been at home.

The defence of Venice

There was nothing novel about the causes of the Venetian Interdict.[3] Venice had in 1603 extended to the Terraferma, the mainland territories, long-established laws preventing land from passing into ecclesiastical possession which had previously applied only to the immediate area of the city itself. Ostensibly she was concerned that an extension of clerical landownership would threaten the state's revenues, for ecclesiastical lands were exempt from most taxes.[4] This was an issue on which Venice was bound to be peculiarly sensitive, since declining revenues from harbour tolls meant that she was increasingly dependent on taxes levied on landed wealth.[5] Almost as important perhaps was the desire of Venetian nobles to prevent the Church from investing its wealth in Terraferma land at a time when large numbers of nobles were moving funds out of trade and state bonds into land: the liquidation of the state debt had recently freed large quantities of money, both secular and ecclesiastical, for reinvestment.[6] This was the central issue of the conflict, but there were others, notably the Venetian state's claim to try clergy guilty of serious crimes.

Just as there was nothing novel about the causes of the conflict, which had been the occasion for tension between Church and state throughout the Middle Ages, so there was no need for Venice to adopt novel arguments in her own defence. The first pamphlet Sarpi issued was a tract by the conciliarist theologian Jean Gerson (1362–1428), while Sarpi's own arguments were correctly characterised by his opponents as being very similar to those of Marsilio of Padua (1270–1342).[7]

It is with surprise then that we find the great bulk of the Catholic propaganda against Venice harping on a single theme: the Protestant character of Sarpi's arguments. The man so recently accused of discussing Machiavelli and Pomponazzi is suddenly presented as plotting a Lutheran Reformation. The truth of the matter, though, is that there is nothing Protestant about Sarpi's arguments during the Interdict. He is quick to admit the supremacy of the papacy in matters of faith, but concerned to maintain that rulers hold their power directly from God, and that therefore the clergy have no authority in matters of secular jurisdiction, being entitled only to freely preach the Gospel. Sarpi's claim was that the Interdict revolved around questions not of faith but of secular jurisdiction: that clerical immunity from secular jurisdiction was a revocable privilege granted by secular rulers, not a liberty protected by divine law, and that the secular ruler's right to pursue the public good entitled him to command his subjects not to make bequests to the Church.[8]

If Sarpi's arguments were labelled Protestant rather than *politique* this was for two reasons. Firstly, the Church's claim was that the dispute involved questions of divine law and papal authority. Much Catholic propaganda had insisted that the root of Protestantism was simply disobedience to the papacy and had attacked any claim that the individual was entitled to judge questions of faith for himself. Disobedience was thus presented as the defining characteristic of heresy. Moreover it was often said that the secular ruler's desire to lay their hands on Church wealth had made it possible for the Reformers to win official support, and Venice's policies were taken to reflect a similar covetousness.[9] But secondly, and most importantly, the central aim of Roman policy was to persuade Spain, and if possible France, to support the papacy. Particularly disturbing was the reluctance of Philip III of Spain to take sides. In face, then, of the Venetian claim to be defending the interests of all secular rulers, the curia had no option but to insist that, far from being intrepid defenders of secular authority, like the *politiques*, the Venetians were Protestants in disguise, and therefore a real threat to the religious and political peace of Italy, and especially of the duchy of Milan.[10] Moreover at the beginning of 1606 Henri IV's influence in Rome was at its height and French relations with Rome particularly close. The papacy stood to gain nothing by pointing out the similarity between the views of the Venetians and those of the Gallicans and risked checking the progress of catholicisation in France. If the Venetian Interdict was to tempt the French into the Counter-Reformation camp, then it must seem to be directed against Protestant and not Gallican heresy.

Such motives could not be avowed, but they need to be taken into account when reading the propaganda of the period. Let us take, for example, Bellarmine's attacks on Sarpi. 'Father Paul', he writes, 'seems to me to resemble a disciple of Luther more than he does a friar of the order of Servites. And I believe that my opinion on such a matter deserves to be taken seriously, for I have spent much of my life reading Lutheran books in order to refute them.'[11] Bellarmine's evidence of Sarpi's Lutheranism is that Sarpi wishes to reduce clerical authority to the preaching of the word of God; that his arguments imply a rejection of all spiritual obligations which are not immediately directed to the soul's spiritual welfare, such as compulsory fasts and the celibacy of the priesthood; that he holds that secular jurisdiction extends over the clergy; and that the abuses of the Church need reform for they stand in the way of man's salvation. Bellarmine had heard other heretics speak of abuses in the same manner as Sarpi:

and when one goes into the matter further and finds out what the abuses they are referring to are, one finds that they regard as abuses the sacrifice of the Mass, the celibacy of the priesthood, fasting at Lent, the invocation of saints, prayers for the dead, the veneration of images, and other practices which they have abolished on the pretext that they are abuses. And don't tell me that the theologians of Venice make no mention of these things, for everything can't be done at once, and in England too no mention was made of these things at first.[12]

Certainly Bellarmine was correct in insisting that Sarpi's emphasis on the spiritual welfare of the individual soul was a threat to the institutions and practices of the Catholic Church. But it was no part of Sarpi's purpose to put forward views which were in any way peculiar to Protestantism. Venice hoped to win, and succeeded in winning, the support of English Protestants and French Huguenots. But, while arousing hopes in these quarters, Sarpi's main objective was to win the support of French Gallicans and all those who wished to resist the progress of the Counter-Reformation. One of the hallmarks of the Gallican and eirenicist school which had so influenced Sarpi was its willingness to emphasise the corruption of the Church and to call in question the theological doctrines which separated Catholics from Protestants. The Catholic Pierre de Belloy, in his *Apologie Catholique* of 1585, had been willing to deny that the Protestants had ever been satisfactorily convicted of heresy and to attack the corruption born of the wealth of the Church.[13] Two years earlier Jacques Faye d'Espesse had with his *Advertissement sur la réception et publication du Concile de Trente* rallied the resistance of the Parlement to the reception of the Council of Trent in France. He had had no hesitation in attacking the doctrinal rigidities of the Tridentine faith:

I ask you how many Catholics there are today...who are completely above suspicion? For all without exception recognise that there are an infinity of abuses in the Church and long for their reformation. Moreover most of us hold that the doctrines which the Council demands we believe as necessary for salvation are either doubtful or indifferent, for if we look into our consciences, how many of us would go to the stake for the doctrines of purgatory, of the invocation of saints, of the withholding of the chalice from the laity, of Corpus Christi, of the veneration of images, for a million different ceremonies, and surely even fewer of us would do so in defence of the primacy of the papacy or of indulgences. Yet all these are laid down as articles of faith necessay for salvation by the Council of Trent. If those who do not believe in them are to be anathematised, then the history of the Inquisition will resemble that of the Thirty Tyrants of Athens. At the beginning they put the guilty to death, and everyone was delighted. A few days later they fell upon the finest citizens, and every one discovered themselves to be guilty.[14]

It was this tradition of argument within which Sarpi's polemics in defence of Venice placed themselves, a tradition of argument which constantly held open the prospect of a break with Rome, without ever committing itself to the Protestant camp. And it was not just Sarpi, but this whole tradition which Bellarmine wished to convict of heresy. In France, indeed, the progress of Catholicisation since the conversion of Henri had placed the Gallicans and eirenicists on the defensive. Even so, the Venetian ambassador in Paris was able to arrange for a number of tracts to be written in defence of Venice, while the upheaval caused by the Interdict was to give Sarpi's French counterparts a new energy and a new, if temporary, optimism.

Bellarmine's attack on Sarpi thus had to be, implicitly, a defence of the fundamental doctrines of the Counter-Reformation. For this purpose the moderation which had characterised his *Controversies* was of little use. Indeed Bellarmine's replies to Sarpi serve to indicate how the Venetian Interdict took place against a background of an increasingly well-defined and intolerant Counter-Reformation theology which had taken form as much in the years after Trent as at Trent itself. The first edition of the *Controversies* had been completed thirty years after the closure of the Council, in 1593. In it Bellarmine had adopted a liberal position on three questions of crucial importance: the authority of the pope over temporal kingdoms, which he held to be indirect, not direct; the authority of the pope over the Council, which he held to be open to debate; and the freedom of the priesthood from secular jurisdiction in temporal matters, which he held to be *de iure humano*, not *divino*. On this last point the Venetians were eager to quote Bellarmine in their defence, although as early as 1599, in a revised edition of the *Controversies*, he had retreated from his earlier position, while by 1606 he was in no doubt as to the authority of the pope over a General Council.[15] He maintained his stand only on the doctrine of indirect power, but he was now little concerned to emphasise, as he had been before, the difference in character between secular and spiritual authority.[16]

Bellarmine had intended the *Controversies* to show the coherence of the Church's tradition teaching as expressed by the great theologians of previous ages, and its conformity with the Bible. By 'resolving' authorities, Bellarmine sought to demonstrate that within what appeared to be a mass of conflicting opinions there existed a single and unquestionable orthodoxy. In the context of the Interdict crisis this conception of an historically and philosophically grounded theology appeared an irrelevance. Bellarmine was forced to substitute for it the view that 'heresies properly speaking have their origin in disobedience to the papacy'.[17] Theological controversy thus gave way to the rhetoric of obedience.

Sarpi had insisted on a radical distinction between secular and religious authority. The one must be obeyed without question and could bind the conscience, the other need be obeyed only in spiritual matters, and only after its commands had been privately considered and were felt to be in accord with the dictates of conscience. Sarpi's argument was based on a double presumption. In the first place he argued on the basis of a concept of sovereignty, which was probably drawn from Bodin, that if the authority of the ruler was not absolute and unquestionable it was effectively non-existent. In the second, he took it that the secular authority was concerned only with the general good, and was thus entitled to override the objections of individuals, while the spiritual authority was concerned only with the good of the individual soul, and must therefore work through the individual conscience. Bellarmine attacked both of these presumptions, insisting that sovereign authorities are not in fact absolute or unchecked, and that secular rulers are sometimes concerned with the interests of individuals, for example when legislating regarding private property, while the spiritual authorities have to take into account the interests not only of individuals, but also of the Universal Church.

Bellarmine may be thought to have had the better of the argument of these two issues, but his purpose in insisting on the similarities between secular and spiritual authority was to stress their common interest in the preaching of obedience, an obedience which, as he had put it in his reply to Venice's state theologians, is

more perfect, and more pleasing to God, when it is unhesitating, without the order being examined, or any attempt being made to establish the superior's reasons for giving it, the mere fact of being commanded being sufficient...and if you object, that if there is any doubt as to whether what is being commanded involves acting sinfully then it is necessary to examine the order if one is not to run the risk of committing a sin, then I will reply to you, with St Bernard, that when the order is not manifestly sinful, then there is no need to examine it, for there is no risk of acting sinfully, for the responsibility lies with the superior, and the subject must presuppose his instructions are good ones.[18]

Despite the responsibility borne by the superior, however, the abuse of power is a lesser sin than disobedience, for the one destroys good government, while the other destroys all government; the one injures the body politic in a limb, while the other injures the head. Sarpi on the other hand, once more trying to draw an unduly simple distinction between the public and the private, the general and the particular, had argued that the abuse of power was more sinful than disobedience, since the one was a public evil, the other a private vice. Certainly he would not have wanted to see such an analysis applied to the relationship between Venice and her subjects.

The Church in Venetian society

Behind the debate between Bellarmine and Sarpi lies the central issue of the Interdict, for Sarpi had not reached the conclusions expressed in his meditations on the *tora* in a vacuum. The view that the state could survive without the support of the Church, and even if opposed by it, had become widely disseminated within the Venetian patriciate. It was, as I have sought to demonstrate elsewhere, the fundamental assumption underlying Venetian policy in 1606. Where the rest of Europe believed in the necessity of cooperation between Church and state Venice was unconvinced of that necessity.[19] Hence her stubborn unwillingness to compromise, which so amazed a pragmatist like Henri IV.[20] Hence her extraordinary refusal – questioned by pro-clerical nobles without effect – to pay pensions to Roman cardinals: such bribes were reserved for the infidel court of Constantinople.[21]

Why was Venice confident that she could afford to ignore Bellarmine's warning that heresy leads to political ruin? Part of the answer lies in the peculiarity of Venetian social institutions. In Venice itself a remarkably high proportion of the population was directly employed by the state, whose power of patronage was enormous, ranging from the nobility to the workers of the arsenal.[22] Although the population of Venice was devout – Confraternities of the Sacred Sacrament had sprung up in nearly every parish – it was well aware that its security in this world derived from institutions – the hospitals, the Scuole Grandi, and the other charitable institutions – which were under lay not clerical control, and subject to state, not episcopal supervision.[23] Indeed Venice had successfully insisted at the time of the apostolic visitation of 1581 that, despite the decrees of Trent, such institutions should be exempt from clerical inspection.[24] Venetian workers were, moreover, relatively well paid, with no urgent reason for discontent.[25] The clergy of Venice, on the other hand, were poor and ill-educated, and were in no position to exercise a decisive influence upon the views of the population at large.

It is true that for some members of the nobility the Church represented an important source of wealth. But bishoprics and other high offices in the Church seemed to be monopolised by a small and powerful group within the nobility: the mass of nobles, far from looking to the Church for advancement, resented the advantages enjoyed by those who had access to clerical office.[26] There was one ecclesiastical institution that did play a crucial role in the life of the nobility: it was the nunnery, where daughters whom the family could not afford to dower were sent. Like the Scuole Grandi the nunneries were closely supervised by the secular authorities, and exempted from the apostolic visitation of 1581.[27] But, strangely enough, it seems that the Venetians did not rely upon the Church to support younger sons.[28] Traditionally brothers in Venetian noble society continued to live in the same household. A high proportion of them could never afford to marry, but they sought to bring wealth to the family by business activities or service to the state, rather than retiring to a monastery or seeking clerical preferment.[29] Only a tiny minority of the Venetian nobility were *papalini*, that is men with brothers or sons holding clerical office: the proportion would surely have been greater for any other ruling nobility in Europe.[30]

The Venetians thus had good grounds for being confident in their own ability to stand firm against ecclesiastical sanctions. But they had no good reason to assume that the peoples of the Terraferma would take a similar attitude. It was widely believed that the Terraferma nobility felt threatened by the expansion of Venetian landholding. They certainly had reason to fear the consequences of the Republic's declining revenues from taxes on trade, and increasingly their local independence seems to have been coming under attack from the Venetian state.[31] It is quite possible too that they were more closely integrated into the Church than the Venetian nobility: the two criminous clerics, a canon and an abbot, whose arrest was one of the causes of the Interdict, were of noble family. Certainly the Church had a much more active role to play in Terraferma society.

It is true that the Venetians sought (although not entirely successfully) to exclude the clergy from the administration of charitable institutions.[32] But the Church had asserted its right to oversee such institutions with greater success than in Venice itself: St Charles Borromeo had visited the hospitals and *monti di pietà* of Bergamo in 1575.[33] Even more important was the innovative role played by the clergy when it came to charitable institutions. Much of the Terraferma lay within the archdiocese of Milan, and looked to Borromeo's reforms for models not only of piety but also of charity.[34] But elsewhere too the clergy had an independent role to play. In Verona for example a number of reforming bishops – especially Giberti and Valier – had proposed reforms in the administration of poor relief to the secular authorities, and had played an active role in ensuring the implementation of their plans.[35]

Above all though – and this was the grievance on which contemporaries laid most stress – the Terraferma nobility were excluded from all important offices under the Republic. The *cittadini originari* of Venice could aspire to posts of high standing in the Republic's bureaucracy. The nobility of the Terraferma, however, were largely excluded from the Republic's armed forces – Venice preferred to employ mercenary troops – and from the highest ranks of the Venetian Church. As a consequence they looked elsewhere for advancement, entering the service of foreign princes or pursuing careers in the Roman curia. It is not surprising that many of them were thought to have concluded that they would be better off under the imperial administration to which large parts of the Terraferma had in the past been subjected.[36]

Venice's failure to foresee the response of the nobility of the Terraferma to the Interdict was the consequence of a curious narrowness of vision. In part the Venetians failed to give full weight to the economic and strategic importance of the Terraferma because they had failed to adjust their outlook to the new situation resulting from the decline of trade and the growing importance of landholding and income from office. In part they could not afford to recognise the grievances of their subjects without making concessions at the expense of the Venetian patriciate themselves. But for whatever reason their eyes seem to have remained fixed on the reassuring institutions of the Dominante until events forced them to look inland. Sarpi himself typifies this narrow, almost parochial outlook. In his polemics he laid much stress on the Church's wealth which, far from benefiting society at large, benefited only a privileged elite. Such arguments were more likely to impress the nobility of Venice than that of Verona, where the Church's charitable intentions had been made clear, or France, where the wealth of the Church was felt in large measure to be at the service of the state. The *Pensieri* are thus the work of a Venetian who had not paused to consider the differences between the lagoonal world of Venice and the *terra firma* of the mainland. The Venetian nobility might increasingly draw their income from land and office-holding, and might increasingly adopt the manners, dress and recreations of a landed nobility, but their relationship to the Church was quite different from that of other nobilities. It was this which made it possible for Sarpi to imagine a society without a *tora*; it was Venice's mainland territories which made the realisation of that dream impossible.

Sarpi and Pierre de Belloy

The social context and the political climate within which the *Pensieri* and the Interdict polemics were written is essential for any explanation of their originality. But Sarpi's thought was also always closely linked to an intellectual tradition. The sharp contrast that Sarpi drew in the polemics of the Interdict conflict between the corruption of the Roman Church, which was seeking to usurp secular authority because its preoccupations were worldly ones, and the poverty and humility of the early Church partly reflected the contrast between the wealth and magnificence of the prelates of the curia and the penury and low social standing of the parochial clergy of Venice, but it was also indebted to a tradition of *politique* argument.[37] The frontispiece of Sarpi's reply to Bellarmine was an illustration of the Biblical text, 'My kingdom is not of this world.'[38] Sarpi's understanding of this text undermined the very concept of an established Church, and in doing so went beyond what was needed in a defence of Venice's claims, and beyond the limits of properly Gallican argument.

We have already encountered a contrast between Church and state, spirituality and worldliness, persuasion and compulsion similar to that drawn by Sarpi in the pair of *politique* texts we examined earlier, *De la vraye constitution de l'estat* and *De la concorde de l'estat*. It is unlikely that Sarpi knew these texts, but he may well have known Pierre de Belloy's *Apologie Catholique*, since it had provoked an important pamphlet debate. If he did know it he must certainly have been delighted by de Belloy's insistence that Christ's kingdom is not of this world. A comparison of de Belloy's views with those of two important Gallican writers, Pithou and Richer, will serve to bring out the distinctively *politique* character of Sarpi's arguments.

Pierre Pithou wrote *Les libertez de l'Eglise Gallicaine* after Henri IV's absolution at St Denis, but before his absolution by the papacy. At this time the schismatic tendencies always fostered by the Parlement were at their most evident, and were supported even by a section of the clergy and by the grand council.[39] Pithou, whose book was approved by the Parlement and the Sorbonne, was opposed in principle to the idea of a schism, hoping instead that it would be possible for pope and king to establish a measure of mutual understanding on the basis of an acceptance of Gallican principles. His task, then, is to give a definition of the minimum principles of Gallicanism which will serve to protect French independence and the king's right to pursue a policy of toleration. To this end he reduces Gallicanism to two fundamental principles:

The first is that the pope can neither command nor order anything, whether in general or in particular, which has to do with the temporal affairs of the lands and estates which owe obedience to and recognise the sovereignty of the Most Christian King. And if he does command or legislate anything of the sort, the subjects of the King, even if they are clerics, are not required to obey him. The second is that although the Pope is recognised as the supreme authority in spiritual matters, even so in France the papacy has no absolute and infinite power, being restricted and checked in its exercise of power by the canons and rules of the ancient councils of the Church recognised in this kingdom, and this in particular guarantees the liberty of the Gallican Church.[40]

The key to this definition is the compromise embodied in the second, and crucial, clause. Three authorities are recognised in questions of spiritual jurisdiction: pope, councils and monarchy (along with the Parlement, which would have to register the reception of the decrees of a Council). But none of these authorities is given absolute power, each being checked by the others.

A much more radical position is that adopted by Edmund Richer in *A Treatise of Ecclesiasticall and Politic Power* (1612). Richer's book was written at the moment of another crisis: after Henri's assassination and during the resultant parliamentary reaction against ultramontanism, Richer's book provided the theoretical justification for the campaign for a *loy fondamentale*, to be based on James I's oath of allegiance, for the persecution of the Jesuits, and for the burning of Bellarmine's *Controversies*. Employing the principles of Gallicanism to establish a general theory of the Church, Richer reached the following conclusions:

[that] all Ecclesiastical power belongs properly, essentially and first to the Church; but to the Pope and other Bishops instrumentally, and ministerially, and only so far as it concerns the exercising,...
[that] since the evangelical law has no other end but everlasting life, and the soul of man for his matter and natural subject, it ought wholly to apply itself about the direction of the inward motions of the conscience, but no ways in any outward force or violence; and therefore judges only of means necessary to salvation, conformably to the essential and spiritual causes of Christian religion; that is, persuasively only, and directively, in preaching of the Word, administration of the Sacraments, and, if need require, exclusion of Communion with the Church,...
[that] since the civil power is the lord of the commonwealth and country, protector and defender of the divine, natural and canonical law, and to that end does bear the sword, it is he alone that has the power of constraining and restraining, by inflicting corporal punishment. Therefore, for the good of the Church and execution of Ecclesiastical canons, he may make laws...[41]

There is no trace of compromise here. All jurisdiction is now monopolised by the monarchy. 'Ecclesiastical power' and 'evangelical law' are not worldly forms of authority. Despite this extension of royal authority, however, ecclesiastical canons continue to be enforced where appropriate. The king has become the protector and defender of every aspect of divine law.

This, however, had not been true in an earlier, *politique* work: Pierre de

Belloy's *Apologie Catholique* of 1585, written before the death of Henri III in defence of the right of Henri of Navarre to succeed to the throne, despite the papal bull excluding him from the succession on the grounds that he was a relapsed heretic. De Belloy's concern to defend the right of a heretic to succeed means that he has to protect religion from state interference. In his view the ruler has the right to employ the goods and property of the Church for the benefit of the state, and to control the Church's charitable activities. He has the right, too, to discipline the clergy. But his sphere of authority is restricted to the protection of his subjects' secular welfare. The moral and spiritual welfare of individuals cannot be protected by compulsion, for faith cannot be forced, and an act ceases to be moral if it is not free. The law of God, therefore, in so far as it is concerned with the salvation of the individual, not the welfare of society, must not be enforced in this world. God must be left to judge for himself what constitutes an infringement of that law.

In short, to put it in a word, there are two sorts of jurisdiction. One of them is worldly and is exercised by kings and princes. To them all sorts of people must obey, of whatever order or quality they may be, laymen or clerics, priests, bishops or popes...The other type of jurisdiction is administered in heaven, and for it we must await the judgement of God.[42]

In 1591, after the death of Henri III, but before Henri IV's conversion, Bellarmine wrote a reply to the *Apologie Catholique*, in which he attacked de Belloy's insistence that God's law, in so far as it is concerned with the spiritual welfare of the individual, is not to be enforced here on earth: 'What is this, if not an outright denial that God has laid down any law at all, properly speaking? And that any commandment of God's can be broken without punishment? Nor can there be any real sin, if only warnings and admonitions, not true laws, are set aside.'[43] For Bellarmine, divine law must be seen to carry penalties. His fear is evidently that if God is simply seen as issuing good advice for the individual's welfare, there will be no justification for hell fire. If God is not to be made to seem unjust, the authorities of this world must be less, and not more, forgiving than he. De Belloy's arguments are thus taken to undermine the whole idea of a providential God, and to justify suspecting him of 'atheism'.[44]

It is de Belloy's position, not Pithou's, nor what was to be Richer's, which Sarpi adopted during the Interdict. He presents the state as being concerned only with the general welfare, not individual interests, and insists that the subject's spiritual welfare is simply a matter for his private conscience. Neither de Belloy's argument, nor Sarpi's, is secular, in that both insist on the divine right of kings. But de Belloy does effectively deny the need for an established, authoritative Church. His position is much more liberal than that adopted in the Edict of Nantes, which recognised two legal Churches, but left heresy and unbelief in general subject to both secular and ecclesiastical sanctions. For de

Belloy, by contrast, the secular ruler is only entitled to punish heresy if he believes it to be seditious. A ruler who oversteps these bounds cannot be deposed, even if he persecutes the true Church. But de Belloy is willing to recognise a certain right of resistance in defence of freedom of conscience.[45]

De Belloy's and Sarpi's arguments can be presented as a defence of freedom of thought and of the independence of religion from politics.[46] But in Sarpi this independence is no more than an aspiration, for he recognises no right of resistance. In his view the state's decision as to what is in the general interest cannot be questioned, so that if the state wishes to control the spiritual lives of its subjects and interfere with their consciences it may do so. This view, implicit in the Interdict polemics, is clearly expressed in two letters which Sarpi wrote to the Gallican Jacques Gillot on the subject of William Barclay's *de Potestate Papae* (1609). Barclay had argued that the pope had no authority, direct or indirect, in temporal affairs, but that he retained full authority in spiritual affairs. The king and the pope were thus two independent authorities, with no rights over each other, but both subject to God. Sarpi objects that if this were the case then there would be no single sovereign authority in the state. There must be, he insists, a single human authority, be it king or parliament, with untrammelled authority, and God cannot be introduced as a *deus ex machina* as a substitute for such an authority. Any form of ecclesiastical authority that may exist must therefore derive from the state.

Alongside the authority of the state, Sarpi recognises the existence of a purely spiritual Church, concerned with the salvation of men's souls through persuasion. This Church is *tutto celeste*, while the state is *esclusivamente terreno*, a terminology which corresponds to de Belloy's. In this context Sarpi insists on a quotation from St Paul which he also employed in the *Pensieri sulla religione*: 'The society of Christians is in heaven.'[47]

But what if the state seeks to interfere in spiritual matters? In the first of the two letters Sarpi dealt directly with this problem:

I deny absolutely and unequivocally that any prince, or any human authority, can present an obstacle to the Church's ministry. 'The gates of hell will not prevail.' The facts themselves show that in the past tyrants have not been able to hinder the Christian faith, although they have made it illegal, have tortured Christians and put them to death, and have employed every possible means against them. Indeed these persecutions led to the expansion of the Church. What need is there to prevent persecution if it benefits the Church? There is no need for the clergy to have the power to prevent things which do their cause no harm. But on the other hand if a clergyman abuses his spiritual authority, think what confusion he can bring about in a state! Think how many obstacles he may place in the way of a wise political administration, of a monarch!...Consequently God, who has given the ruler the task of ruling the state, has given to him all the power he needs to restrain ecclesiastics who seek to abuse Christ's authority to the detriment of the state.[48]

In principle, then, religion and politics deal with quite separate issues, but in practice the state must be given complete authority over the Church. In order to defend this position Sarpi has to appeal to a providentialist view of history: persecutions directed against the true Church are doomed to failure, while those directed against the abuse of spiritual authority are liable to succeed. The position Sarpi adopts on the question of the jurisdictional authority of Church and state can be interpreted in two ways. Sarpi might have come to believe in the purely spiritual Christianity portrayed in the *Pensieri sulla religione* as being characteristic of the Church of the apostles, and have come, in addition, to accept a providentialist view of history which is quite incompatible with the views expressed in the *Pensieri*. Or else Sarpi is seeking in his letters to Gillot to give veiled expression to two of the central principles of the *Pensieri*: on the one hand the state must be free to employ religion for political purposes as a medicine; on the other the state need not rely on this medicine, and if it chooses not to, doctrinal, authoritarian religion will be superseded by a spiritual and natural religion, a religion which will provide few obstacles to the truths of philosophy. In the second case, which seems to me the only likely one, it is evident that Sarpi would indeed have wished to persuade Gillot to reject the arguments of Barclay, who admitted the existence of two parallel types of jurisdiction, and to reject even the view of the medieval defenders of imperial authority, the view which Richer was to adopt, which gave the sovereign authority in spiritual matters. Instead he was bound to uphold the view that the sovereign has absolute authority in all matters, but that that authority is in no way spiritual. If this is the case, Sarpi's appeal to the values of the primitive Church was founded in a conviction of their polemical force, and of their relative compatibility with philosophical truth.

Our study of the polemical position adopted by Sarpi during the Interdict crisis suggests then that he had a triple purpose. In the first place, his aim was to rally as wide a body of opinion as possible to resist the pretensions of the papacy. In the second place, he may well have wished to prepare the ground for a schism between Venice and Rome: he was certainly not aiming to make a negotiated compromise possible. In the third place, though, and much more cautiously, he may have been seeking to cast doubt on the need for an established, authoritarian Church, and to suggest the possibility that the state might choose to allow a complete freedom of conscience in spiritual matters. In short, there is nothing to suggest that the author of the Interdict polemics differs in any way from the author of the *Pensieri*.

Campanella's *Antiveneti*

Although the great majority of Catholic polemicists followed Bellarmine in concentrating on the theological problems posed by Venice's refusal to recognise the Interdict, there were three Catholic polemicists who addressed themselves to political as well as theological issues: they were Possevino, a prominent Jesuit who had been expelled from Venice along with the rest of his order; Campanella, whom we have already encountered; and an otherwise obscure figure, Balthasar Nardi. These authors were convinced that the Venetians' preoccupation with politics and reason of state made it necessary to confront them with the political consequences of disobedience to the papacy. As a conseqence their polemics touched on many of the issues which were of actual concern to Venetian politicians, and, in the case of Campanella, who, as we have seen, knew something of Sarpi's real views, of concern to Sarpi himself.

Possevino was concerned to exploit the discontent of the Terraferma nobility: amongst his publications was a letter urging revolt which masqueraded as being from the city of Verona.[49] Possevino, having lived in Venice, was well placed to identify and seek to exacerbate the most serious of the tensions within Venetian society. Nardi and Campanella, on the other hand, sought to provide what were in large part conventional analyses of the political factors that the Venetian patriciate should take into account. If both emphasised the danger of revolt it was not because their intention was to bring about a revolt, but because they wished to persuade the Venetian senate to change its policies. Nardi argued that there was a real danger of a revolt in Venice itself. There the people had been corrupted by the coming and going of men of all nations, while the citizen class had good reason to be aggrieved that they were excluded from high office, and were capable of providing effective leadership for a revolt.[50] Campanella, who had himself once sought to organise a popular uprising, believed that the real danger came from the peasantry.

It seems likely that Nardi, even if his sense of the social tensions in Venetian society was less acute than Possevino's, had excellent up-to-date political information, for he stressed the divisions within the patriciate caused by the gap between the wealthy and the poor nobles, and the rise of a faction of relatively poor, relatively young men associated with the doge, Leonardo Donà, and capable of dominating the senate. Indeed his attack on Donà mirrors those in circulation in Venice at the time: he emphasises, along with the threat of revolt, the danger that Donà will employ the militia under his brother's command to give himself absolute authority.[51]

Campanella and Nardi also emphasised a number of other topics which were highly relevant to the debates taking place within the Venetian senate during the Interdict crisis. Both were concerned to stress that Rome was the bulwark of Italian liberty, for without her Italy would fall under Spanish domination, and to argue that Venice would be unable to obtain adequate support from other powers to wage an effective war. Both too were concerned to defend ecclesiastical wealth, Campanella going beyond a defence of the Church's charitable role to claim – inaccurately, unfortunately – that ecclesiastical wealth was in effect the common property of all Venetian nobles, for all their families stood to benefit from the incomes that could be derived from ecclesiastical appointments.[52] For us the real interest of these tracts, however, lies in Campanella's treatment of the question of the political role of religion.

Both Campanella and Nardi were concerned to make the most of a commonplace of anti-Machiavellian polemics: the need for the secular ruler to respect the Church if he is to retain a secure hold on power. Nardi committed himself to the providentialist arguments which had been pioneered by Bellarmine and taken up by Possevino and Ribadeneyra in their well-known attacks on Machiavellism. On the one hand Machiavelli was rejected for implying that religion was to be subordinated to Utilitarian considerations, while on the other it was claimed that God guaranteed worldly prosperity to the faithful ruler, or, as Nardi claimed, that Christ would repay one hundred times, even in this world, all gifts to the Church.[53] As in many other polemics of this sort, the ancient Romans were presented as an example of astute piety, and both Campanella and Nardi insisted, as others had done, that God had punished the Romans when they had turned against their Gods, Campanella claiming that their sin lay in rejecting what they believed to be true. But while Campanella agreed with Nardi in arguing that providence was concerned to protect faithful rulers, his argument implied that providence simply cooperated with natural political forces, thus bringing him in line with the essentially rationalist tradition of reason of state argument pioneered by Botero, who had argued the need for cooperation with the Church in largely secular terms, stressing the political importance of religion in general, and the political superiority of the Catholic Church to other Churches.[54] Campanella, indeed, was concerned to present his arguments in a rationalist, if far from secular form. He justified the use of astrological predictions suggesting that the times were unfavourable to republics on the grounds that astrology was a science unreasonably neglected by the Machiavellians, while he defended his application of Biblical prophecies regarding Tyre and Egypt to Venice by appeal to 'the principle of physics' that like conforms to like.[55]

Campanella's argument is of particular interest, however, because he is concerned to attack not just Machiavellian reason of state but also atheism. He insists that if Venice breaks from Rome she will be driven into the arms of the Protestants and forced to accept the Protestant doctrine of the servitude of the will. This will cause her subjects to revolt, for a change in religion always brings about a change in government, which is something Venice's subjects already have sufficient reason to long for:

You are no saints, and the nobility treat the common people like slaves. Little by little, by one method or another, all the farms and wealth of the Terraferma have fallen into the hands of the Venetian nobility, and the peasants look at you with a jaundiced eye, and while you are sleeping comfortably in your villas or your boats, the peasants say: 'See how fat they have become, and how thin we are. O God, what can we do! Is it not shameful to serve such sluggards!' Then they go to confession, and the priest tells them off, and says that they must let things be and obey their superiors, even if they are wicked, as St Peter has commanded, and that in the next world it is they who will be the masters, and their present masters will be subjected to them. But you Venetians now tell them not to believe what the priests tell them, and they, losing hope of Paradise, will want to have the wealth and estates of this world, like you, and will do their best to bring about a change, for to the peasant any change seems to be for the better.[56]

Campanella, however, was not concerned merely to insist on the need for continuity in religion. He wanted to insist on the peculiar dangers of the doctrine of the servitude of the will, which Bruno before him had singled out as incompatible with good government.[57] To teach the servitude of the will is to teach that men are not responsible for their actions. This has evil consequences both for religion and for politics. It makes God the author of sin, and this eventually leads to the rejection of any providential deity. Such atheism is indeed to be preferred to belief in an evil God: Campanella here formulates the paradox which was to the starting point of Bayle's *Pensées diverses*. But in politics the consequences are equally disastrous. For if people are told they are not responsible for their actions, then they no longer see any reason to obey the constituted authorities. A society in which this doctrine is acceptable must tend therefore either to tyranny, which will alone suffice to keep the populace in place, or else to a disordered popular government in which the very principle of subordination is denied. It is true that these consequences may be offset by the stupidity of the people – this has happened in northern Europe – or by their fear of neighbouring states, but such factors will not be at work in the case of Venice. The Venetian Republic, which is in fact a narrow oligarchy, can thus only hope to avoid denegrating into a despotism or a democracy by insisting on the truth of Catholic doctrine.

Campanella's argument is based on a premise which Sarpi would have accepted: that the doctrine of free-will is a necessary precondition for the effective exercise of clerical control over human behaviour. It was precisely for this reason that Sarpi insisted so strongly on the servitude of the will and on the need to have a low opinion of human nature.[58] Where Sarpi and Campanella differed was over the question of whether an acceptable political regime could be sustained where the authority of the clergy had been undermined.

Part of the reason for this, I have suggested, lay in the fact that Campanella had foremost in mind the society of the Terraferma, Sarpi that of the Dominante. Campanella was less astute than Possevino and Nardi in identifying the social tensions that would force Venice to make concessions – albeit limited ones – to the papacy. But, perhaps because he knew Sarpi's real views, he alone identified the central problem as being that of the role of religion in maintaining social order, and he alone insisted that Venice's policies must logically culminate in the creation of a society of moral atheists – an outcome he viewed with horror.

Campanella's argument thus centres, like Bellarmine's, on the question of obedience to authority. For Bellarmine the authorities of Church and state are interdependent, for to question either one is to undermine authority in general. But in the last analysis the authority of the Church is superior, for it alone derives directly from God and concerns itself with the welfare of man's immortal soul. Campanella, confining himself to political arguments, insists that it is the Church's promise of heavenly bliss in return for good behaviour which is alone capable of sustaining political authority. Venice had failed to take account of this, and it was this general error, rather than any particular set of grievances on the part of Venice's subjects, which would be her undoing. Campanella was not alone in regarding this as the moral of the Interdict crisis. Shortly after the Interdict ended, Antonio Querini, one of Venice's leading politicians, and the only Venetian noble to publish a tract in defence of the policies which had given rise to the Interdict, wrote a history of the Interdict crisis. Querini's conclusion was that Venice had seriously miscalculated in failing to give due consideration to the Church's role in preserving political stability, but he, like Campanella, failed to link the general question of the Church's moral authority to the particular problem of the grievances of the nobilities of Venice and the Terraferma, grievances which had been so clearly identified by Possevino and Nardi.[59] To historians of our day, at any rate, it must seem that Querini, Sarpi and their associates had erred not in failing to give due weight to the fear of hell as a factor in politics, but in failing to give due consideration to the conflicts which existed within Venetian society.

Sarpi: isolated intellectual or representative Venetian?

That an error had been made was apparent by December 1606, nine months after the proclamation of the Interdict. War between Venice and Rome was at hand, and each was hoping for international support. Venice's resolve, however, was dangerously undermined by the growing realisation that she could not trust the nobility of the Terraferma. Were the pope to release them from their obligation of obedience, as he was entitled to do once the Interdict had been in force a year, Venice might well lose control of her Terraferma dominions, as she had in 1509 when attacked by the league of Cambrai.[60] In those days, however, the Venetian nobility had drawn its wealth primarily from the sea: to lose the Terraferma now would be to lose a great part of the nobility's income and the prospect of further economic expansion.

Faced by this development, the nobility, which had hitherto been largely united in its hostility to the papacy's claims, split into opposing camps. On one hand were those who, for all their opposition to the papacy's views on clerical immunity and ecclesiastical acquisition of land, saw the Church as a guarantor of political stability and Rome as a potential ally against Spain. On the other were the *malestanti*, the poorer and less well-placed nobles, who aspired to earn a living from holding state office, and who sought to improve their position through war and and the expansion of state power.[61]

Sarpi's *Pensieri* on the *tora* had their origin in concrete social and political realities, in particular the secular control of charitable institutions in Venice and the existence within the Venetian nobility of a substantial group of discontented nobles, committed to anti-clerical policies and to the expansion of state power. It was these factors which made it seem that the state could survive even in the face of ecclesiastical opposition. It was the weakness of Venice's grasp on the Terraferma, however, which more than anything else made Sarpi's ideals unrealisable. In April 1607 Venice and Rome agreed to a compromise which satisfied neither of them. At first there was the prospect that the conflict would imminently recommence, but as this prospect faded Sarpi had to look to international developments to bring about the destruction of clerical authority, and this in turn meant that the defence of Venice, such as he had undertaken in the Interdict polemics and in the *History of the Interdict*, rapidly ceased to be Sarpi's main preoccupation. The peculiar detachment which one encounters in the *History of the Council of Trent* is the product of this disappointment. The political defeat of the anti-clerical *giovani*, whose power base lay amongst the *malestanti*, freed Sarpi of the obligation to defend a 'Venetian' view of the Church. Had Sarpi not seen the world from a narrowly Venetian point of view he could never have written the *Pensieri*. Had he not come to feel that Venice no longer epitomised the struggle against clerical authority he could not have come to write the *History of Trent*.

Was this process of emotional estrangement a mere reflection of Sarpi's progressive detachment from the Venetian ruling elite? Certainly the Interdict crisis divided the anti-clericals against themselves. The doge, Leonardo Donà, and his close associate Antonio Querini had been in the forefront of the opposition to Rome, but it was they who came to be the leading exponents of a policy of, at the least limited, concessions. But it is doubtful if Sarpi had had much in common with Donà and Querini to begin with: Donà at any rate was fiercely anti-Protestant and even pro-Spanish.[62] What the crisis of the Interdict did do, far from cutting Sarpi's ties with the Venetian patriciate, was establish a close alliance between him and a number of prominent Venetian politicians who had inherited from Donà the task of leading the anti-clerical forces.

Most prominent among them was Nicolò Contarini, one of the leaders of the intransigeants in 1607. As a young man he had written a philosophical study which emphasised the extent of human ignorance and the weakness of man's intellectual capacities, but which expressed a firm commitment to doctrinal orthodoxy.[63] In the years before the Interdict Contarini had been less anti-clerical than Querini, but after the Interdict he was the leading exponent of Sarpi's policy of alliance with the Protestant powers.[64] There is some evidence that he had undergone a change of heart: he seems at any rate to have wished to disown his youthful expressions of orthodoxy.[65] It may be that he had come to believe that only the Protestants were likely to provide unwavering support against Spain, whom he had regarded as a more serious threat than Rome in the years before the Interdict.[66] In favour of the first view is the approval he expressed in the History he wrote as official historian of Venice for the fatalism of Islam, an approval which is reminiscent of Sarpi's advocacy of the doctrine of predestination.[67]

Second after Contarini amongst Sarpi's allies was Pietro Priuli, Venetian ambassador to France at the time of the Interdict. Priuli was a whole-hearted supporter of resistance to Rome, and when he returned from his embassy he summarised for the benefit of the senate the principles of French Gallicanism in terms which could only serve to emphasise the similarity between Gallicanism and the views propounded by Sarpi during the Interdict. Priuli, however, unlike Contarini, was not unconditionally in favour of alliance with the Protestant powers.[68]

This cannot be said about the third of Sarpi's associates, Antonio Foscarini, who replaced Priuli as ambassador to France and was then posted as ambassador to England. Foscarini was a young man who looked to Sarpi for political guidance. Unfortunately he lacked Sarpi's astuteness and his gift for dissimulation. His dispatches from France were transparent in their intent to foster alliances between Venice and the other anti-Habsburg and anti-curial powers, while his close association with Protestants lost him the trust of the French court. He was later to be accused by his chaplain of scoffing at religion and of being an atheist. Perhaps he was, although there is no evidence that he and Sarpi confided in each other on such matters. In the end he was strangled on suspicion of collaboration with Spain. The suspicion was unfounded, but the trial had been in secret and there was no appeal. His body was found dangling by the feet in St Mark's Square one morning, before it was known that charges had been brought against him.[68]

Nicolò Contarini, Pietro Priuli and Antonio Foscarini were all members of the political elite. Contarini was to become, late in life, doge. Others amongst Sarpi's associates were less prominent. Particularly interesting is the case of Giovanni Francesco Sagredo, a friend of Galileo's and a determined opponent of Aristotelian physics. He was also committed to the defence of the Republic's jurisdictional rights and shared Sarpi's loathing of the Jesuits. When he was on his deathbed he refused to say confession, and his anxious brother turned to Sarpi in an attempt to persuade him to change his mind.[70] Three years later Sarpi himself was to die, having refused, his friends claimed, to say confession or to receive extreme unction.[71]

Others amongst Sarpi's friendships are indicative of a network of shared values. Sarpi had Montaigne's essay on friendship translated, for example, for two friends whose devotion to each other was famous.[72] But it is impossible for us to tell how far such friendships were based on shared philosophical views and a common attitude to religion. We know that a number of nobles attended the discussion group which met at the house of Gerhard Nis, but who they were, and to what extent they shared Sarpi's values, we cannot tell. Certainly it would be wrong to think that everyone with whom Sarpi was in some way associated shared his views. He corresponded, for example, on the most amicable terms with Francesco Priuli, ambassador to Spain at the time of the Interdict. But Priuli was sympathetic to Spain and keen to establish better relations with Rome.[73]

Any attempt to discuss Sarpi's political allies and intellectual associates must stop short of definite conclusions. But it might be thought that the correct approach towards an understanding of Sarpi lies in attempting a more general appraisal of Venetian political and intellectual life. It has been argued that Venice, in standing firm against the absolutism of Spain and the intellectual totalitarianism of Rome, was defending republican values. These values were particularly cherished by the *giovani* who were radicals only in the sense of being militants in the defence of established values, and it was these values to which Sarpi, as spokesman of the anti-clericals, gave expression during the Interdict crisis. Sarpi thus comes to be identified with Venice, his private beliefs with his public obligations.[74]

What is notable, though, is that the evidence we have regarding the views of otherwise anonymous politicians who supported the intransigeants during the Interdict – 'L.B.', for example, a speech of whose was published in French, or 'B.M.' who wrote a chronicle of the period – suggests that many of the supporters of anti-clerical policies had little interest in questions of religion or sovereignty.[75] They simply wished to see Venice pursue 'noble' and 'generous' policies and relished the thought of war. It is the common dependence of men like Donà, Contarini and Sarpi on the support of such men which explains how the pious Donà and the infidel Sarpi could have been the most prominent representatives of the Republic's views in 1606, for what held the *giovani* together as a group was not a community of values but a common willingness to appeal to the prejudices of the poorer nobles. One of those prejudices was anti-clericalism, but equally important was the commitment of the ordinary nobles to the expansion of state power. What made Sarpi an acceptable spokesman for the group as a whole was not only his uncompromising opposition to the papacy, but also his willingness to adopt the rhetoric of absolutism, not republicanism.

Venice was a republic, and was widely regarded as a model of republican liberty.[76] Because there was a widely held 'myth of Venice', it is easy to assume that the Venetians shared the view others held of them. But the days when Contarini could portray the Venetian constitution as an ideal combination of democracy, aristocracy and monarchy had passed. Foreigners were struck by the inadequacy of the traditional myth of Venice as they became aware that many young and poor nobles were adopting the manners of the nobilities of the great absolutist states, going about armed, riding horses, engaging in duels.[77] Nardi and Campanella in 1607 saw the Venetian nobility as a narrow and selfish interest group. In 1612 the anonymous *Squitinio della libertà Venetiana* was published, which portrayed Venice as a despotic government which granted no liberty to its subjects.[78] The marquess of Bedmar, erstwhile Spanish ambassador to Venice, expelled in 1618 for supposedly plotting against the Republic, wrote several famous accounts of Venice in which he emphasised the petty tyranny exercised by the nobility over their subjects.[79] The change in the mores of the nobility clearly reflected the shift from investment in trade to the purchase of estates. This was not sufficient to completely destroy the myth of Venice amongst foreigners: it was kept alive by Boccalini for example. But it does seem to have almost entirely destroyed among the Venetians themselves. The *Tract on the Venetian Republic*, on which Acton placed such emphasis, seems to have been written by a Venetian, yet it advocated a despotic government of precisely the kind that Venice's opponents had come increasingly to portray, and it is only with difficulty that one can find evidence of the survival of republican ideals amongst the Venetian nobility of the early seventeenth century.[80]

Sarpi's political polemics in 1606–7 were expressed in terms of princes, not republics, and although they in no way attacked the idea of a corporate prince, they certainly implied a Bodinian contempt for any theory of a mixed constitution. Moreover the absolutism of Sarpi's political philosophy cannot be separated from its political context. Prominent anti-clericals were suspected on at least two occasions – Donà in 1606 and Renier Zeno in 1627 – of seeking to appeal to the disaffected minor nobility in order to undermine the Republic and establish a dictatorial government.[81] In such a context the rhetoric of absolutism must have seemed like an attack on traditional values. The nobles who appealed to those traditional values, invoking the nobility of old, who were peaceful, sea-going and frugal, were the opponents of the *giovani*.[82] The nearest thing to a republican political gesture I have come across is attributable to one of them, Ottaviano Bon, who had contempt for the manners of the young nobles and took the traditional values of the Republic seriously. Bon, having served a six-month term of office as a *savio del consiglio*, refused to continue to wear the insignia of his former status, as had become the custom, insisting on dressing like an ordinary noble. Where Donà had been accused of Caesarism he was accused of putting himself in the role of Cato. His reward was to suffer the indignity of election to an inferior office.[83]

Historians have not taken account of the threat to republican values posed by the *giovani* because the *giovani* had in 1582 'reformed' the Council of Ten, taking power away from a narrow oligarchy and returning it to the senate and the Maggior Consiglio.[84] This attack on oligarchy may have been accompanied by a temporary espousal of republican values, but it depended for its success on those nobles who stood to benefit from the adoption of authoritarian policies towards the Terraferma. It was absolutist sovereignty, not republican liberty, to which the *giovani* committed themselves in 1606, and some nobles at least feared that this would lead to the exercise of despotic authority, not merely over the subjects of the Terraferma, who had traditionally been protected from the exercise of any untrammelled sovereign authority by a whole network of municipal assemblies and independent courts, but even over the nobility themselves.

Sarpi's Interdict polemics suggest that he was concerned to win the support not only of the monarchs of Europe, but also of the discontented nobles who, it was suspected, might have preferred a dictatorship to a republic. If this is so Sarpi's polemics were works of party propaganda which must have horrified the traditionalist *vecchi* and the nobility of the Terraferma towns. They may indeed have contributed to the collapse in the unity of the Republic which took place in December 1606, when the nobility turned on each other, and the Terraferma turned on the Dominante. In this situation the polemics of Nardi and Campanella, who claimed that Venice was faced with the prospect of dictatorship or anarchy, must have seemed more to the point than those which concentrated on the supposed threat of Protestant Reformation.

As Campanella had suspected, it was not simply Sarpi's espousal of a Bodinian concept of sovereignty which gave an absolutist tone to his thought, for the ideal of a secular state formulated in the *Pensieri* had been expressed in absolutist terms. Sarpi's insistence that there could be no objective standard of ethics had meant that he had had to present the law as a set of arbitrary commands which must be obeyed in the end out of fear.[85] Moreover the supremacy of the state as the mechanism for the correction of human defects meant that every aspect of life, including religion and ethics, ought to be brought under political control. It was only because Sarpi conceived of the state in such absolutist terms that he believed it could effectively exercise authority without the support of the *tora*. What we do not know, though, is whether Sarpi had ever asked himself whether the complex, interlocking mechanisms of the Venetian constitution were adapted to the exercise of such arbitrary power.[86] Nor, at this point in time, can we hope to judge whether the fears of the *vecchi* were justified or misplaced. What is clear is that Sarpi's definition of sovereignty was calculated to appeal not just to men like Pietro Priuli, but also to the hotheads like 'L.B.'. Sarpi may thus be seen to have written as a party politician, even though his ideas and aspirations went beyond those of his party.

Tacitism

Because all adult male Venetian nobles were entitled to engage in political activity – and most of them, indeed, were engaged in the pursuit of political office – political life in Venice was more intense than anywhere else in Europe. A natural consequence of this was a nearly universal preoccupation with *ragione di stato*, reason of state.

The principles of reason of state theory were often explicitly invoked by Venetian politicians, above all the simple principle that rulers must act according to the inflexible rules of self-interest.[87] Sarpi could not have moved in Venetian political circles without learning to think and argue in terms of reason of state. Despite this, it is difficult to place Sarpi in an adequate context when it comes to the literature of reason of state, for although we know some of the books he read, there is little evidence as to what he thought of them.[88] There need be little doubt, though, as to the tradition of political discussion by which Sarpi must have been most deeply influenced. When it was a question of political philosophy, Sarpi drew his inspiration from the *politiques*. When it was a question of political analysis we may safely assume that Sarpi drew part of his inspiration at least from the Tacitists.

The term Tacitism is one which needs to be used with care. In the first place it refers to those who commented upon, and drew inspiration from, Tacitus. But the popularity of Tacitus, in the years after the publication of the first books of the *Annals* (first published in 1515) and above all after the publication of Lipsius' classic text in 1574, owed much to two factors, aside from the availability of a complete and comprehensible text.[89]

First, the attacks on Machiavelli mounted by both Protestants and Catholics meant that those who wished to discuss the topics he had dealt with had to do so while appearing to be independent of him. Tacitus provided the best disguise for covert Machiavellism, for Machiavellian precepts could be found in Tacitus, especially in his account of the policies of Tiberius, or, where they were lacking, could plausibly be attributed to him. But Tacitism was something more than covert Machiavellism. The decline of the Italian republics, the growing domination of Spain over the Italian peninsula, and the consolidation of the petty absolutisms of the Medici, of Savoy, Modena, and so forth, meant that Machiavelli's authority, Livy, no longer seemed to speak to the times. It was Tacitus, the moralising historian of a corrupt despotism, not Livy, the historian of the republic, who seemed to provide an appropriate model for imitation.[90]

The predominant importance of Tacitus within Italian, and indeed European, discussions of reason of state in the late sixteenth and early seventeenth centuries has made it seem possible to identify Tacitism with reason of state theory in general, and to claim, on the one hand that Tacitism was the political philosophy of the Counter-Reformation state, and on the other that it was the philosophy of those who admired Venice and hated Spain.[91] Such generalisations pay scant attention to who was, and who was not, willing to call himself Tacitist. For our purposes Tacitism may be identified with the views of three of the most distinguished of Tacitus' admirers, who may be said to constitute the main stream of Tacitism: Lipsius, Ammirato and Boccalini. A very brief exploration of the views of these three writers will serve to bring out the similarities and the contrasts between Sarpi and the Tacitists, and will cast further light, both on Sarpi's irreligion, and on the decline of Venetian republicanism.

Sarpi would have known of Lipsius' Christian stoicism, which had influenced Charron. Lipsius did not influence Charron, however, only when it came to his treatment of religion. Much of Charron's extensive discussion of politics and reason of state was drawn from Lipsius' *Six Books of the Commonwealth* (1589). This book may be said to have three central themes: the seditious character of the populace; the dangers of religious dissension; and the need for politicians to obey, rather than flout, the law of nature. Lipsius was willing, however, to recognise that in the face of a seditious and potentially heretical populace, the ruler might have to employ methods which Machiavelli would have approved. Even so, 'we must enterprise these matters with fear: God, even God, does he not oppose himself openly?' Moreover the willingness of rulers to lay aside the principles of natural law certainly exacerbated the natural unruliness of the mob:

And surely I do freely confess that whereas Europe is troubled with so many commotions, that kings and kingdoms do burn with the flame of sedition and war, peradventure the true and just cause is that the government of the most part of them is not just and right. They corrupt public laws, they drive justice from them, not fearing the word of God, therefore does He rightly foresake them that leave him, and for these causes does He daily send to them woe and will not cease to afflict them.[92]

It was because he found a similar combination of moralism and realism in Tacitus that Lipsius admired him.[93]

Lipsius does not hesitate to appeal to the word of God, but it is piety in general, not Christianity in particular, that Lipsius believes provides the only basis for political stability. God rewards piety – witness the history of the Romans – and what is required of the politician is not that he should seek out the true religion but that he should remain loyal to the religion of his ancestors, which will encourage unity and obedience in his subjects. For Lipsius, as for Charron, the true religion cannot be expressed in outward observances. Indeed the central principles underlying Charron's treatment of religion – the distinction between superstition and true piety, and the secular analysis of cults and creeds – derive from Lipsius, who insists that superstition is

an utter enemy to religion. Whereunto (being inclined by default of nature) we are the rather drawn by those, to whom it brings profit and commodity. Neither do great ones hinder this because they are certainly persuaded nothing has more force to range the multitude in better order than superstition, which we ought to eschew and avoid, for after it has once seized on our hearts, we are never at rest, this difference being between religion and superstition that the religious person does love God, the superstitious dreads Him...Imprint this golden sentence in your mind, the best sacrifice we can offer to God is a pure heart. And yet we must not altogether condemn external things, although the most part of them (as one will have it) pertain rather to custom, than to the substance of religion. But a wise man will observe them as enjoined and commanded by laws (not as acceptable of themselves to God) if they be not manifestly wicked and impious: otherwise we ought to yield to religion, and not stubbornly reject the use and custom allowed of in the commonwealth wherein we live. Moreover, take not too much delight in vain words and frivolous questions, but set forward in the way of well-doing, for the whole religion of Christians consists in living without blame and reproach.[94]

Here, as in his discussion of stoic philosophy, it is a natural, non-providential religion that Lipsius might seem to have in mind. It is not surprising that he was often accused of atheism, an accusation to which his own frequent and almost casual changes of religious affiliation leant support.[95]

If we turn to Ammirato, we find he shares the central preoccupations of Lipsius. He too is a humanist, though where Lipsius was one of the greatest scholars of his age, Ammirato's humanism is often no more than a device for self-protection, since his determination to confine himself to examples from Roman history and to avoid any reference to current events makes it very difficult to pin him down. He too fears the common people and is willing to make concessions to Machiavellian methods, while at the same time warning of the 'dolcezza di dominare' which leads rulers to do whatever they like without concern for right and wrong, and insisting that rulers who object to the criticisms of historians like Guicciardini have only their own misconduct to blame. Above all he too praises the piety of the Romans, as if there was little to be gained from a knowledge of the truths of Christianity, and he too comes close to advocating a natural rather than a revealed religion. In his chapter 'Dell'antica religione umanamente parlandone' Ammirato argues that all men have a natural knowledge of things divine. All peoples agree on God's existence, His inestimable goodness, his providence, on man's free-will, God's enforcement of a moral code, and the prospect of punishment and reward in a life after death. Indeed the precepts of natural law are agreed on by all religions. Whoever looks at the question historically will see that all religions share a common origin, and can be traced back to the first times. In essentials, the worship of images aside, the religions of the Jews and the gentiles are in conformity with each other, and the decrees of Numa coincide with those of Moses. The same consent is to be found regarding the person of Christ. There may be disagreement regarding Christ's divinity, but all, even the Mohammedans, agree that he was good, wise and endowed with miraculous powers. There would then seem to be, humanly speaking at any rate, nothing special about Christianity.[96]

In Boccalini too we find these same characteristics.[97] He too fears the common people, for popular disorder merely leads to tyranny and Caesarism. He too criticises the immorality of the absolutist governments of Europe – indeed he is by far the most savage critic of absolutism. And he too betrays a certain religious scepticism, which is apparent in his treatment of Protestantism. Boccalini's account of Protestantism was part and parcel of his unremitting – in print at least – hostility to the Habsburgs. In his view Spanish power rested upon the gold of the Americas and upon Spain's ability to associate her own imperialist interests with those of Catholicism. In order to avoid being oppressed by the emperor the German princes invented 'the pitch of heresy, which makes the fires of rebellion blaze up so fiercely that they cannot be put out'. They were then imitated by William of Nassau, who was faced with the prospect of the effective establishment of Spanish absolutism in the Netherlands.[98] But even though they were the cause of the Reformation, the Habsburgs had still managed to take advantage of it. They had given support first to the Huguenots and then to the League in France, so debilitating the French crown that they had long been in a position to exercise as much authority in Rome as in Milan. The roots of Protestantism were thus not religious discontent but imperial oppression. One might deplore the *ateismo politico* which led to the abuse of religion for political purposes, but both sides were equally guilty of this. And on the merits of the political conflict there could be no room for hesitation: the German and Dutch Protestants were deserving of uninhibited support. Were they to be successful in defeating the Habsburgs, Protestantism would lose its reason for existence and the Protestants would become amenable to rational argument.[99] Indeed it would be possible to solve all religious disagreements by persuasion, were it not for the tendency of religion to be employed to legitimise purely political discontents.[100]

Boccalini is thus willing to give a purely secular account of religious disagreement. What he longs for is the reunification of Christendom and the depoliticisation of Christianity, but this goal can only be attained if Spain is defeated and Italy liberated. Boccalini does not cast doubt on the unique importance of the Christian revelation, but he does insist, like many of the *politiques*, that Christianity is not a religion designed to fulfill political purposes: the one truly political religion is Islam, which is tailor-made to the needs of the government.[101]

Lipsius, Ammirato and Boccalini are debating the same issues as the Gallicans and *politiques*. Like Charron, Lipsius seems to doubt whether belief in divine punishment may not be superstitious though necessary. Ammirato on the other hand adopts the position of the *Vraye et légitime constitution de l'estat*: the principles of natural law and divine providence are common to all men, and predate the idiosyncracies of any particular religious creed. Boccalini, as we shall see, also holds this view, but in addition his arguments are reminiscent of those of de Belloy, who had treated the Catholicism of the Council of Trent as no more than a device to conceal Spanish political interests, and who had insisted that heresy should be tolerated except in so far as it constituted a political threat. Their views are not identical, but each of them is willing to adopt a detached and sceptical attitude to Christian doctrine, though not to question the necessity of piety for political stability.

The association of Tacitism with religious scepticism is difficult to explain. In part it seems to derive from the persistence within Tacitism of a Machiavellian view of religion as a political device to be subjected to political analysis. In part it may derive from a wider tradition of pagan humanism and of esoteric scholarship which regards Christianity as only one religion amongst many.[102] But in part too the mainstream of Tacitism may represent a continuation of Erasmian political philosophy and of Erasmian piety within the altered circumstances of the post-Reformation world.[103] Like Erasmianism Tacitism subjected governments to moral criticism whilst admitting that a moral political order is almost inconceivable. Like Erasmianism Tacitism placed emphasis on piety and morality at the expense of doctrine and revelation. But the Reformation had made the position of the Christian humanists untenable, and Tacitism was not nourished by the Gospel message in the way that Erasmianism had been. The Tacitists are perhaps best seen, then, as the heirs of a number of different humanist traditions, all of which were hostile to doctrinal religion.

Because the Tacitists demonstrated that rulers were bound, out of political necessity, to occasionally employ the techniques of Machiavelli, they were felt to be a threat to stable government. Their moral criticism of absolutism might encourage revolt, while their reluctant defence of Machiavellism could only weaken men's confidence in government. Tacitism was thus quickly subjected to the same barrage of criticism as had been directed against Machiavellism.[104] In 1627, for example, Boccalini's posthumous *Commentaries on Tacitus* were ruled to be unsuitable for publication by the Venetian Council of Ten, on the grounds that not only would individual governments, especially Rome and Spain, take exception to Boccalini's account of their policies, but all governments would be endangered by the public discussion of the secrets of reason of state.[105] Boccalini's book was held to be suitable only for restricted circulation amongst those employed in giving counsel to rulers, and this indeed reflected a process whereby Tacitism became the secret wisdom of government circles. French libertines like Naudé, for example, were Tacitists.[106] Thus just as deism was held to be subversive if popularly disseminated, but acceptable as part of the philosophy of men of state, so Tacitism lost its critical associations as it became an esoteric doctrine, confined to the proponents of absolutism.

Sarpi must surely have been drawn to Tacitism by its association with stoicism and religious scepticism. But evidently he would have accepted the view that it was wrong to expose the motives and methods of rulers. Late in life he expressed his adherence to this viewpoint in a memorandum to the Venetian senate, justifying it in terms of the divine right theory of kingship: 'a ruler, who has no superior apart from God, is not required to give an account of the reasons underlying his actions, and everyone is bound to believe them to be just and reasonable; for those who wish to condemn rulers and sit in judgment upon them offend God, usurping what He has reserved to Himself, for He is the sole judge of sovereign rulers'.[107] In the *History of the Interdict* and the *History of the Council of Trent*, Sarpi thus avoided giving any detailed analysis of the motives or characters of secular rulers. On the other hand, Sarpi was keen to apply the methods of Tacitism to the history of the Church, exposing the motives and methods not of secular rulers but of the papacy and the prelates. It was precisely because Tacitism was held to encourage one to distrust the established authorities that its methods must have seemed to be so well-adapted to Sarpi's purposes when it came to the writing of Church history.

Sarpi as a historian of the Church stands in a tradition descending from Tacitism. Sarpi's attitude to secular governments on the other hand is one of respect. Here the strongest contrast has to be drawn between Sarpi and his contemporary Boccalini. Boccalini had been an official in the papal administration. After he came to Venice and accepted a Venetian pension to write in praise of the Republic he continued to recognise Borghese, the nephew of Paul V, as his patron. Apart from the praise of Venice and the analysis of Venice's legendary stability, the central theme in his *Ragguagli di Parnaso*, reports on events in Parnassus, was provided by his hatred of Spain.[108] Nevertheless, he continued to be on close, even compromising, terms with the Spanish ambassador. Boccalini is a complex and a contradictory character. Increasingly, however, he has come to be presented as a fatalist and a pessimist, a man whose love of republicanism was flawed by his conviction that nothing could in practice be done to bring about the liberation of Italy. I believe, though, that this emphasis on the strain of resignation in Boccalini's writings has distracted attention from his most original contribution to the defence of republican liberty.

Boccalini's resignation had its origin in his belief that it was impossible for monarchies to reform themselves. There was quite simply no such thing as a good king:

Good kings, who deserve the title of God's lieutenants on earth, who *sint instar Deorum*, are longed for, and are portrayed by authors, but they are like the Sirens, the Hipographs, the Tritons and the Unicorns, who are also described and depicted. They are fabulous and do not exist.[109]

All that one could hope for therefore was the destruction of monarchy itself. In the context of this ambition Venice was a source of disappointment. She might be the model of republican stability, far superior to ancient Rome, but she was too conservative to declare war on the principle of monarchy.

Boccalini's originality lay in his belief that in northern Europe a quite new type of democratic republicanism had been born. The democracies which horrified Campanella were the objects of Boccalini's admiration:

The Germans, who are as skilful and excellent in the art of constructing republics as they are in those of inventing and constructing mechanical instruments, are the first and only people in the whole human race to have been able to discover the amazing knack of making a peaceful democracy, one which is governed prudently and according to the law.[110]

Those German republics which have provided a model for the Dutch are likely to provide an inspiration for all peoples to throw off monarchical rule. Republicanism, by controlling ambition at home and the urge to imperial conquest abroad, transforms politics and, consequently, the principles of reason of state. On the first day that a people acquire their liberty 'foreign nations become their compatriots, and the subjects and citizens of enemy states become their dear friends'.[118]

The only hope for absolutism then, in face of the internationalism of democratic republicanism, is that all princes should unite in its defence. But such a unity cannot be attained, for the fundamental principle of absolutism is individual ambition, and the conflicting efforts of princes at self-aggrandisement necessarily prevent them from recognising their common interests. The princes are in any case at a disadvantage, for no mercenary army, no matter how large, can defeat free men fighting for their liberty. Moreover, the democratic republics offer not only liberty but also equality. Absolutist governments, in order to stay in power, have to foster inequality and ignorance. Republican governments have to encourage equality and learning.[112] Republicanism also brings in the rule of law in place of government by arbitrary decree, and opens up the prospect of an authentic freedom of conscience, for since there are no suppressed political discontents within a democratic republic, religion ceases to be employed as a pretext for sedition.[113] It is not surprising then that the two social systems are irreconcilable, nor that the prospects for the victory of republicanism are good, for 'what more cruel and pernicious enemy could a monarch encounter than he who attacks him with the most powerful of all weapons, the claim to have the intention of granting their liberty to an enslaved people...liberty which all men so greatly love, as by an instinct of nature'.[114]

The only weakness of republicanism is the success of absolutist governments in nurturing a debased populace. The seditious mob, which Boccalini fears as much as the next man, is itself the product of the corruption of absolutist government.[115] Its lawlessness does not prove the impracticality of democratic citizenship.

Boccalini's vision of a militant, democratic republicanism was one he was unable to hold to consistently throughout his work. But it was a unique and valuable ideal. All Boccalini writes reflects his longing for political liberty. He thus presents a most striking contrast to Sarpi, whose objective is not political but intellectual liberty. Like the author of *De la vraye et legitime constitution de l'estat*, and like Bayle, Sarpi believed that only by bolstering up the arbitrary power of the state could one create the conditions for intellectual freedom. Boccalini's conception of liberty would have meant nothing to Sarpi. For Sarpi the Germans and the Dutch were to be admired for their assault on papal tyranny, not on monarchy. In his view the nature of man necessitated the etablishment of an arbitrary authority if social life was to be possible. Ideally that arbitrary authority would not depend upon a superstitious Church. Ideally too it would impose its will no more than was necessary to ensure stability, for otherwise it would be tyrannical. But even the well-adjusted state could not be characterised as free.

For Sarpi there were two alternatives: anarchy, which would be ideal if men could cope with it, and government founded on the principle of absolute sovereign authority.[116] That there might be some difference between political freedom and political servitude, he, the inhabitant of a republic (although a man, of course, without political rights), seems never to have paused to consider. But, as Boccalini realised, it was impossible to combine any serious consideration of such problems with unquestioning loyalty to Venice. Even the defence of the rule of law would have seemed subversive in a state where the partiality betrayed by tribunals was notorious, and where secret courts regularly sent people 'for a drink', that is to say drowned them, without even informing their friends and relatives.[117] Boccalini might pretend to see the rule of law upheld in Venice, but he knew that in reality the republican ideal and Venetian practice did not coincide. In writing of Venice it was the ideal, rather than the reality, which he sought to keep before his readers' eyes, for the ideal of liberty he pursued was one incompatible with arbitrary and absolute government. He deserves, in fact, a rather more prominent place in the history of freedom than he has generally been given. All too often he has been overshadowed by Sarpi, who deserves a place in any history of free thought, but none in a history of political liberty.

CONFIRMATIONE
DELLE
CONSIDERATIONI
DEL P. M. PAVLO DI VENETIA
Contra le oppositioni.

DEL R. P. M. GIO. ANTONIO BOVIO
CARMELITANO.

Di M. Fulgentio Bresciano Seruita.

OVE SI DIMOSTRA COPIOSAMENTE
qual sia la vera libertà Ecclesiastica,
& la potestà data da Dio alli Principi.

VT SIT SICVT MAGISTER EIVS. ET SERVO

SVFFICIT DISCIPVLO

SICVT DOMINVS EIVS.

Matthæi. 10.

IN VENETIA, Appresso Ruberto Meietti. 1606.
Con Licentia de' Superiori.

3

Sarpi's place in Europe

Sarpi and the early Church

The ancient fervour of Christian charity not only moved princes and private individuals to give away worldly goods to churches, but also moved the clergy to devote those goods to pious uses. Now that this fervour has grown cold, it is no wonder that the clergy are no longer generous, but are diligent only in acquiring goods and in retaining what they have acquired. And so it has become necessary to pass laws controlling excessive acquisitions, and pious men feel a strong desire to see the use made of ecclesiastical property return to the ancient model, or at least to a tolerable compromise with it.

The defects that can be seen today did not affect all the clergy together nor all at once. From a state of absolute or divine perfection, the clergy descended step by step to that imperfection now obvious to all, which they themselves admit and which some of them consider beyond all remedy. Yet if it pleases our Lord God to give as much grace to the faithful now as He gave to our ancestors, we ought not to despair of seeing the same marvels in our age as in theirs. It was by steps that the situation became so serious, and it is by steps that it is necessary for it to improve, in order to return to the primitive perfection of the Holy Church. This cannot happen unless it is known how temporal goods were administered in the beginning, and how this administration came to degenerate...[1]

With these words Sarpi commenced his *History of Benefices*, a brilliantly concise work which does far more than trace the history of the administration of the Church's wealth through the ages. Sarpi's purpose is to show that the Church's wealth is the key to its moral and social character. He who understands the history of clerical wealth is in a position to understand Church history as a whole.

Sarpi shows how the early Church owned no landed wealth, and how the income it received in the way of gifts from the faithful was spent entirely on charity and on pious uses. The wealth of the Church was thus the wealth of all Christians, and to this economic order corresponded a democratic form of Church government. Under Constantine the Church was for the first time permitted to acquire landed property. At the same time the secular ruler began to take control of appointments to Church offices. Moreover, when the authority and wealth of secular rulers declined in the period after the collapse of the Roman empire in the west, rulers were tempted to grant bishoprics to courtiers and administrators. The politicisation of the episcopacy was a serious mistake, however, for the bishops soon claimed that their jurisdictional authority came by virtue of their episcopal status, not by delegation from the monarchy. Similarly, the clergy began to claim the right to control the appointment of ministers, attacking secular interference in such matters.

It was the papacy that led this campaign for clerical independence, supported by the monasteries, which wished to be independent of their bishops, and which, as the only centres of learning, were in a crucial position to give legitimacy to papal claims. As a result the status of the papacy was so greatly enhanced that it was able to usurp the right of appointment from local chapters and bishops and claim it for itself. With the right of appointment it gained the right to levy taxes of one kind or another on all appointments and on all clerical incomes, insisting that what was simony when done by others was no sin when done by the papacy. It claimed the right too to dispense with the regulations of the canon law, making possible pluralism and non-residence. Finally it claimed the right to set aside the declared wishes of testators who had left land for specific purposes, insisting that the Church's wealth belonged not to individual chapters or monasteries but to the successors of St Peter.

Thus the history of ecclesiastical wealth is the history of the decline of secular and the growth of clerical, and above all papal, authority. Just as the changing pattern in the administration of the Church's wealth reflects the changing pattern of power within the Church, so the growth of the doctrinal authority of the papacy must stem from its control of the Church's finances. The first Councils of the Church were democractic, and made no distinction between clergy and laity. Later councils were controlled by the secular rulers, and later ones still by the papacy. Thus one would naturally expect the Church's doctrines to reflect the changing distribution of power. Sarpi, of course, cannot elaborate upon this thesis, for it would mean providing a critical history of what have come to be established as the fundamental doctrines of Christianity. He confines himself to showing how the doctrines relating to clerical wealth have changed, for example the Church's teaching with regard to tithes, and to showing how the whole vocabulary of Christian discourse has been corrupted: all the faithful were once referred to as *santo* and *beato* while now only the pope is; the word 'pope' was originally applied to all the bishops; at one time every Church, that is to say, every Christian community, had its own 'patrimony', while now all ecclesiastical wealth is referred to as the 'patrimony of St Peter'.[2] Such changes in vocabulary, however, are merely reflections of an underlying reality: the process whereby the Church's wealth, which formerly was employed to the benefit of the poor and the community of the faithful, has come to be monopolised by the clergy and the court of Rome.

Sarpi's history of clerical wealth is a history of clerical corruption, of the progress of greed, simony and non-residence. If the corruption of the Church has taken place by stages – the replacement of the authority of the laity by that of the ruler; of that of the ruler by that of the clergy; and of that of the clergy by that of the pope – so, Sarpi seems to suggest in his opening paragraphs, this process should now be reversed. The first step would be to make the papacy's control of the appointment to benefices subject to the provision of canon law, and this Sarpi clearly recommends. The next would be to restore the authority of bishops and chapters. Both these reforms had only recently seemed possible. Pope Adrian VI had planned to reform the curia, while many bishops at Trent had claimed that episcopal rights and obligations were *iure divino*, and thus, by implication, that the bishops should not be subordinated to papal authority. But Sarpi's scheme is interesting because it does not stop there, just as in his *History of the Council of Trent* his sympathy with Adrian VI and with the bishops never leads him to suggest that their views deserve unqualified support. Indeed Sarpi's scheme does not even stop with the restoration of secular authority: it points to a distant goal, the restoration of the authority of the laity. It is true that that goal may not have seemed so distant, in that the parochial clergy of Venice were democratically elected.[3] But to restore the principle of popular election to all ranks of the ecclesiastical hierarchy would be to make religious doctrine subject to popular determination. By implication it would make religion in the end, as it had been for the early Church, a private, voluntary, non-political affair. Thus it would serve to disestablish the Church.

Sarpi's *History of Benefices* thus points clearly at an unavowable objective. Once take note of that objective, and its incompleteness immediately becomes evident. It does not, as I have already remarked, discuss the extent to which clerical and papal authority have perverted Christian doctrine. Equally lamentably, it does not attempt any serious discussion of Church–state relations. The period in which the state was dependent upon the episcopacy is explained in terms of the state's weakness and the Church's wealth. The same factors could be employed to explain the Church's success in winning independence from the state. But why had Constantine originally taken the disastrous step of creating an established, landed Church? In the *Pensieri* this was presented as the great turning point in the history of Christianity. In the *History of Benefices* Sarpi confines himself to showing that the Church has been corrupted by the clergy. He makes no attempt to raise the question of how far it may have been corrupted by the state's need for a *tora*, or how far the original other-worldness of Christianity, its presumption of the imminence of the Second Coming, made it unsuitable for its new role as a guide to social and political life.

In the *History of Benefices* we thus find the ideals and preoccupations of the *Pensieri* reflected not just in Sarpi's condemnation of clerical wealth, but also in his implicit criticism of the attempt by secular rulers to make use of ecclesiastical authority for their own purposes. Just as Sarpi's polemics during the Interdict pointed beyond Gallicanism to the views of a *politique* like de

Belloy, so the *History of Benefices* hints that it may be necessary to transform not only the Church, but also the state which brought it into being. What it does not do is discuss the difficulties involved in such a transformation, and this is presumably partly because such a discussion would be subversive of political order, as Tacitism was supposed to be, and partly because Sarpi's first priority is to concentrate attention on the need to attack clerical wealth and papal authority.

So far then the *History of Benefices* fits fairly neatly with the *Pensieri*, and appears to be a natural development of the analysis of Church history presented in the *Pensieri sulla religione*. But there is of course one central problem yet to be tackled. In the *Pensieri* the early Church is assessed in terms of standards drawn from elsewhere, and shown to have virtues and defects. In the *History of Benefices* it is presented as the ideal towards which all Christians must strive. Had Sarpi been converted to Christianity in the meantime? Was the critical view of Christianity adopted in the *Pensieri* no more than an intellectual exercise? It is difficult to rule out either of these possibilities completely. But it is possible, I believe, to make them both seem highly unlikely, and to suggest that Sarpi's appeal to the early Church was no more than a polemical device.[4] In order to do so we will only need to look at one striking example of Sarpi's reaction when the early Church was presented in all sincerity as an ideal to aspire to, an institution to be reconstructed in this world. But since Cardinal Jacques Davy du Perron was largely responsible for the importance the history of the early Church had come to have, and since his views provide such an exact contrast to Sarpi's, it will be worthwhile pausing to trace the career of the man who perhaps did more than any other to prevent the realisation of Sarpi's ideals.

Jacques Davy du Perron played a central role in many of the major events of French politics during the period between the death of Henri III and the acceptance by the Assembly of the French Clergy in 1615 of the decrees of the Council of Trent.[5] He instructed Henri IV in preparation for his conversion; he was the senior French representative in Rome for the negotiations for Henri's absolution by the pope; he established himself as the champion of Catholicism by his victory at the conference of Fontainebleau over Du Plessis-Mornay, 'the Huguenot pope'; he was the most influential Frenchman in Rome from December 1604 to May 1607, during which period he sought to bring the papacy into an alliance with France against Spain; and he was the leading opponent of the *loy fondamentale* proposed by the Third Estate at the Estates General of 1614 (which would have made it illegal to hold that the pope has the authority to depose a secular ruler), and an architect of the clergy's acceptance of the decrees of the Council of Trent, in defiance of the Gallicans, in 1615. This wide range of activities discloses two central preoccupations: opposition to Spain and support for the Catholicisation of France. He was thus well placed to mediate between Henri's leading ministers, the Catholic Villeroi, keen to establish good relations with Rome and willing to seek a rapprochement with Spain, and the Huguenot Sully, keen to support the Dutch and defend the interests of the Calvinist minority. But du Perron was a convert to Catholicism, and his political links were with Sully, not Villeroi, despite his reputation as Catholicism's most dangerous propagandist.[6]

Du Perron was said to be the most eloquent Frenchman of his age, and could certainly claim never to have been defeated in public theological debate. At the age of twenty-two he had preached the funeral sermon for the poet Ronsard. Then he lamented the immeasurable superiority which the Protestants had long had in religious propaganda, attributing it to their willingness to write in the vernacular and their humanist scholarship. Ronsard had been the first to make it evident that 'all the elegance and sweetness of letters' was not on the Protestant side, and it was in his footsteps that du Perron sought to follow.[7] As a young man he had taken pleasure not only in Ronsard, but also in Montaigne, Rabelais and Guicciardini. As the years went by his curiosity and his eloquence faded. His energies were devoted to a single task: the accumulation of historical evidence vindicating the authenticity of Catholic traditions. His masterwork was intended to be his book on the Eucharist which sought to show that the early Church believed in transsubstantiation.[8] But his occasional polemics are of greater interest: for many years he had his own private printing presses which he seems to have kept in almost constant action, writing as fast as they could print.

Despite du Perron's commitment to the task of Catholic propaganda, contemporaries were not slow to accuse him of hypocrisy. It is true that his conversion to Catholicism came at an opportune moment for the advancement of his own career. More damaging, and much reported, was the occasion on which, having delighted Henri III with a proof of God's existence, he immediately offered to prove God's non-existence, an offer Henri rejected in horror.[9] A Huguenot satirist went on to accuse him of being as willing to defend the Koran or the Talmud as the Christian faith.[10] Certainly his scholarship, which was genuine and laboriously won, was employed in the service of a party, not the truth. He was well aware that it would have been as easy to expose the errors of Bellarmine or Baronius as it had been to reveal those of Du Plessis-Mornay.[11] It is thus not entirely surprising that he – like so many of his famous contemporaries – was the subject of entirely conflicting accounts regarding the attitude he expressed towards the sacraments on his deathbed.[12]

Du Perron's polemics suggest more a man who took satisfaction in a job well done than a man who wrote out of personal conviction. Even his correspondence never suggests that his relations with his colleagues were ones of affection rather than mere politeness. But whatever du Perron may have believed or cared about, of one thing he was, of course, convinced, and that was that 'experience has taught us too well that human laws only, and apprehension of temporal punishments, can never serve for sufficient remedy to such evils as proceed from a perverse and corrupted imagination of religion. We must have therefore laws of conscience such as work on our souls, and keep them in fear of eternal torments.'[13] The problem with Protestantism was that it provided no adequate principle of certainty on the basis of which such laws of conscience could be founded. Because it left everything to private conviction it led to Arianism, Mohammedanism, atheism.[14] In place of the subjectivity of Protestantism du Perron presented Catholicism as a guarantor of order and stability because it was soundly based upon the traditions of the early Church, and, more important, because it was a visible, authoritative community.[15]

Du Perron's propaganda, however, emphasised stability more than it stressed authority. Authority was the only possible foundation for stability because private individuals could never hope to agree on the interpretation of the Scriptures. They had to be persuaded to accept, in addition to the Scriptures, the traditional teachings of the Church, and if they were to be convinced by the Church's explanations of the internal contradictions to be found within the Scriptures, they must first be persuaded to adopt a submissive attitude to authority.[16] Even so, what mattered to du Perron was membership of the Church, rather than agreement with its teachings. Wherever possible he dwells on the dangers of schism, not the errors of heresy. Just after the death of Henri III, du Perron's friend and associate Henry Constable had written a remarkable work entitled, in its English translation, *The Catholic Moderator*, in which he had argued that what was important was not that one should agree with the Church on all matters of doctrine, but that one should believe one's views to be Catholic: it was implicit faith, not explicit faith, which gave unity to the Church.[17] Du Perron never attempted such a rash formulation, but he was convinced that it was easier to persuade men that they were not members of the visible Church than that they were wrong. Moreover once people accept the security offered by the Church, the intellectual problems which troubled them before they joined it disappear: 'It seems to those who are outside the Church that it wanders, wavers and vacillates. But those who are within it know that it remains fixed, stable, and rooted in the doctrine of the Fathers.'[18]

Sarpi might mock du Perron's 'sofismi rossi e barbati' but he was the most formidable of the opponents of the French *politiques* and Gallicans, Sarpi's allies, and he had played a decisive role in settling the Interdict crisis of 1606–7, contrary to Sarpi's hopes for an irreconcilable rupture with Rome.[19] Since arriving in Rome in 1604 du Perron had campaigned tirelessly to establish an anti-Habsburg bloc. He was handicapped by Henri's grant, in the treaty of Lyons, of the marquisate of Saluzzo to Savoy, for this meant that France no longer had a secure route by which to bring troops into Italy.[20] Even so, his initial achievements were remarkable, especially in Rome. There Aldobrandini, nephew of Clement VIII, cast in his lot with the French, but many other cardinals were eager to see Rome freed from the domination exercised over it by the Spanish. Baronius, an implacable exponent of papal temporal authority, cried out 'Vive le Roy' at the sight of a portrait of Henri IV.[21] Bellarmine, and indeed almost the whole Jesuit order, were drawn into the French camp.[22] An ample supply of funds for the payment of pensions to loyal cardinals meant that the French were able to select Leo XI as pope in April 1605.[23] A month later, though, Leo died. French hopes of securing an unshakeable majority in the college of cardinals were shattered. Nevertheless, when Borghese was elected Paul V it was on the instigation of the French cardinals.[24] Despite the fact that Borghese, having been a nuncio in Spain, was in receipt of a Spanish pension, the French cardinals were eager to claim that he was their man. In September 1605 the papal nephew became a French pensionary.[25]

This newfound French influence was to be exploited to build up an anti-Habsburg bloc. Savoy was enthusiastic. Cardinal Delfino, once a leading Venetian politician, was willing to act in association with du Perron. The Florentines were sympathetic. It seemed the thing could be done.[26] These plans, however, were destroyed by the Interdict, which cut right across the lines of French policy. Had Paul V been convinced of the importance of the anti-Habsburg struggle, the Interdict would never have taken place. Had the Venetians, they would have been willing to make concessions. But Paul was more interested in asserting the authority of the papacy, and the Venetians were more interested in pursuing anti-clerical policies.

There were naturally conflicting counsels among French politicians as to how the Interdict should be handled. Sully was keen to see a war in Italy if it would take the pressure off the Dutch.[27] Villeroi wanted France to favour the papal cause.[28] Du Perron urged the need for strict neutrality, and it was this policy which Henri sought to adopt.[29] But du Perron had further ambitions which met with Henri's disapproval, but which he hoped, acting in concert with Canaye de Fresnes, the French ambassador in Venice, and also a former Protestant, to put into effect. For perhaps it might be possible at the same time as a settlement was achieved to draw Venice and Savoy into an alliance against Spain, even if the papacy would have to be left out. Perhaps the Venetians, having spent so much money on an army, could be persuaded to put it to another purpose.[30]

Such suggestions were rebuffed in Venice. It was the conflict with the papacy which took strength from the internal tensions within Venetian political life, between rich nobles and poor, Dominante and Terraferma. The *giovani* were not to be distracted from this conflict to pursue a policy acceptable to Delfino and Aldobrandini. The Duke of Savoy's attempts to come in person to Venice, ostensibly to act as a mediator, were thwarted.[31] Later some of the *giovani* like Nicolò Contarini were to favour such an alliance, but by then the diplomatic balance of forces had changed. For as early as September 1606 the French position in Rome was showing signs of collapsing. In that month the pope created a congregation of Italian cardinals to organise the campaign, both military and diplomatic, against Venice. All were associated in some way with Spain; none had French connections.[32] Where du Perron had previously felt that it would be easy to sustain French influence in Rome he now began to be doubtful. The pope's relatives were bound to be inclined toward Spain, after all, because the Spanish could offer them estates in Italy, where France could offer them only money.[33] Indeed the tide had turned. The French had lost the ability to control appointments. In the coming months the nuncios appointed to Venice, to the empire and to Savoy all had Spanish connections.[34] In May 1607 du Perron was recalled. The diplomatic assault on Rome was abandoned. France was so weak that Aldobrandini was now known as a Savoyard.[35] It was not Rome, but the crisis in the Grisons which now dominated French thinking. And France was faced squarely with the necessity of a Protestant foreign policy. Her objective henceforward was to ensure papal neutrality rather than to win papal support.

Neither the pope nor the *giovani* had responded to the alluring prospect of an anti-Habsburg alliance. Du Perron had, however, managed to prevent either of them obtaining the satisfaction of winning a victory over the other. Mistakenly, he believed that once the conflict between them was settled both would rediscover their old affection for France. But on the Roman side the settlement was agreed to only under extreme pressure and quickly regretted. On Sunday 25 March 1607, du Perron was sent to the pope after the failure of representations by Baronius – ironically the most bitter of the anti-Venetian polemicists – by the procurator-general of the Jesuits, by the French ambassador, and by the cardinal de Joyeuse to persuade him to accept the terms that de Joyeuse had brought back from Venice. Told by du Perron that war would lead to the establishment of twenty Genevas in Italy the pope acquiesced. By the next Sunday it was rumoured that he had changed his mind again, and by Tuesday 3 April he was closeted with his military advisers. It took two further interviews for du Perron to win him round.[36] Then when the Venetian announcement of the terms of the settlement was received in Rome the pope was only persuaded not to repudiate it by a further round of interviews.[37] Victory was hard won, but the war itself had been lost. Soon the pope was trying to persuade the Spanish to enter into an alliance with him against the Venetians.[38] Rome had become convinced that Spain was her only reliable ally. Sarpi and the *giovani* leaders had lost control of the senate, and with it had gone their hoped-for opportunity for war against the papacy. The new coldness between France and Rome, and the popularity of anti-Habsburg feeling in Venice, meant that they, however, were well-advised to swallow their discontent at French policy. Where the *vecchi* would only enter an anti-Habsburg alliance if it had papal support, the *giovani* now sought to urge on the senate and on Henri IV the forward policy of du Perron.[39] It is thus probable that but for du Perron there would have been war between Venice and Rome and Sarpi's dream of seeing Venice break with the papacy would perhaps have been realised.

Du Perron was responsible on another occasion for inflicting a crushing and permanent defeat on the forces of anti-clericalism. In 1614 the Third Estate in the Estates General sought to assert the independence of the secular authority from clerical interference by passing of the *loy fondamentale*.[40] Du Perron's own respect for political stability meant that he had no taste for papal policies which appeared to encourage sedition. In Rome he had consistently opposed Spanish attempts to foment rebellion in England. But the *loy fondamentale* opened up the prospect of schism, which must lead to atheism and sedition.[41]

The *loy fondamentale*, however, was supported by groups with diverging views. Richer, as we have seen, put forward an orthodox Gallican position which ascribed religious responsibilities to the king. An anonymous reply to du Perron's speech against the *loy*, however, took up a viewpoint close to that of de Belloy and Sarpi...It quoted Du Tillet's *Libertés de l'Eglise Gallicane* as saying that

the spirituality is committed to the prelates and ministers of the Church alone, for they have the highest responsibility, which is that of the care of souls, and with this kings and secular rulers are forbidden to concern themselves. Nevertheless their temporal authority covers the whole field of public order, the first priority of which must be the protection, guard and conservation of the order and discipline of the Ecclesiastical estate of their territory.[42]

The king's solicitude for the Church must be subordinated to 'the supreme law of the state', the preservation of the ruler and of his kingdom.[43] The author of the *Response* was quite happy to admit that the clergy were an indispensible mediator between man and God – which Sarpi and de Belloy would have denied – but on the other hand he did not claim, as Richer did, that the authority of the ruler over the Church was to be exercised for other than secular purposes.[44] Thus du Perron's opponent was keen to confine the state to purely secular objectives, while du Perron on the other hand liked to contrast Christianity with paganism of this sort:

for among the pagans religion was a part of the state and a subordinate accessory to it, while among Christians the state is subordinate to religion, which holds the highest place, and to which the state is an accessory whose task is to make it possible for its subjects to pursue their temporal welfare without sacrificing their spiritual and eternal welfare.[45]

Du Perron had played the leading role in seeking to persuade the Third Estate to reject the *loy fondamentale* and the clergy followed on from this by urging them to accept the Decrees of Trent. Here the *politiques* came to their aid against the Gallicans. The Gallicans had always insisted that the Church's decrees had no force for Frenchmen until they were adopted by the king. But the president of the Third Estate, Miron, told the clergy that the decrees of Trent were about matters of faith and so of no concern to the lay authority. This was the view of the *politiques*, that Church and state had quite separate spheres of interest, and it was quickly exploited by the clergy, encouraged by du Perron, for they decided to impose the decrees of Trent on the whole Church of France through an assembly of the clergy.[46] The division between the *politiques* and the Gallicans had led to a serious defeat for Gallicanism, but also for the whole anti-clerical movement. In 1607 and 1614/15 du Perron thus played a central role in defeating the principles Sarpi stood for. But du Perron's story is not only important for any account of the defeats suffered by anti-clericalism in the years when Sarpi was perhaps its most distinguished exponent. For it was du Perron's efforts to convert the Protestant scholar Isaac Casaubon which forced Sarpi to reveal something of his real attitude towards the early Church, and so provide a key to the interpretation of the *History of Benefices*.

Casaubon had been one of the judges at the conference of Fontainebleau, and his failure to intervene to prevent the defeat of Du Plessis-Mornay had earned him the ill-will of his co-religionists.[47] But Casaubon was a scholar, and his loyalty to Calvinism was less strong than his love of the truth. Although at this time he retained a horror of Catholicism, he had probably already begun to feel dissatisfaction with regard to the Calvinist account of Christian doctrine, an account which could so easily be shown to be at variance with the historical evidence regarding the beliefs of the early Church. The real crisis in Casaubon's relationship to Calvinism came, however, with du Perron's return to France from Rome. Throughout 1609 and the early months of 1610 Casaubon was engaged in intense private theological debate with du Perron, who had hopes of persuading him to enter the Catholic Church.[48] Casaubon's friends reached the conclusion – which was transmitted to Sarpi – that he was certain to succeed. In fact Casaubon was not emotionally attracted to Catholicism, and continued to retain a Protestant distaste for superstitious practices like the cult of the Madonna.[49] But he had indeed been convinced that the Protestant doctrine of the eucharist did not conform to the views of the early Church, that auricular confession was practised in the early Church, and that the Protestant view on predestination and salvation by faith alone was unsatisfactory.[50]

Casaubon's position was untenable. Committed neither to Protestantism nor Catholicism, he desired only to practise a Christianity in conformity with the doctrines of the early Church. His great hope was the reunification of the Church, and he responded favourably to the eirenicist views of the Arminians.[51] But in the absence of any movement towards reunification he had to attach himself to some Christian community or other. With this in mind he turned his thoughts towards Venice, where he would be able to study the doctrines of the Greek Church, and where he could collaborate with Sarpi, who had done so much to attack the unhistorical accretions to the Christian faith which had become part of Catholic doctrine, without attaching himself to the fallacies of Protestantism. On 1 April 1610, however, after a year's consideration of this plan, he opted for the only alternative: he decided to go to England. He had already made progress with learning the language, and he soon settled happily into the Church of England, forming close contacts with those who were opposed to Puritanism.[52]

It was from England in 1612 that he wrote an open letter in defence of anglicanism in reply to du Perron, who had criticised his conversion, and in doing so had attacked the beliefs which James I had propounded in his *Apology for the Oath of Allegiance*. In his reply Casaubon struck at the heart of du Perron's position by insisting that it was not communion with Rome – it was the danger of schism which du Perron had, predictably, emphasised – but belief in the authentic doctrines of Christianity which could alone guarantee salvation.[53] Moreover the doctrines necessary for salvation were all to be found in the Scriptures, the rest being adiaphora, to be settled according to the wishes of the prince. As for du Perron's claim to be able to show that the beliefs of the Counter-Reformation Church coincided with those of the early Church, Casaubon pointed out that his real motives were betrayed by his insistence on taking the Church after the conversion of Constantine as his model. The Church of the period of persecution was none the worse for lacking power and wealth.

Casaubon's preoccupation with the beliefs of the early Church was essentially a private and spiritual one, a matter of conscience. Even so, he was clearly aware of the political significance of the doctrines of the early Church, doctrines which stood contrary to papal primacy, and which vindicated the authority of secular princes against papal usurpation. During the Interdict Pietro Priuli had persuaded him to write a defence of Venetian policy, and this had led him to read Sarpi, whose views had greatly impressed him. Casaubon had commenced work on an authoritative study of the early Church's views on ecclesiastical 'liberty', on clerical rights. The publication of *de Libertate Ecclesiastica*, however, was interrupted by Henri IV, who was urged by du Perron to prevent this Protestant interference in a Catholic affair.[54] The incomplete text was republished after Casaubon's conversion to Anglicanism. In it Casaubon insisted that Sarpi's views were not Protestant, even though the Catholics seemed to be determined to push the Venetians into alliance with Protestantism, thus further dividing Christendom, rather than working towards its longed-for reunification. That his views were *politique* he could not deny:

Behold what is now stil'd the Liberty of the Church... This is that Liberty, against which if any Man, induc'd by the love of his Country, dare but to mutter, he is immediately call'd a Politician, as though no longer deserving the name of a Christian. And indeed this was the only thing wanting to fill up the Scandal of our Age, that as though the Church of God were not at this time rent into parts enough, that new Name should be likewise found out by some turbulent Ringleaders of Sedition, who are sworn Enemies to the publick Tranquility, to alienate from each other such as otherwise agree in the Doctrines of Faith.[55]

Casaubon's approach was thus locked within a Christian and theological frame of reference. An awareness of this partly explains Sarpi's response when he received a letter from Casaubon in the second quarter of 1610, a letter in which Casaubon appealed for his help in deciding what to do in face of the Protestant failure to conform to the doctrines of the early Fathers. But Sarpi's response was also influenced by the fear that the reports that were circulating were true: that Casaubon was planning to convert to Catholicism and come to Venice. In a letter to Castrino, he was to give frank expression to his unease at the prospect of having to collaborate closely with Casaubon:

With regard to what you write about Mr Casaubon, I beg you to put it to him that he will not find in Italy either that erudition, or that merit which he expects, and least of all will he find sincerity; indeed I myself will prove to be quite different from what he imagines...Coming to Italy is of no use unless one wants to become a hypocrite.[56]

Sarpi's goal therefore was to disabuse Casaubon of the view that in Venice the doctrines of the early Church were revered, and that there was a possibility of the state reforming the Church in the light of those doctrines.[57] In his reply to Casaubon's letter he insisted that Casaubon, in his desire to prevent the preaching of novel and dangerous doctrines, had betrayed an aspiration to belong to a perfect Church, one which accepted only the doctrines of the early Fathers.[58] But there can be no perfection on this earth. Moreover the early Fathers are not always to be trusted. They often spoke rhetorically, and made excessive concessions to western prejudices. In any case, their words can be made to bear almost any meaning. In addition, they were discussing different problems from those which concern us now. All that matters, as St Paul made clear, is the fundamentals of the faith. The non-essentials can be allowed to be false or corrupt. One's attitude to religion should be determined by sentiment, not reason: this is what is meant by those who say one should subject the intellect to faith. Reform is dangerous, for any rejection of the established faith is likely to give rise to new and greater errors and corruptions: one should live happily with those faults to which one has become accustomed.

In a second letter, provoked by Casaubon's reply, Sarpi returned to the same theme.[59] However the faith of the early Fathers may have been distorted, the fundamentals of the faith must by definition remain intact, for this God has promised. Only the external aspect of the Christian faith can change. Casaubon is thus wrong to worry about the distortion of the true faith: the fundamentals of the true faith will survive. And he is wrong, too, to fetishise the opinions of the early Fathers, for they did not take themselves so seriously. Above all he is wrong to try and correct the errors of the public:

No wise man tries to cure public ills. It should be enough for you if you manage to correct my faults. A wise man recognises that he who cannot put up with the idiocy of the public but gets angry at it and believes that it can be corrected is not himself healthy. If God has permitted you to see the truth, imitate Timothy, see to yourself and to the muses, for the just man shall live by his faith. Let everyone else go their own way, for you will have a large enough audience in yourself. If only I was the sort of person to be able to give you good advice, I would give myself over entirely to the task, but he who you think is healthy is perhaps more dangerously ill than you...

What is the significance of these letters? There is no need to emphasise how they reflect the views expressed in the *Pensieri medico-morali* on the need to conform to the foolishness of others, and on the impossibility of learning from books. But they contain no suggestion that it might be practicable to attempt to change people's views, a possibility Sarpi had explored in the *Pensieri*. And they seem at first sight to amount to an attack on the very ideal of ecclesiastical reform with Sarpi had spelled out in the *History of Benefices*.

On other occasions, however, Sarpi remained faithful to the viewpoint expressed in the *History of Benefices*. Writing to the Gallican jurist Jacques Leschassier in 1608 he had stressed that it was marvellous 'how much a knowledge of the structure and values of the early Church could help to ensure public tranquillity',[60] while in September 1610, writing again to Leschassier, he wrote

We study every aspect of the writings and doctrine of the early Fathers, but we have changed the meaning of all the words they used. For us words like pope, cardinal, deacon, church, Catholic, heretic, martyr no longer have the same meaning that they had for them. What more can be said? We have transformed everything, and while we claim to be publishing the works of the early Fathers we are in fact disseminating our own.[61]

This, although so similar to what Sarpi had had to say to Casaubon, was intended not to demonstrate the uselessness of reading the early Fathers, but the urgency of studying them in the spirit of the *History of Benefices*. This indeed is the nub of the matter. The study of the early Church was for Sarpi of value if it was a study of the corruption of the clergy and the papacy. But if it was undertaken, not with the goal of establishing a healthier political order, but with that of restoring the *beliefs* of the early Church, then it simply amounted to an attempt to replace one form of superstition by another, an attempt carried out without reference to contemporary social and political needs. In such circumstances the value of theology itself must be called in question, and Christianity must be presented as a purely spiritual, entirely otherworldly religion, involving no clearly articulated set of beliefs. If it was recognised to be no more than that, then there would be ample scope for religion to be moulded to society's needs.

Sarpi's anxiety to persuade Casaubon that he is not what he takes him to be, someone who wishes to restore the beliefs of the early Church, is sufficient evidence as to the purely polemical nature of the programme laid down in the *History of Benefices*. Sarpi's objective was the establishment of a healthy state, not a perfect Church. There is another occasion on which Sarpi revealed a similar reluctance to discuss faith, and the same determination to present Christianity as a religion without any essential doctrinal content. In 1613 he was requested by Sir Dudley Carleton, the English ambassador to Venice and a close associate, to supply an assessment of the works of Conrad Vorst for James I, who had been leading an international campaign against a man accused of denying the Trinity, of regarding God as a natural entity existing in time, and of denying His omnipotence and prescience.[62] Not surprisingly his views had been generally condemned, and Carleton hoped to win James' favour by supplying yet another learned refutation. It was with some dismay that Carleton took delivery of what he recognised to be an attack on all innovators – and reformers – in matters of religion.

At the beginning of his criticism of Vorst, Sarpi explains that 'I have made two assessments of these doctrines taken overall. First I have assessed them from a religious point of view, and then I have judged them from a secular point of view.'[63] In discussing Vorst's views from a religious point of view Sarpi starts off by claiming that a discussion of the nature of the divinity is a discussion of something that is 'indifferent', not essential to salvation. There is, then, in Sarpi's view, nothing 'heretical' about Socinianism. Sarpi concentrates instead on the question of the attitude Christians should adopt to the discussion of theological problems, taking as his text St Paul's command that one must not scandalise one's weaker brethren with one's opinions. On the basis of this Sarpi maintains that theological questions, even questions concerning adiaphora, can only be discussed when the *opportunità* presents itself. Consequently, such questions may *never* be discussed in print, for one can never tell who may read a book, and so one can never ensure that it will not cause scandal. The magistrate can forbid any discussion of new theological opinions, and, even more certainly, can prevent any publication of such opinions.[64] One should always bear in mind 'the importance of the danger of offending Christ by bringing about the destruction of one's brother, for whom he died', and one must accept St Paul's advice that 'if you are certain of something keep it to yourself before God'.[65]

Sarpi then turns to discuss Vorst's views from a secular point of view. Only at this point does he discuss the merits of Vorst's view of God, which he holds to be unsatisfactory because it presents a picture of the Divinity less elevated than the normal one. It is possible that Vorst's arguments are not intended to have the significance that Sarpi and others might give to them, but as Plato has shown in the *Parmenides* contrary conclusions can easily be drawn from a single premise, and so arguments mean only what they are taken to mean. Vorst has no right to complain if people take him to be saying scandalous things. Since he has failed to observe the existing conventions in theological debate his book represents 'an infinite field' of possible meanings until such time as a conventional account of it has gained ground. Vorst's mistake lies in his unwillingness to accept the imperfections of the conventional view:

If one is certain of not being able to cure oneself of all disease, what's the point in troubling oneself, instead of accepting the complaints one has inherited, and which have become natural to one through the habituation of one's forebears and oneself? On questions concerning God all mortals will always talk with a stutter, and there is no use in struggling to make the stutter affect one syllable rather than another, for then speech may become impossible.[66]

There is much that is puzzling about the *Scrittura su Vorstio*. For why should Sarpi have chosen to emphasise the difference between a religious and a secular attitude to theological debate, and in doing so expose the unorthodoxy of his own position? In the case of his letters to Casaubon it seems clear that he was provoked by the prospect of Casaubon's coming to Italy. In the case of the *Scrittura su Vorstio* it seems likely that he was provoked by the knowledge that the text was likely to be read by James I, for not only was James' attack on Vorst dividing the opponents of Rome amongst themselves, but his earlier defence of the Oath of Allegiance had had even more serious consequences for international opposition to Rome. The Huguenots had been distressed by the criticisms levied against the Puritans in that work, but worse still James' decision to send a copy to every major ruler in Europe had brought his views to the attention of the Venetian senate and had served to undo much of the effort put in during and after the Interdict by Sarpi and the then English ambassador to Venice, Sir Henry Wotton, to nurture close relations between England and Venice.[67] The *Scrittura su Vorstio* was thus as much a rebuke to James as to Vorst, for, as Sarpi had put it in December 1609,

The king of England in trying to stimulate us may have served his own interests, but he has certainly not served ours. He, in trying to give an account of his beliefs and an explanation of the Apocalypse, has attacked doctrines which are held here to be the foundations of the true faith, which has given rise to the saying that his object was to destroy the faith, not to make men think about the tyranny (of Rome). Oh how useful it would have been if only he had confined himself to political arguments...[68]

James was thus as guilty as Vorst of offending Christ by bringing about the destruction of his brother.

Sarpi should not, however, be taken as denying, in the letters to Casaubon and the *Scrittura su Vorstio*, the value of any sort of ecclesiastical reform or religious reformation. What he is insisting is that no such reformation should be carried out for *religious* reasons. And reform for secular reasons must recognise the dangers of innovation: the cure may be worse than the disease, which is at least well-established and predictable. If the presumption should normally be in favour of conservation rather than reformation, still it would be necessary to do something about any disease which threatened to be fatal to the patient, and this, in Sarpi's view, the doctrine of papal absolutism was bound to be for the secular state. Sarpi never hesitated to insist on the need to reform the papacy, and he believed that if the papacy's authority was destroyed then it might be possible to aspire to a state of relative health, in which the doctrines of Christianity were not taken seriously, but a socially and psychologically useful view of God and of man's nature was fostered.

The motives underlying Sarpi's campaign against the papacy were always in the end secular, rather than religious. Even his insistence on the need to have a conception of the perfection of God which stood in sharp contrast to the inadequacy of man was presented, in the *Scrittura su Vorstio* as in the *Pensieri*, as being motivated by human, secular considerations. Yet Sarpi felt the failure to preserve this contrast between the divine and the human was the main defect not only of Vorst's doctrines, but also of those of Catholicism. Sarpi's attack on Vorst could, in its main outlines, have equally well been an attack on Counter-Reformation theology. From it we learn something of the theological views of which Sarpi approved, but also, more significantly, how little his approval had to do with a concern for theological truth.

Sarpi and the Protestants

Some few months after the end of the Interdict Sir Henry Wotton wrote to Giovanni Diodati, a Calvinist pastor in Geneva who was in the process of completing an Italian translation of the Bible, inviting him to come to Venice and lay the foundations for the establishment of a Protestant Church there. Hopes were high, Diodati was informed, for the Reformation of the Venetian Church, towards which the establishment of a Protestant congregation would be a first and vital step. Diodati was assured that the invitation was being issued with Sarpi's approval, and that the new congregation would have support in the highest quarters in the Venetian senate. Diodati for his part informed Du Plessis-Mornay, 'the Huguenot pope' and the man best able to ensure the support of the international Calvinist community for the project, of the exciting turn of events.[69]

The move to introduce Protestantism into Venice was accompanied from the beginning by efforts to bring Venice into closer contact with the Protestant powers. Arrangements were made, through Diodati and through Johann Lenck, a German Calvinist living in Venice, for a representative of the prince of Anhalt, Christoph von Dohna, to come to Venice, ostensibly to take care of some financial arrangements for the prince. In fact von Dohna's mission was delicate and secret. Anhalt was the architect of the recently established Protestant Union of German princes hostile to the Habsburgs, and he managed the foreign policy of the most important of these princes, the elector Palatine. His mission was to see if there was any prospect of bringing Venice into the Protestant Union, and to find out if there was anything which could usefully be done to advance the cause of Protestantism in Venice. In the carrying out of this mission he was to accept Sarpi's advice implicitly.[70]

Thus there was set in train a Protestant policy which had both a political and a religious aspect. In Venice the key figure was Sarpi, who was the intermediary between an anonymous group of established Venetian politicians and the foreign Protestants, Sir Henry Wotton in particular. Sarpi and his friend and amanuensis Fulgenzio were in almost daily contact with Wotton and his chaplain Bedell.[71] They were able to count on the support of Diodati and Du Plessis-Mornay, of the leading members of the Protestant Union, and of the Venetian ambassador in Paris, the ill-fated Foscarini, but their plans were dependent upon the shadowy figures within the senate with whom Sarpi was cooperating. The first fruits of this policy were the visit of von Dohna to Venice in late July and early August of 1608 and of Diodati in late August and early September.

There could be nothing more embarrassing for any account of Sarpi as a reforming Catholic than this close collaboration with Protestants, a collaboration which was not confined, certainly as far as men like Du Plessis-Mornay, Diodati and Bedell were concerned, merely to the common pursuit of political ends, but had as its object the establishment of Protestantism in Italy. Two conflicting historiographical traditions have, however, laid great stress upon Sarpi's collaboration with Protestants. One group of historians has seen it as clear evidence of Sarpi's secret conversion to Protestantism, while another has argued that Sarpi's goals were essentially political ones, that he avoided as far as possible compromising himself on religious questions, and that he was forced to present himself as sympathetic to Protestantism in order to win for Venice the confidence and practical support of the Protestant powers and to create the preconditions for a movement of Catholic reform.[72] Neither approach does justice to the complexities of Sarpi's Protestant policy.

The first problem to be resolved is that presented by a conflict in the evidence as to what arrangements were actually made in Venice preparatory to Diodati's visit. Diodati had clearly formed the impression that Venetian nobles were to be members of the Protestant congregation, and was horrified on arrival to discover that no attempt had been made to distinguish between those nobles willing to make vague offers of support and those willing to make a decisive break with Rome and to join a Protestant Church. When, after his arrival, the sympathetic members of the nobility were questioned they all expressed reluctance to take such a step. In view of this it was suggested that Diodati should set up a Protestant Church amongst the foreigners resident in Venice, an enterprise he rejected as involving risks which outweighed the likely benefits.[73]

Bedell's account is quite different. According to him a number of Protestant merchants, all of them foreigners, had been approached and had been told that were they to form a Protestant Church the enterprise would receive the blessing of the senate. Bedell's account implies that Venetian nobles had never been considered suitable to be founder members of the Church.[74] Sarpi, for his part, assured von Dohna that specific commitments had been entered into by those approached, at least to the extent of providing guarantees of financial support.[75] What then went wrong? According to Bedell the merchants backed out when they discovered that the senate was in fact likely to be hostile to the enterprise. Was the intention, in the spring of 1608, to set us a Protestant congregation of foreigners resident in Venice, or one of Venetian nobles? The first seems to me much the more plausible, for it is clear that Sarpi himself had no intention of openly breaking with the Catholic Church and joining a Protestant congregation. He argued that any such action would appear to justify the excommunication the pope had placed upon him during the Interdict, and would make it impossible for him to continue to influence government policy towards the papacy. Moreover, in face of Diodati's insistance that one could not find salvation within the Catholic Church, he maintained that all that mattered was that the individual should be in a correct relationship to God. Salvation could not depend upon membership of a Church, or participation in certain ceremonies. This was, therefore, more than a lame effort at self-justification, for in a striking passage in the *History of the Council of Trent*, Sarpi was later to take pains to show that there could be no coherent theory of how one entered into membership of a Church.[76]

If salvation was possible within the Catholic Church, then only reasons of public policy, not private conviction, could justify the break with Rome. But considerations of policy pointed to the necessity of maintaining an appearance of orthodoxy, not only in Sarpi's case, but also in that of the leaders of the anti-clerical faction within the senate. It is not surprising then that Diodati had occasion to lament that Sarpi and Fulgenzio had failed to urge their followers to convert.[77]

It is also worth considering the fact that it would have been very hard for anyone who accepted Sarpi's political philosophy to justify a decision to reject the religious practices authorised by the sovereign, particularly since Sarpi held that no doctrine necessary for salvation was in question. If one accepted the right of rulers to regulate the affairs of the Church, then the only legitimate policy would be one of trying to persuade the ruler to change his confessional allegiance, or else of trying to persuade him to introduce some measure of religious toleration. As long as the first option remained closed, it was natural for Sarpi and his associates to hope to persuade the senate to tolerate the establishment of a Protestant congregation among foreign merchants, for this could be presented as being no more than an extension to Protestants of the rights already conceded to those who belonged to the Greek Orthodox Church.[78]

Diodati's assessment of the situation in Venice before he arrived there was felt by others to be over optimistic.[79] It seems likely that when he arrived he was under the misapprehension that promises of senatorial support were promises to convert to Protestantism, and that a tactful fiction was employed to disabuse him. Perhaps he had been misled as to the real nature of the proposed Protestant congregation: this may, as we shall see, have been because there existed contingency plans not for the establishment of a Protestant congregation, but for reformation of the Venetian Church. In any event, Bedell's testimony must be preferred to Diodati's: he was on the spot and knew Sarpi well. Bedell, as we shall see, understood that Sarpi's approach was primarily political; Diodati expected him to act as a minister of the Gospel. Above all Bedell describes a plan which might conceivably have won substantial political support within Venice; Diodati's would have been universally opposed.

But what went wrong with the plan to establish a reformed Church for foreigners? If it is right to suppose that this plan did not run counter to the fundamental principles which Sarpi had upheld during the Interdict, then it must have come unstuck because it was realised that it would be impossible to persuade the senate to give even tacit approval. Even in Bedell's account the question of the senate's attitude is introduced as if it was primarily of interest to the merchant community, when it must in fact have been the central preoccupation of Sarpi and his associates, not only because unless the senate took a benevolent attitude it would be impossible to ensure the nascent congregation's survival, but also because the whole purpose of establishing such a congregation was to familiarise the Venetian nobility with Protestantism and persuade them that it was not inherently subversive. Nothing would be gained if they were simply provoked into prejudiced and unthinking hostility.

Quite separate from the attempt to establish a Protestant congregation was, according to Bedell's description, a project to persuade the Venetian nobility of the merits of Protestant doctrines. This project was to centre on the translation of a work of Protestant apologetics, but, before Diodati's arrival, Sarpi had managed to successfully transform it so that it became a platform for the expression of his own fundamental convictions. Bedell reported that

it has been considered that to propound [the knowledge of the truth] in its own naked simplicity to men, either blinded with superstition, or that by the only light of reason discerning the vizor of that religion which is among themselves, have thereupon closed their eyes to any representation of that sort, it were but to expose it to contempt, and as it were to demand a repulse: these same men read gladly discourses of policy, so as under that name if religion could be conveyed, it were likely to find much better entertainment...Agreeably whereunto it would perhaps be very convenient in our times to convey the reproofs of the abuses and errors of the papacy in politic discourses discovering the greater drifts thereof, which in truth should be very just also before God and man, that as they have a great while propounded, and set forth to the world their own politic devices under the mask of religion, so might men see now at last their religion in the true and natural shape of policy; in this kind there is extant already in our tongue a work so proper to that purpose, as if God had directed the pen of the author to that special end to do him service in this place: it is the relation of Sir Edwyn Sandys that I mean.[80]

Sarpi thus extricated himself from the obligation to preach Protestantism to his associates, and instead found a justification for presenting religion 'in the true and natural shape of policy', an undertaking which was likely to win the approval of the many 'atheists' Sarpi said were to be found in Venice.[81] Sarpi improved on Sandys, whose hostility to Puritanism made him unnecessarily tolerant in his account of Roman Catholicism, by supplementing his work with a number of bitter attacks upon the papacy.[82] He then informed Bedell that his presence would not be welcome at discussions of religious questions attended by the Venetian nobility.[83] It seems likely that Sarpi's motive was to ensure that such discussions could concentrate on questions of policy, not doctrine, and to forestall any attempt to persuade Venetian nobles to break with the established Church.

The most important part of the Protestant policy though, according to Bedell, lay in the efforts being made to build up Venice's contacts with the Protestant powers and to exacerbate her relations with Rome, in the hope that the sort of conflict which had given rise to the Interdict would once more break out, but would lead this time to a complete break with the papacy.[84]

This aspect of Sarpi's Protestant policy casts light, I think, upon the other two. Sarpi's closest associates must have been disappointed, as he was, that the French had managed to bring about a settlement in the conflict with Rome. But, quite apart from those who actively wanted to break with Rome, more conservative Venetian politicians had reason to fear an attack from Rome and Spain with the opening of the new campaigning season in the spring of 1608, for Roman hostility to Venice was scarcely concealed, while the object of Spanish military preparations was the subject of much speculation.[85] Spain was, moreover, in the middle of seeking to negotiate a truce with the Dutch, and were this to be successfully concluded she would be free to fight a war in Italy.[86]

Had Rome attacked Venice in 1608 the government would have had to choose between humiliating concessions and a Protestant alliance. What was being proposed in the early months of 1608 was, I believe, just such an alliance. Venice's ability to obtain troops from Germany had been a crucial issue during the Interdict. Equally important must have been the question of what Venice could do should the pope absolve Venice's subjects from the obligation of obedience. The only effective answer would have been to establish a schismatic Church. Sarpi's efforts to prepare an Italian liturgy, and Wotton's request to Diodati that he have a special pocket edition of his translation of the New Testament printed may have been intended as preparations for such an emergency. In the early months of 1608 Sarpi would thus have been able to muster political support for an opening to the Protestants. Once the campaigning season had begun without incident, however, such support would have rapidly declined, which goes some way towards explaining the attempts made in August to put off Diodati's visit, Sarpi's failure to disseminate a work of Protestant apologetics, and the senate's unwillingness to allow freedom of worship to foreign Protestants.[87]

The central problem in interpreting Sarpi's contacts with Protestants is thus that of determining whether Sarpi was – as Bedell's account implies – pursuing policies which he hoped would prove acceptable to the senate, or whether he was – as Diodati hoped – planning to urge Venice's subjects to adopt heretical and illegal beliefs. One reason for trusting to Bedell's account rather than Diodati's is that it seems evident that Sarpi must have had governmental permission for some at least of his contacts with Protestants. It was strictly illegal for Sarpi to meet the representative of a foreign power without official permission. Had he not had such permission his meetings with Wotton – which were not a well-kept secret – would have been severely punished by the Council of Ten.[88] This is not to say that Sarpi was acting simply as an agent of the Venetian government in his dealings with Protestants. He was keen to conceal the full extent of his correspondence with Protestants from the *Collegio*, and he sought to employ the English ambassador to persuade the *Collegio* to adopt anti-clerical policies.[89] On such occasions he was acting with the knowledge of, or in support of, leading anti-clericals like Foscarini, Nani and Nicolò Contarini. He was dependent on the protection of these men who, in Rome's view, continued to nurture hopes of establishing a congregation of Protestant merchants in Venice after the failure of Diodati's visit, but some of his actions must have had the approval not just of a faction, but of the established authorities.[90]

There were widespread rumours that Sarpi's dealings with Protestants had official authorisation.[91] Moreover, Sarpi's activities in 1608 form part of a larger pattern. At least three Venetian diplomats were at the same time acquiring themselves reputations for philo-Protestantism.[92] By 1609 both France and Rome were convinced that in the event of another Interdict Venice would break with the Church of Rome: a conviction that played no small part in dissuading the pope from introducing sanctions against Venice.[93] Rome was keen to prove the Venetians were heretics, not mere defenders of secular sovereignty, in order to win support for sanctions against Venice; the Venetians on the other hand had to threaten the papacy with heresy if they were to persuade the pope that they had no intention of compromising.[94] Seen in such a context, Sarpi's contacts with Protestants served the interests not just of a faction within Venetian politics, but of the government itself.

Sarpi, of course, could not claim to have the government's approval, but he did insist that he had the support of leading politicians.[95] He told von Dohna that he was in contact with the doge himself, on whose approval, he insisted, the success of any policy depended.[96] It is of great interest then that he describes a conversation with Donà on the effect of changes in religion. Donà had raised the classic objection that any change in religion must lead to a change in government. Sarpi's reply was that the present state of affairs threatened the overthrow of the government, for the Jesuits and others taught obedience to Rome, not the Venetian state, while no religion which taught the subject to obey his ruler could be a threat to the state.[97] Sarpi has thus put the case to Donà both for limited religious toleration and for a complete break with Rome. But Donà showed no signs of being convinced: he may well have felt that it was no use introducing a religion which taught due obedience to the secular authority if its introduction was likely to provoke the revolt of the Terraferma.

Sarpi told von Dohna that he had never been able to learn anything about Donà's religious views, for he had always kept them to himself, seeming to be concerned solely with matters of state.[98] A few months before it had been possible to claim, presumably on Sarpi's authority, that the doge was favourably disposed towards the new religion, so that it seems possible that the disarray which met Diodati on his arrival in Venice was the result of a shift in Donà's position, resulting from a growing conviction of the unlikelihood of war.[99] It is clear from Sarpi's correspondence that despite the fears of most Venetian politicians he himself had never been convinced that war was likely, and that he entertained no illusions about the strength of those politicians who wished to provoke a war with Rome.[100] Nor did he share the hopes and the illusions of Bedell and Diodati. He was convinced, though, that the policies employed during the Interdict had proved inadequate. The presumption had been that no settlement would be reached, that war would ensue, and that with war would come a break with Rome. If war was now unlikely, in Sarpi's view, simply because Rome and Spain stood to lose more than they might reasonably hope to gain, yet it was still necessary to make what preparations one could in the hope that war could be brought about. During the Interdict, Venice had insisted that her concern was simply to defend secular authority, not to interfere in questions of religious belief. Rome on the other hand had not only insisted that questions of faith were at stake, but had also shown herself to fear the advance of heresy into Italy more than anything else.[101] In the light of this Sarpi reached the conclusion that the mere defence of secular sovereignty was insufficient, unless it was accompanied by an attack upon those religious views which tied men to the papacy. After the Interdict, then, he came to believe that it was necessary to foster Protestantism in Venice.

The reasoning that lay behind the adoption of this policy is made clear by a letter Sarpi wrote to Groslot de l'Isle in April 1608:

this world of ours [Venice] has been sick for a long time, and indeed the illness was believed to be incurable. But there was a small crisis in the progress of the disease, which led people to think that it could be cured. The doctors thought they could cure the patient with good food and without medicines, forgetting Hippocrates' warning that nourishing food is dangerous for a sick man. If, at that point, action had been taken in accordance with the scientific principle that serious diseases require extreme remedies perhaps the outcome would have been better. The situation is dangerous...the patient's body is now accustomed to being ill...one might say, in the words of the comic, that health itself cannot save it.[102]

Thus it is not healthy food but medicine that the sick man needs. This had been a theme at the heart of the *Pensieri*: of the *Pensieri filosofici* where food stood for philosophy and medicine for religion, and of the *Pensieri medico-morali* where Sarpi had insisted that people with false ideas had to be told, not the truth, but a medicinal falsehood. It is thus the need for religious propaganda which Sarpi is thinking of here: this is the extreme remedy which had not been tried during the Interdict crisis, when Sarpi and his associates had sought to provoke a war by appealing to the secular principles which would convince a healthy society, not the religious ones which would transform a sick one.[103]

A few months later, though, Sarpi's view had changed. Writing to Groslot just before von Dohna's arrival, Sarpi, hesitatingly, returned to a defence of the policy pursued during the Interdict, a policy which had confined itself to attacking papal tyranny, and avoided preaching new dogmas:

perhaps God wishes to extinguish the [Roman] tyranny in this century by employing a more delicate method than that which was tried last century [i.e. with the Reformation]. Then an attack was made upon the foundations [of papal power], but the sappers were unable to finish the job; who knows whether by beginning with an attack on the head, as is being done at the moment, we may not see a more satisfactory outcome?[104]

Had Sarpi chosen to retreat from the Protestant policy, or had he been forced to by Donà and the other senators who had given their initial approval to it? It seems likely that he may have been reluctant to give up plans for the formation of a Protestant church for foreigners in Venice, but relieved to free himself of any obligation to disseminate falsehood. Certainly he admitted to Diodati that he was temperamentally unsuited to the task of inspiring religious enthusiasm, and he must have felt happier persuading people of the demerits of the papacy, as in the additions he made to Sandys, rather than seeking to demonstrate the merits of Protestantism. It evidently occurred to him too that though it was the weakness of the anti-clerical party in Venetian politics which made necessary this present retreat, yet even if they were in the future to gain an effective grip on power it would still be unwise for them to be too closely associated with Calvinism, for he believed that if the state were to break with Rome it would need at first to retain as many aspects of the old religion as possible, as had been done in England. To seek to advance Calvinism in Venice would be to risk committing oneself to a policy of subversion. Perhaps then it would indeed be possible in Venice to proceed by offering food for the healthy, not medicine for the sick, only providing that the Protestant states continued to grow stronger and established themselves as Venice's natural and potentially effective allies in the event of war with the papacy.

Thus it seems that Sarpi's hesitations and Donà's reservations put paid to the Protestant policy of the spring of 1608. But they did not render useless the contacts that had been established, or put an end to all forms of religious propaganda. When they came to Venice Diodati and von Dohna were urged to persuade the Protestant princes of Germany to send agents to Venice, men who would be able to educate the ignorant Venetian nobility as to the realities of German politics. As a result the elector Palatine sent Sarpi's friend Lenck to Venice as his agent. Then when Spain and Holland eventually agreed on a truce, in April 1609, Sarpi wrote to Du Plessis-Mornay urging him to have the Dutch send a special ambassador to Venice to inform the senate of the terms of the treaty. Du Plessis-Mornay complied, and Venice responded to the Dutch gesture by initiating an exchange of ambassadors. From these diplomatic contacts, brought about by Sarpi and Du Plessis-Mornay and opposed by the papacy, were to come first the recruitment of 2000 Dutch troops by the Venetians during the war of Gradisca, and then the formal alliance between Venice and Holland of 1619.[105]

The effects of Sarpi's Protestant policy were thus more striking in the political than in the religious field. Even so, Sarpi's Protestant allies continued to nurture hopes of Reformation in Venice. It was Sarpi's often reiterated belief that war would bring Reformation, for it would destroy the power of the Inquisition, which alone sustained the papacy, and so make possible freedom of worship and the preaching of the Gospel.[106] The progress of the Reformation thus depended on seizing the political opportunities which might lead to war. Sarpi's Protestant allies reproached him for his *fredda prudenza* (undue caution) which prevented him breaking from Rome.[107] He for his part preached to them the pre-eminent importance of *opportunità*, the queen of all sciences.[108]

After July 1608 there was no real prospect of undertaking a campaign of specifically Protestant propaganda in Venice. But something remained of the religious aspect of the Protestant policy in the preaching of Fra Fulgenzio Micanzio. Where Sarpi wished to further the Protestant cause, Micanzio certainly appeared to wish to commit himself to Protestantism. Bedell was evidently impressed by his fervour, and when Diodati insisted on the need to break with Rome Micanzio exclaimed that he would willingly go into exile if Protestant worship continued to be impossible in Venice.[109] In 1609 Micanzio preached a series of Lenten sermons to packed audiences. The series was prepared in close collaboration with Bedell, but even so the sermons were formally orthodox: the nuncio was unable to find any explicit heresy in them, although Micanzio's stress upon the teaching of the Gospels made it easy for his audience to identify those doctrines which were not to be found in the Gospels but which were taught by the Catholic Church.[110]

In 1610 three factors combined to prevent Micanzio's preaching again, and so put an end to any lingering hopes of a Reformation in Venice which was not the side-effect of war. At the same time they made it unlikely that war in

Italy would lead to a conflict between Venice and the papacy. The first development was a change in the papacy's attitude to Venice. In the years after the Interdict there had been a constant series of minor conflicts between Venice and Rome, and the Republic's determination to stand by the principles it had expressed in 1606 was symbolised by its regularly imprisoning offending clerics.[111] The papacy, for its part, hoped to persuade Spain to join in a war against Venice once it had reached a settlement with the Dutch. It was finally disillusioned when, in April 1609, the Spanish announced that, despite the truce with the Dutch, they had no desire to go to war with Venice. From this date the papacy had to give new consideration to a policy of conciliation with Venice.[112] Two events helped make such a policy feasible. In August, as we have seen, the king of England provoked disquiet in the senate by presenting it with a copy of his defence of the Oath of Allegiance, and, although the rift between Venice and England was soon patched up, the senate had demonstrated its unwillingness to enter into relations of complicity with Protestantism. Finally and decisively, in September 1609, Henri IV had released the text of an intercepted letter between Diodati and Du Plessis-Mornay concerning their hopes for a Reformation in Venice, and had gone on to urge the Venetians to put a stop to the preaching of Micanzio. Henri's purpose was probably to give evidence of his commitment to Catholicism and so to persuade the papacy to stay neutral in the event, which was increasingly likely, of a war between France and Spain. To attain this end he was willing to sacrifice the hopes of those who had worked to draw Venice into the Protestant camp. As in the past, the establishment of good relations with Rome had been given priority over efforts to bring Venice into the anti-Habsburg camp.[113] As far as Henri was concerned, it was better to have Venice and Rome neutral than to have the support of Venice and the hostility of Rome. Consequently, he was happy to weaken the anti-clerical party in Venice, and to demonstrate his support for those who were concerned to establish close relations with Rome and would be unwilling to pursue a foreign policy unacceptable to Rome. As a result, by November 1609 it was clear that the papacy wished to establish better relations with Venice, and that the anti-clerical faction was now not strong enough to persuade the senate to pursue provocative policies of a sort which would make it impossible for the papacy to moderate its stance.[114]

Thus Sarpi, who had always insisted that the struggle against the Habsburgs was identical with the struggle against the papacy, was once more misled by his dogmatic conviction that anti-Habsburg policies must needs be anti-papal ones. On the strength of this he had persuaded himself not only that war would bring Protestant troops into Italy, but that this would mean the end of the Inquisition and the spread of Protestant worship.[115] Yet Venice herself was soon to fight a war against the Austrians with the aid of Dutch troops, despite which the Inquisition continued to operate and Sarpi's longed-for *opportunità* failed to materialise.[116]

The Protestant policy initiated after the Interdict thus suffered a first set-back in the summer of 1608, when Diodati failed to establish a Protestant Church in Venice, a second in the autumn of 1609, when Micanzio was silenced, and a third and final one in 1616, when it became apparent that Protestant troops would not necessarily bring freedom of worship to Italy. The first phase of the policy may never have had Sarpi's full backing, but certainly Sarpi was committed to the advancement of the Protestant cause. Can one then conclude that he was, as Bedell claimed, 'for the substance of religion wholly ours'?[117] The evidence, it seems to me, does not justify such a conclusion. Rather Sarpi seems to have been attracted to Protestantism merely as an antidote to Catholicism. Even when most involved with the Protestant cause he remained loyal to his conception of a spiritual religion. It was in the name of this religion that Sarpi justified to Diodati his continuing to say Mass, and it was this spiritual religion that Sarpi meant to refer to when he spoke of the Gospel. It must be remembered that Micanzio had managed to preach the Gospel without once expressing an explicitly Protestant doctrine: the Catholic doctrine he seems to have been most concerned to undermine was the doctrine of the confessional, the foundation, as it seemed, of clerical authority.[118]

The truths of Sarpi's Gospel touched only indirectly on the questions at issue between Catholic and Protestant. Late in life Sarpi was unwillingly obliged by the senate to grant an interview to the prince of Condé, one of the political leaders of French Catholicism. Sarpi's replies to Condé's questions were evidently intended as much for the education of the senate as the prince, and Sarpi seized an opportunity to defend his interpretation of the text 'My kingdom is not of this world' as meaning that there could be no conflict between the true religion and the state: only a false religion could have worldly interests to defend. But on this occasion he went on to maintain that this was indeed the central message of the Gospel: 'all the preaching of Christ Our Lord and of the apostles has no other purpose but to demonstrate that the temporal promises of the Old Testament are to be understood as referring to spiritual and not worldly things. Nowadays however preachers are solely concerned with giving a worldly meaning to the spiritual things Christ promised to the Church.'[119] The real conflict, in Sarpi's view, was thus between a worldly and a spiritual conception of the Church.

The victory of a spiritual conception of Christianity must depend upon the victory of Protestantism, both because Protestantism was the only available antidote to Catholicism, and because the Protestants respected the teaching of Christ and the apostles, while the Catholics suppressed it. Sarpi supported the Protestant cause because it was a spiritual kingdom he wished to see preached, not because he was convinced by Protestant doctrine.[120] But if he wished to hear such a kingdom preached, it was not necessarily because he believed in the truth of the Gospel, any more than he believed in the doctrines of Protestantism: the merit of an otherworldly Christianity may merely have lain in the fact that it corresponded reasonably well to the 'best' religion which Sarpi had found in Charron and had described in the *Pensieri sulla religione*.

Sarpi and the *History of the Council of Trent*

Sarpi's greatest work has always been held to be his *History of the Council of Trent*.[121] As a work of history it is amongst the greatest, perhaps the greatest, of its day. It has three qualities which give it this status. In the first place, it is never a chronicle or mere narrative: Sarpi quite consciously determined to give events only such space as they deserve in his story, and this story is not simply the story of Trent, but the story of the failure of the reform movement at Trent. Sarpi's history is thus problem-centred history, and in this respect stands as a representative of a new type of historical writing.[122] Secondly, Sarpi is keen to impress upon the reader that he has made an exhaustive study of all the available documents. His is supposed to be a critical history which goes beyond the myths regarding what happened at the Council and exposes the real course and logic of events. To achieve his goal Sarpi has to adopt a new ideal of scholarly history.[123] Finally Sarpi sees Trent as a tragic history of hopes and expectations disappointed, of corruption and the abuse of power triumphant. He claims to be writing the Iliad of contemporary times.[124] And this means that his history has to attain the status of literature: he has to let events and men speak for themselves, whilst at the same time inspiring in his reader the strongest feelings of disquiet, dismay and disgust.

There is no doubt that the *History of Trent* is a marvellous piece of writing, although it would be aside from our purpose to give an account of Sarpi's style here.[125] As to Sarpi's claims to scholarly accuracy, these are much debated. The problem is essentially a technical one: what sources were available to Sarpi, and can he claim to have given careful consideration to the evidence available in those sources? Hubert Jedin, the great modern scholar of Trent, was in no doubt that Sarpi's history was tendentious and irresponsible.[126] In the seventeenth century Sarpi's history was subjected to an exhaustive refutation by Cardinal Pallavicino, who had the advantage of having access to documents which had not been available to Sarpi.[127] The problem is complicated by the fact that it seems likely that Sarpi, for his part, had access to some documents which have not survived, so that on occasion his argument may be soundly based in evidence which is no longer available. The likelihood of this has been much enhanced by the recent identification of a source – the letters from the papal legates at Trent to Pope Paul III and the cardinal nephew – which Sarpi had relied on in a passage which Jedin had singled out for attack. Reassessed in the light of the evidence available to him, Sarpi's account appears surprisingly exact and careful, and to be based indeed, as he had claimed, on careful research in the original documents.[128]

This does not mean that Sarpi's history was in anyway impartial. Sarpi's purpose was to draw up an indictment of the modern papacy, not to look for ways of giving a favourable account of its actions. But it does seem to me reasonable to hold that Sarpi's *History of Trent* is essentially an honest work. His purpose was not simply to produce propaganda, but also to explain to himself what had really happened. His task was to explain how the wrong side had emerged triumphant, and there was no question of his taking an impartial view of the merits of the opposing forces. But, within the limitation imposed by his definition of the problem, his purpose was to learn as much as possible from the available evidence.

This honesty, it must be stressed, is not a characteristic of all of Sarpi's work. In the *History of the Interdict* he fails to give any hint of the disagreement between the doge and the senate, presenting Donà merely as the incarnation of the Republic's official views, and the *Trattato della pace et accomodamento* contains similar suppressions and even falsifications.[129] But these, like all of Sarpi's secular histories, were works intended to justify official policy, and this purpose meant that where necessary the arcana of government must be hidden from the reader: to do otherwise would be to expose the ruler to an illegitimate scrutiny. It is true that the *History of the Interdict* has the appearance of being a private undertaking, while the *Aggionta* and *Supplimento* to the *Historia degli Uscocchi* and the *Trattato della pace et accomodamento* were probably written to an official brief. But then in the months after the Interdict the Venetians could scarcely authorise a provocative restatement of the Republic's view of the conflict with the papacy. Nevertheless, the *History of the Interdict* is no more than an account of the official Venetian view of the conflict, an account which was not intended for publication, but which it was hoped would be used by Jacques de Thou in writing the relevant section of his influential *History of His Own Times*. It was undertaken with the tacit approval of the government, and Sarpi dared not send it to de Thou when relations between Venice and Rome improved and it became apparent that the government would no longer approve of such an action by one of its councillors.[130]

The *History of Trent* is private in a quite different sense from the *History of the Interdict*. Written under the (transparent) pseudonym of Pietro Soave Polano, it expresses Sarpi's personal views, not the views of Paolo Sarpi, *Consigliere di Stato*. Indeed it was written under conditions of the greatest secrecy, and had it claimed to be published by a Venetian or in Venice it must necessarily have incurred the disapproval of the senate. Not long after the publication of the *History of Trent* the Council of Ten refused to permit the publication of Boccalini's *Commentaries on Tacitus*, a work full of praise of Venice, on the grounds that it would be likely to anger certain princes, including the pope, by its exposure of the real motives and actions of rulers.[131] Sarpi's works of official propaganda are careful not to stray far from matters of public record even in describing the motives and actions of Venice's enemies. In the *History of Trent* all such caution is laid aside. The work is a ruthless exposure of behind-the-scenes intrigue and dishonest motivation. Of course, Sarpi's attack is directed at the papacy as an ecclesiastical, not secular, ruler: it is this which justifies him in his own eyes in adopting the techniques of Tacitist history, but such a view could scarcely have been officially condoned by a state which had been amongst the first to accept and enforce the decrees of Trent.

The *History of Trent* is thus quite different in character from Sarpi's other narrative histories, and it is the only one of which one can be sure that the views expressed are Sarpi's own. Just as one turns to the *Pensieri* for evidence of Sarpi's private convictions, so too one naturally turns to the *History of Trent* expecting to find there a forceful expression of Sarpi's views.

But Sarpi's history is not of that sort at all. His method is reminiscent of Fulgenzio Manfredi's description of Sarpi's and Micanzio's propaganda on behalf of Protestantism amongst the Venetians as being conducted 'cautiously, as if they were engaged in some other activity, so that people do not realise what they are up to'.[132] Sarpi presents with care all the proposals for the reform of the Church and dissects the conflicting views of the theologians. He always conveys the impression that the minority view within the Council is the better one, and that things would have been better if any or all of the reform proposals had been accepted. Thus he is evidently hostile to non-residence, to indulgences, to the Index, and willing to approve divine right episcopacy and communion in both kinds. Above all, of course, he conveys the view that a true Council should be superior to the pope, that the Council should determine its own agenda rather than having one imposed upon it by the papal legates, and should not depend upon papal ratification for its decrees. But Sarpi expresses approval or disapproval indirectly, through his portrayal of events, and so he avoids committing himself to particular arguments. And at each point it is clear that he is simply concerned to imply approval for those policies which would reduce the authority of the pope or improve the standing of the laity. He does not commit himself to the view that divine right episcopacy and communion in both kinds are intrinsically right: he merely presents them as preferable.[133] And similarly in his treatment of those decrees of the Council which are directed against the doctrines of the Reformed Churches he avoids claiming that the theological arguments of the Reformers are valid. Indeed if Sarpi conveys any overall impression at all it is that theological arguments are all specious and are to be interpreted simply in the light of the policies they are designed to justify.

The purpose of the *History of Trent* thus appears to be to attack papal absolutism, not to defend any particular theological standpoint; to show why this Council was not a true Council, not to prejudge what a true Council would have decided. Sarpi's purpose is to prevent the decrees of Trent from being established as a mere fact of history, and to show them as the outcome of controversy and conflict, thus preserving the memory of, and a commitment to, the reforming policies which were rejected. His objective is to present arguments which would rally all the opponents of the Council, both Protestant and, in so far as any survived, Catholic; not to defend any religious truth. Sarpi's *History of Trent* is thus a curiously detached work. It does not provide us with the insight into Sarpi's personal convictions that we might have hoped for. It is thus hardly surprising that the circumstances of the publication of the work have come to be treated as casting as much light on its significance as anything that Sarpi actually says.

It was Marc Antonio de Dominis, archbishop of Spalato, who had apostasised and left Italy for England in 1616, who first edited Sarpi's work for publication. De Dominis was an eirenicist who was eventually to leave England for Rome in pursuit of a hopeless project for the reunification of Christendom. Surely, then, a work recommended by such a man must itself be eirenicist, dedicated to demonstrating that Trent had failed to carry out the reforms which would have made possible the reunification of Christendom?[134] Indeed it was long thought that the manuscript of the *History of the Council of Trent* had been entrusted to de Dominis by Sarpi himself, and that it was he who had smuggled it to England: a myth which dramatised an eirenicist interpretation of the work.

However, in 1956 Gaetano Cozzi demonstrated conclusively that the manuscript was in fact smuggled out of Venice after de Dominis' departure, at the instance of George Abbot, the Puritan archbishop of Canterbury, and with the assistance of a network of Dutch merchants. He argued that these circumstances surrounding the publication of the work conformed to a picture of a Sarpi who was in substance a convert to Calvinism, and indeed he was able to show that the publication of the work had been intended to coincide with the publication of the Decrees of the Synod of Dort and thus, it would seem, to play a part in a general reinvigoration of militant Calvinism.[135]

Certainly the *History of Trent* falls within the ambit of the Protestant policy analysed in the last chapter, but it shares all the ambiguities of that policy. This is not to say though that the *History of Trent* takes us no further towards an understanding of Sarpi's views, for it confirms and deepens our knowledge of them in two respects.

The first arises from what is perhaps the only occasion on which Sarpi in the course of his narrative commits himself to a theological position – although significantly it is not in his view a position which is peculiar to Protestantism.[136] Sarpi chooses to reveal his own views when describing the debate in the Council over Zwingli's doctrine of double predestination. He explains that the more distinguished theologians held Zwingli's doctrine to be Catholic, and to conform to the views of St Thomas Aquinas and Duns Scotus. It was the less distinguished ones who dismissed it as inhuman and impious in that it convicted God of injustice:

The first opinion makes God's ways mysterious and incomprehensible, encouraging man to be humble and resigned in the face of God, placing no confidence in his own merits, but recognising the deformity of sin and the excellence of divine grace, while the second is plausible, popular, and encourages human presumption and trust in appearances; it was approved by those friars who were dedicated to preaching, rather than by those who were dedicated to theology, and the courtiers regarded it as the more likely, since it conformed to the requirements of government... The defenders of the second view prevailed over the others as long as human arguments were in question, but when it came to discussing the testimony of the Scriptures they were evidently defeated,

although of course they succeeded in having the Zwinglian view declared heretical.[137]

In this passage Sarpi is concerned to stress not just predestination, but also trust in God. One is reminded of what are almost the opening words of the history:

I will recount the causes and events of an ecclesiastical convocation which lasted twenty-two years, during which time it pursued varying ends and employed varying means. I will show who established it and desired it, who resisted it and postponed it. I will explain what happened during the total of eighteen years when it was in abeyance, how it finally came to be concluded, and how out of the varying goals pursued within it there emerged a conclusion and a settlement which was quite contrary to the plans of those who brought the Council about and in no way corresponded to the fears of those who sought at all costs to disrupt it: which will be a clear demonstration of the need to trust oneself to God, and not to rely upon human prudence.[138]

It is thus no accident that Sarpi expresses his support for the Zwinglian doctrine of predestination, for distrust in man and trust in God are intended to be the lessons to be learnt from the history as a whole. And if one looks across the whole scope of Sarpi's writings this is really the only theological issue on which he expressed a clear commitment. For example, the two letters which are most compromising in terms of implying that he has committed himself to Protestant doctrines are one to Heinsius in which Sarpi expresses his approval of the decrees of the synod of Dort regarding predestination and free-will, and one to van Meurs in which Sarpi appeals to the teaching of St Paul against his correspondent's Arminianism.[139]

Sarpi's approval for the orthodox Calvinist, or Gomarist, position adopted at Dort does not demonstrate, however, a commitment to Protestantism in general. In the *History of Trent*, as we have seen, he stresses that the predestinarian position is that of Aquinas and Duns Scotus, and in 1609 Sarpi had written for the senate an assessment of the contemporary conflict at Rome between the Jesuits, who wished to defend the Tridentine doctrine of free-will, and the Dominicans, who wished to defend, as far as possible, the teachings of Aquinas. In this *consulto* Sarpi asserted his firm opposition to any attempt to give man a role in his own salvation, and he adduces reasons similar to those presented in the *History of Trent*: the doctrine of free-will is condemned by the schools and by the theologians, yet 'in sermons and through the confessional it is taught to the people, under the pretext that they are incapable of grasping the truth, and in reality because this doctrine alienates man from God and makes him dependent upon other men, and because it conforms with the needs of government, to which religion is now subordinated'.[140]

Sarpi's commitment to the doctrine of the servitude of the will is thus a continuing one. Fulgenzio Micanzio had preached, in his Lenten sermons, 'la miseria umana e la virtù della divina grazia' ('the sinfulness of man and the power of God's grace') and Sarpi's letters are full of references to the need to have faith in the ways of God not man.[141] What is harder to determine is whether this commitment, like Sarpi's commitment to the idea of a spiritual religion, to which it is closely allied, is essentially religious or secular in origin. Sarpi told van Meurs that his sole concern in clinging to the Pauline doctrine was 'to know Christ and the virtue of his resurrection', and in the *Pensieri sulla religione* he presented the doctrine of salvation by works as something imposed upon primitive Christianity in order to make it compatible with political and social life.[142] Sarpi's concern might thus have been simply to cling to the teaching of the New Testament, though it must be said that the religious language of the letter to van Meurs is highly uncharacteristic, especially in its reference to the resurrection. Much more characteristic of Sarpi's way of thought is his insistence that the doctrine of free-will gives authority to the clergy, who are in a position to declare which acts will meet with God's approval and which will not. Such arguments seem to suggest that Sarpi's uncompromising theological commitment derived partly from his anti-clericalism, partly from his conviction, expressed in the *Pensieri*, that the best religions are those which have the highest conception of God and the lowest of man, and partly from his philosophical opposition to the idea of free-will.[143]

The approval Sarpi expresses for the doctrine of predestination thus does not constitute incontestable evidence that his views had changed since writing the *Pensieri*. What it does provide is striking evidence of the continuity of Sarpi's thought between the *Pensieri* and the *History of Trent*: the *History of Trent* advocates an attitude to God similar to that recommended in the *Pensieri*. There is a difference of course in that the Zwinglian doctrine of predestination is a doctrine which condemns the majority of mankind to damnation, while Sarpi in the *Pensieri* maintains that good religions either convey no sense of sin, or else make expiation easy. But the recurring theme in Sarpi's treatment of this question is that of the need to trust God not man, of the need to recognise the limitations of human nature. The whole objection to the doctrine of free-will and salvation by works is that it gives the clergy the opportunity to inculcate a sense of sin and so to control men's behaviour. The doctrine of predestination frees men from personal responsibility and so from guilt, requiring only that they place their trust in God.

Sarpi claims to show the need to trust in God by showing how events fail to take the course expected to them. This, however, is very different from showing the hand of God at work in history. Sarpi was capable of writing in a letter to Groslot de l'Isle: 'God oversees all things, and ordains them to his glory, even though men's plans run counter to his', but it is striking how there is no attempt in the *History of Trent* to suggest that things are indeed ordained to the glory of God.[144] In a famous passage Sarpi mocks the idea that this Council, so tightly under papal control, was a true Council of the Church, under the guidance of the Holy Spirit, by repeating (or inventing) the joke that it was evident that the Holy Spirit travelled back and forth between Rome and Trent in a despatch box.[145] Sarpi's history is in fact a determinedly secular one, and his concern is to demolish one account of the divine significance of Trent, not to substitute another. Thus the trust in God he advocates becomes merely a willingness to await the outcome of events, a recognition of the limitations of human activity and understanding. Indeed the opening words of Sarpi's *History of Trent* recall, presumably intentionally, those of Guicciardini's *History of Italy*, where Guicciardini describes how those who invited the French armies into Italy were unable to control the events that followed from that.

Guicciardini thus portrays history as being dominated by accident, fortune and fate. Great events are heralded by miraculous portents, and God's justice manifests itself as an inexplicable destiny.[146] Sarpi, by contrast, provides in the *History of Trent* a perfectly clear explanation of why the outcome of the Council proved contrary to expectations. With the aid of hindsight, human misconceptions are shown to result from a failure to understand the institutional context within which political conflicts take place. Within a narrative directed to this end there could be no place for the miraculous or the portentous.[147] Sarpi does not advocate trust in God because historical events lie outside the grasp of human reason, but because men, at the mercy of forces outside their control, are not responsible for their own success or failure.

The best example of Sarpi's characteristic method of historical explanation is his treatment of the pontificate of Adrian VI, who was elected pontiff in 1522 with no previous experience of curial affairs, and who longed to reform the faults of the Church, ingenuously admitting that it was the corruption of curia and clergy which was the cause of the Lutheran revolt. Adrian's proposals for reform, however, came to nothing. One of them, for example, was the suggestion that the harsh penances customary in the Middle Ages should be reintroduced as a means of restoring discipline, and of giving meaning to papal indulgences,

which could be defended as providing absolution from the penalties imposed
in the confessional, rather than those imposed at the Last Judgement. This
proposal was, however, unanimously rejected by Adrian's advisors, who argued
that penalties which were accepted without question in the Middle Ages would
not be tolerated now. The remedy would thus prove too drastic for the diseased
patient, and far from recovering Germany Adrian would lose control of Italy.
Adrian's pontificate was a short one – as Sarpi remarks ironically, it pleased God
that he should pass on to another life, since the curia was not worthy of such
a pope – but in that short time he became completely disillusioned. Sarpi reports
that he told his closest associates that the position of pope was a miserable one,
for it was evident that he could do no good, even though he wished to and
struggled to.[148]

Sarpi seems to have drawn this last anecdote from the diary of Francesco
Chierigati, which he claims to have read, but which no longer survives.[149]
Whatever he may have found in his sources, Sarpi's presentation of Adrian's
pontificate differs markedly from most of those which would have been available
to him in print. The great Sleidan, author of a history of Germany during the
Reformation, presents Adrian's promises of reform as a cynical attempt to delay
calling a council.[150] Guicciardini attacks Adrian as politically inexpert.[151]
Panvinio and Giovio reflect the viewpoint of the Roman court. They emphasise
his ignorance of the affairs of Italy and the papacy, and concentrate on his
financial economies and his lack of generosity towards his relatives (which, as
they take pleasure in pointing out, contemporaries held to be occasioned by
avarice), rather than on his attempts to reform the Church: they give as much
or more attention to his efforts to put an end to blasphemy, usury and sodomy
in the City of Rome.[152] Sarpi's approach does coincide though with that of the
author of the *Revision du Concile de Trente*, a Gallican work concerned to defend the liberties of the Gallican Church as the surviving remnants of the
ancient liberties of the whole Church, and to demonstrate the decrees of Trent
to be invalid both in substance and in form. In this work Adrian's pontificate
is mentioned at the beginning, and he is described, as in Sarpi, as 'honest
Adrian...the only pope with right intentions'. But his hopes of reform had come
to nothing, for 'the popes turned the cat in the pan, and carried the matter so
handsomely, that instead of a natural birth the Council was delivered of a
monster'.[153] There is no suggestion here, however, that Adrian's hopes were
dashed in his own lifetime: it is his successors who prevented reform, not the
institution of the papacy or the curia.

Sarpi's account of Adrian's pontificate is not remarkable simply as an example
of how events turn out contrary to expectations. What is truly remarkable is
his insistence that it is institutions not individuals which determine events.
Adrian might long for reform – might continue to long for it until his death – but
as pope he could not undermine papal power, nor threaten the income of the

curia. Sarpi wishes of course to drive home the degeneracy of the Roman Church, which can now only be reformed from without, by the destruction of papal power, but he is also seeking to exemplify the workings of what is for him a fundamental law of history: that events are dominated by the interests of corporate groups and institutions, not by the wishes of individuals.

In order to grasp the novelty of Sarpi's historical understanding we need to see it in relation to two complementary traditions of explanation. The first is the tradition of seeing history as a study in the workings of self-interest concealed by hypocrisy. This approach is at the heart of the Tacitism of a writer like Boccalini. For him politics is to be explained in terms of the working of an inexorable political law, that politicians are bound to pursue self-interest in terms of the maximisation of power at all times. They thus act as if in the grip of an evil force outside their own control. Of course they do not admit their real motives, but hypocritically conceal them. The present age is peculiarly hypocritical because politicians have increasingly come to appeal to religion as a justification for their actions.

The same approach had characterised the work of the founding father of Gallican historiography Charles Dumoulin (1500–1566) who was one of the sources for Sarpi's *History of Trent*. Dumoulin, we are told,

described in clear and vivid terms the pattern of ecclesiastical corruption, [but] he was less successful in analysing it historically. He did not overlook the degeneration of doctrine...He realized, too, that the disease, whatever it was, had invaded the Church from top to bottom. But for Dumoulin it was primarily a disorder of the head – proceeding not from the complications of bureaucracy and finance but from papal policy, *de motu proprio*.

He was thus led to praise Machiavelli – long before the massacre of St Bartholemew gave Machiavelli such a bad name – as having 'depicted marvellously well the origin, rise and growth of the papacy and the ruses of the popes by which they were achieved'.[154]

Much of what Sarpi has to say falls squarely within this tradition. Peter Burke, who has followed Milton in describing Sarpi as 'the Great Unmasker', has noted that a form of reductionism is involved, but one which moves not from individual opinions to economic structures, but rather from one level of motivation to another, from the outward appearance of piety to the 'reality' of political self-interest.[155] Thus Sarpi writes, very much in the manner of Boccalini, 'everything conceals itself behind the mask of religion...In other centuries hypocrisy was not uncommon, but in this one it pervades everything, so that no true piety remains. God have pity on us!'[156] Much of the *History of Trent* is concerned with exposing the hypocrisy of the papacy, and indeed as far as Sarpi is concerned the whole of scholastic theology is no more than an elaborate mask devised to conceal papal self-interest. As he explains in his notes to Sandys, it was because the absolute authority of the papacy was obviously absurd and contrary to true Christianity that 'schools were instituted in the monasteries, where they could study how to accommodate Christian doctrine to the interests of those in power. However, such an obvious contradiction could not be successfully overcome.'[157] Theology was only of interest to Sarpi in so far as it masked abuses in the accumulation of power and wealth. Aside from this, theological differences were merely verbal, and of no importance. Thus the eirenicists who sought to reunite Christendom by seeking doctrinal reconciliation had failed to recognise the roots of theological disagreement. As Sarpi wrote, politely, to Hotman, who was engaged in just such an enterprise:

The real obstacle to such a valuable undertaking, is the advantage which those in power obtain from [religious] disagreement... The religious orders benefit financially from the conflicts, and the Jesuits do so in particular, for they have grown so rich and so powerful through them, that they give orders to kings... while rulers have no interest in breaking with people who can give them the right to break their oaths and to commit incest. It is these which are the insuperable problems at issue...[158]

Sarpi's exploration of hypocrisy, however, is nearly always a study of the hypocrisy bred by official, rather than purely personal, ambition and it is thus wrong to suggest that he is not concerned with structural factors.[159] Sarpi's portrait of the excellent Adrian fails to mention that he did not lavish gifts on his relatives: it is Giovio who notes this striking example of Adrian's 'avarice'. So, too, when dealing with corrupt popes, it is their efforts to defend institutional corruption, not their private vices, which Sarpi delineates.[160] The *History of Trent* is not a portrait of the foibles of the popes as men, but of their astuteness as rulers.

For Boccalini reason of state demands the pursuit of personal self-interest. For Sarpi the logic of power requires the defence of bureaucratic authority and entrenched privilege: men are simply the agents of the institutions they serve. The *History of Benefices* after all had been concerned to trace not the progress of moral corruption within the clergy, but the process by which they came to have a corporate interest which conflicted with that of the laity and of the secular authorities.

It seems to me that Sarpi's historical understanding in this respect was deeply influenced by another convention of political analysis which we may term the republican myth. Machiavelli in his *Discourses* had portrayed the vigour and energy of the Roman Republic as arising from political conflict between different social classes and constitutional institutions. Internal disunity had acted as a check on individual ambition and a spur to territorial expansion. In *The Prince*, on the other hand, he had portrayed absolutist government as dependent upon hypocrisy and deceit to won popular consent.[161] Thus republican virtue which subordinated individual self-interest to the defence of institutional rights was contrasted to absolutist hypocrisy, based on a recognition that power derived from personal not institutional authority. Machiavelli's view of course is a complex and ambiguous one, but someone like Boccalini could draw upon a Machiavellian heritage when contrasting the constitutional order of Venice, which served as a check upon the untramelled pursuit of personal self-agrandisement, with the absolutist court, where the pursuit of personal power led to deceit and mutual distrust.[162]

What Sarpi was doing, then, in emphasising the institutional constraints governing political activity was applying to absolutist political systems the methods of analysis which had previously been reserved only for republics. Sarpi had no doubt that papal government was absolutist – the pope had 'un imperio assoluto sopra tutti', ('an absolute sovereignty over all'), and papal plenitude of power had become a papal 'totality' of power.[163] Yet nevertheless the pope was incapable of acting contrary to the interests of the curia, and power lay with the institution not the man. On the death of Donà Sarpi, exceptionally, adopted the traditional rhetoric of republican mythology:

it has no effect whatever on the office of the prince. His death has caused not the slightest change in affairs of state, for the Republic is so well ordered. The same government, the same objectives, the same opinions: all these things continue. The Romans entertained some hopes that they had made a gain, but they were soon firmly convinced that this polity is ruled by the whole body of the nobility, which remains unchanging.[164]

Yet Sarpi could have said almost the same about Rome, substituting merely curia for nobility. Indeed his conviction that Rome always did remain the same made him refuse to give weight to temporary shifts in papal policy.[165]

Sarpi's historical understanding distinguishes him from his contemporaries, for in his case 'unmasking' does not mean simply moving from one level of motivation to another, but also means moving from the world of private hopes and delusions to that of institutional constraints.[166] Sarpi's history is in the end about structures and not simply about motives. It is this, I think, which makes Sarpi so strikingly modern an historian. He does not have a sense of history having its own internal motor, of the past as being different in kind from the present. Such a sense of progress in history emerges only with the Enlightenment, and in particular with Turgot, whose *Essai* of 1750 influenced Gibbon, Voltaire, Robertson and Hume.[167] What he does have a sense of is man as being as much the creature as the creator of social institutions. Sarpi's sense of the role of institutions in history makes it easy to see why he was so admired by the philosophical historians of the Enlightenment.[168] Lord Dacre has described philosophical history as being characterised by the belief that 'history's course, though it may be affected in detail by human decisions, is fundamentally determined by the structure of society, that is (in Robertson's words), by "the division of property, together with the maxims and manners to which it gave rise"'.[169] Sarpi may never have articulated so general a principle of historical explanation, but he certainly held that it was the division of property within the Church which had determined the 'maxims and manners' of Catholic Christianity.

This feeling for institutional constraints went far beyond a mere grasp of *opportunità* as traditionally understood to refer to the realm of contingency, of unpredictable political conjunctures, for while Sarpi always hoped that the anti-clericals would be granted an appropriate political opening, he saw that this was only likely to happen if the institutional interests controlling political activity were transformed. There was no point in matching one's intellect against an institution like the papacy, unless one could also counterbalance it with a countervailing set of institutions and a countervailing ideology. When Sarpi writes of the importance of *opportunità* it is to stress not the vast potential for action open to he who knows how to seize the time, but rather the forces working to delimit and restrict the effective actions of individuals. Sarpi's conception of history led him to a new pessimism regarding the possible impact of political action, including his own.[170]

Sarpi's weakness was that he was not capable of creating new institutions or ideologies in the manner of a Luther or a Calvin. His strength was that he understood exactly the weakness of the intellectual or the political conspirator who could not depend upon the backing of Church or state. His associates might accuse him of *fredda prudenza*, but he realised clearly that the papacy could be transformed only by a shift in the balance of power in Europe and by armed struggle, and never by the wishful thinking of a Hotman or a de Dominis. Sarpi was thus a revolutionary seeking to overthrow not only the papacy, but clerical power in general, and he was a true revolutionary in that he had a sense of the past as weighing upon the present, restricting his freedom of expression, his freedom to agitate, making his aspirations hazardous and improbable.

Sarpi's sense of the past was rooted in his anti-clericalism. It was this which had led him to insist on the absolute authority of the state, and in the process to treat republics and absolutist monarchies as one. His philosophical treatment of sovereignty thus opened the way to a new sociological understanding of the distribution of power in society. But even before that his view of the limited role of religion as a set of internalised values, a *tora*, in maintaining social order had opened the way not only to a new conception of the significance of religion for the state, but also to a new understanding of social structures in general. Indeed it may not be far-fetched to claim that Sarpi's recognition that history is primarily the record not of private desires but of institutional and structural constraints is a corollary of his recognition that 'atheists' are capable of living together in society. Both depend upon an understanding of the density, the constant pressure, the compelling force of ordinary social relations. Once admit that the wills of 'atheists' are subject to social constraints, and it becomes evident that so are the wills even of princes.

Sarpi's sense of history as the embodiment of intersubjective, not subjective, realities and of material interests not spiritual ideals marks the birth of modern historical understanding. And it is doubtful if history could have been written in these terms by anyone who had not rejected the conventional view of the role of purely subjective, internalised fear in preserving society from chaos, and who had not, at the same time, been able to draw on a tradition of 'republican' mythology. If Sarpi had abandoned his belief in the sociability of 'atheists' his account of Adrian's pontificate would surely have, as a consequence, sought some explanation for Adrian's failure in his character, rather than placing such stress upon institutional constraints. As it is, the Sarpi of the *History of the Council of Trent* is at one with the Sarpi of the *Pensieri* in stressing the prime importance of man's relationship to other men, mediated by social institutions, rather than their relationship to God or their conscience. The *History of the Council of Trent* thus reflects the originality of the *Pensieri*, both in its failure to put forward an account of true Christianity, and in its perception of the role of social institutions and structures in political and ecclesiastical life.

Sarpi's view of politics, however, is not entirely without precedent, even outside the republican tradition. It is striking that in the *De la concorde de l'estat* of 1599, a tract which we have seen to parallel Sarpi's outlook in a number of respects, the *noblesse de robe* are presented as being the embodiment of the state, without whose support Henri IV will be powerless.[171] This is political propaganda, not political analysis: it is some distance from providing an account of the interests of the *noblesse de robe* as a group, or the extent to which the crown's dependence on them will act as a constraint upon royal policy. But here perhaps we have an indication of how the new secular account of religion which is to be found in works such as this was made possible by a new understanding of social institutions in general, a new picture of power as being widely distributed throughout the political elite, and of the world of politics as being distinct from the world of constitutional and legal authority. Perhaps it was precisely because authority was seen as having its roots within society, rather than as being imposed on it from without, that it was possible to argue that social order depended not upon revealed religion, but only upon natural piety.

Sarpi's portrait of Adrian VI shows that he could have been the first great historian of modern times. But, neither in the *History of the Council of Trent* nor in his other histories, is there a portrait of a secular ruler to set alongside it. We can only regret that Sarpi's secular histories were all concerned with the defence of legal authority, not the analysis of political power. Had he applied the methods of the *History of the Council of Trent* to a wider range of subjects his influence would have been the greater. His commitment to absolutism, however, stood in the way of such an undertaking. The *History of the Council of Trent*, although the greatest historical work of its age, remains a work limited by the reticence imposed upon Sarpi by the need to address a diverse audience and by Sarpi's own inability to contemplate the limitations, the fallibility of secular authority. When he attacked secular powers, as in the *Aggionta* and *Supplimento* to the *Historia degli Uscocchi*, it was in order to show that they were in the wrong and Venice in the right.[172] Such questions of guilt and innocence at no point involved an analysis of the the concrete nature and practical limits of secular political authority.

We have to turn to Micanzio's correspondence to find a portrait of a king – James I of England – who might be forced by circumstances or by pressure from the political community to act contrary to his own desires. Such a ruler, Micanzio argues, is unlikely to act with the skill and determination of someone who is following his own instincts.[173] He thus implies a view of individual politicians as the agents and interpreters of forces outside their own control, ascribing to them a certain, circumscribed ability to affect the course of events. It is an irony of history that Micanzio's letters should survive in a translation by Thomas Hobbes, their addressee's secretary, for in them is to be found in embryo an analysis of real political power which stands in sharp contrast to any absolutist account of legitimate political authority.[174] In Sarpi, unlike Hobbes, we find both an absolutist theory of authority and a sociological analysis of power. Certainly there is an unresolved tension between the two, especially since Sarpi's absolutism is presented in divine right terms. Was Sarpi unaware of this tension? The two arguments, although formally at odds, serve a common purpose. Sarpi's divine right absolutism legitimises the view, presented in naturalistic terms in the *Pensieri*, that there should be no independent clerical authority. His analysis of political power goes a step further in implying that clerical power is not only properly subordinate, but may also be unnecessary. Thus the unresolved tension between Sarpi's publicly expressed views on authority disappears once these are recast in the terms employed in the *Pensieri*. It is not Sarpi's convictions which are internally inconsistent, but the forms of argument to which he has recourse in his attempt to give them public expression.

PAX VAN
TIBI GELI
MAR STA
CE MEUS

4   The lion of St Mark holding a copy of the Gospel, as it appears at the head of the
doge's proclamation to the clergy of the Venetian territories in reply to the papal Interdict
(6 May 1606)

4

The man and his masks

A gross error it is, to think that regal power ought to serve for the good of the body, and [not] of the soul; for men's temporal peace, and not for their eternal safety: as if God had ordained kings for no other end and purpose but only to fat up men like hogs and to see that they have their mast?

(R. Hooker, *Of the Laws of Ecclesiastical Polity*,
bk VIII: written C. 1593; 1st edn, London, 1645)

Stimò sempre la Republica di Venezia che il fondamento principale d'ogni imperio e dominio fosse la vera religione e pietà, et ha conosciuto per grazia singolare di Dio l'esser nata, educata et accresciuta nel vero culto divino.

(Paolo Sarpi, *Considerazioni sopra le censure della santità
di Papa Paulo V contro la serenissima Republica di Venezia*, Venice, 1606)

(The Venetian Republic has always held that the most important support for all government and authority comes from true religion and piety. By singular grace of God Venice was born, educated and has developed to the present day in the practice of the true worship of God.)

Images of the man

Ego eius ingenii sum, ut, velut Chamalaeon, a conversantibus mores sumam; versum, quos ab occultis, et tristibus haurio, invitus incordio: hilares et apertos sponte ac libere recipio: personam coactus fero, licet in Italia nemo sine ea esse possit. (Letter to Gillot, 12 May 1609)[1]

(My character is such that, like a chameleon, I imitate the behaviour of those amongst whom I find myself. Thus if I am amongst people who are reserved and gloomy I become, despite myself, unfriendly. I respond openly and freely to people who are cheerful and uninhibited. I am compelled to wear a mask. Perhaps there is nobody who can survive in Italy without one.)

The Bodleian Library portrait of Sarpi graphically depicts the man as he was seen by his contemporaries in northern Europe.[2] It portrays Sarpi as a man of letters, yet the pen in his hand is gripped resolutely, suggesting a man of action. Moreover the large patch on his cheek is a reminder that he had been singled out as a target for political assassination, while the caption – EVISCERATOR CONCILII TRIDENTINI – reinforces this impression of violence. The message is clear: Sarpi, the man who survived the assassin's dagger, has with his pen delivered a mortal wound to the soft underbelly of Catholicism. Thus Wotton arranged for Sarpi to be held out as an inspiration to a future generation of scholars. Others too admired Sarpi for these reasons: John Donne when Dean of St Paul's had a portrait of Sarpi, a fellow enemy to the Jesuits, in his parlour.[3] Even in recent years it has been possible for the Catholic historian Hubert Jedin to describe Sarpi as the papacy's greatest enemy after Luther.[4]

Sarpi would have been pleased at this image of himself, but it should not blind us to the ambiguities of his life. He himself dismissed the *History of Trent* as a work which would be of only passing significance: he had not sought to deal in it with subjects of lasting importance.[5] What were those subjects for Sarpi? According to the conventions of seventeenth-century biographers it was on their deathbeds that men betrayed their real convictions. It is with dismay that we discover that Fulgenzio Micanzio, Sarpi's closest associate, was responsible for two contrasting accounts of his death. One, for domestic consumption, claimed he had died a pious Catholic. The other, to be sent abroad, suggested he had died a Protestant.[6] Search as one may, it is hard to locate the man behind the masks, even in death. But the meaning of the *Pensieri* is clear enough, just as it is evident what Sarpi's reputation was before he became a public figure.

We have now surveyed Sarpi's life in its different aspects, and are in a position to attempt an overall assessment of the evidence regarding his beliefs. In this chapter I want briefly to argue that the evidence strongly suggests that the *Pensieri* represent Sarpi's true convictions, that if the last years of Sarpi's life were directed at any goal it was at the realisation, in this world, of the philosophical ideals sketched in the *Pensieri*. There is, however, no remotely plausible account of Sarpi's life which has not at some time been propounded, and it will be helpful at this point if we survey the most important of these interpretations.

According to Taucci, himself a Servite with the honour of his order to defend, Sarpi was always an orthodox Catholic. His collaboration with Protestants was motivated by the need to win political allies for Venice, not by any hostility to the Catholic religion, and he sought as far as possible to avoid committing himself on questions of doctrine in dispute between Catholics and Protestants.[7] This line of argument, however, now commands little support. Taucci did not know of Sarpi's letter to Heinsius welcoming the decrees of Dort, nor of the circumstances of the publication of the *History of Trent*. Sarpi's association with Protestants was obviously intended to serve political purposes, but there was clearly more to it than that: his intention was to use Protestantism to destroy the power and authority of the papacy, and, at the least, he found the Protestant Churches more attractive than the Catholic.

If Sarpi was not an orthodox Catholic, perhaps he was a Catholic reformer? It might be possible to present him as being in some sense Catholic rather than Protestant if he was willing to accept the authority of tradition in addition to that of the Bible. As a Catholic reformer Sarpi might have been concerned to restore the pure teaching of the early Church, to seek some kind of moderate religious settlement such as that embodied in the Anglican Church, or merely to return to the doctrines of pre-Tridentine Catholicism. Each of these interpretations has been put forward. A recent study of Sarpi by da Pozzo has argued that the 'myth' of the early Church is at the very heart of the *History of Trent*. Frances Yates has sought to assimilate Sarpi's views to those of the Anglican Church, while one of the first English historians to do research in Venice, Horatio Brown, compared Sarpi to the Old Catholics who had refused to accept the decrees of Vatican I.[8]

Each of these interpretations of Sarpi as a Catholic reformer, however, is supported by inadequate evidence. In the first place there is no evidence of Sarpi accepting any characteristically 'Catholic' doctrines: the authority of tradition, divine right episcopacy, salvation by works, and so on. In the second, two of these interpretations were rejected by Sarpi himself: he insisted to Casaubon that the early Church could not be re-established in the present, and he made clear to Dudley Carleton, the English ambassador to Venice, that he had no time for the view that the doctrines of the Church before Trent had been authentic.[9] The view that Sarpi was at heart an 'Anglican' is at first sight more plausible. Certainly, had Venice broken with the pope, he would have wanted the senate to adopt the Anglican Church as its model, but this was because, as he explained to von Dohna, any reformation introduced from above would need to appear to be as conservative as possible if it was not to endanger political stability.[10] His own support, however, was given to the Calvinists: the circumstances of the publication of the *History of Trent*, much relied on by Yates, point to a desire to further the cause of the Gomarists within international Calvinism, and do not suggest any particular feeling of affinity for the Anglican Church.

Perhaps Sarpi was no sort of Catholic at all, but a Protestant? This was the view that Pastor found most convincing, in view of Sarpi's intimate collaboration with Protestants. More recently this view of Sarpi has been revived as a result of the early researches of Ulianich, who discovered the letter to Heinsius, and of Cozzi, who showed the relationship between the publication of the *History of Trent* and the decrees of Dort.[11] Of course Sarpi presented himself, when writing as adviser to the senate, as a pious Catholic.[12] Even more damaging for this interpretation, though, is the fact that Sarpi continued to the end of his days to say Mass, and that he told Diodati that salvation could be found within the Catholic Church.[13]

Of the various attempts to attribute to Sarpi a consistent and articulated religious viewpoint only one remains. According to this Sarpi must be understood as an eirenicist who clung fast to the fundamental truths of Christianity, but who was keen to avoid superfluous doctrines. In an article on Sarpi Bouwsma has portrayed him in such terms, and this was certainly how Sarpi presented himself to Groslot when he attacked Protestant efforts to treat the identification of the pope with Antichrist as an article of faith.[14] Ulianich, in a careful survey of the evidence relating to Sarpi's opinions on questions of ecclesiology, was reduced to the conclusion that Sarpi must be presumed to have believed at least the doctrines of the Creed.[15] But precisely this presumption must be thrown in doubt by any study of the *Scrittura su Vorstio*.[16]

Sarpi, however, may not have been primarily concerned with questions of religious doctrine. Chabod believed that Sarpi was first and foremost a politician, concerned to defend Venetian sovereignty and to strengthen Venetian independence. Bouwsma, in his book on the Interdict crisis, presents Sarpi as primarily a political ideologue, concerned to defend traditional Venetian (and Renaissance) values against the totalitarianism of Counter-Reformation theology.[17] As we shall see, Sarpi was certainly willing to present himself in this light, and an informed contemporary like Casaubon was eager to present him as someone driven by love of country, rather than theological conviction, to ally with Protestantism.[18]

To see Sarpi in this light, however, one has to concentrate on those things he wrote in his capacity as state theologian, in which capacity he was required to defend Venice's theological orthodoxy while insisting on her right to political independence. It is true that one may present Sarpi's alliance with Protestantism as an alliance directed against Venice's main enemies, Spain and Rome. But Sarpi clearly went beyond the requirements of political intrigue when he urged upon Gillot a view of secular authority which conflicted with the one which he had defended in public, or when he declared his support for the decrees of Dort. Above all the *History of the Council of Trent* can only be understood as a private undertaking, one which had little prospect of furthering Venice's political interests, and which scarcely refers to the central theme of so many Gallican attacks upon the Council: the threat it posed to the independent authority of the secular ruler. The *History of Trent* is clearly intended to educate Protestant Europe rather than to win its support for Venice, and if the principles it seeks to inculcate are tantalisingly indefinite, nevertheless they clearly originate in a view of the Church rather than of the state.

The best recent scholarship, above all that of Cozzi, has thus been concerned, while giving due weight to Sarpi's defence of secular authority and his alliance with the *giovani*, to emphasise his private preoccupation with questions of religion. But since Sarpi is evidently neither Protestant nor Catholic, and not even, perhaps, an orthodox Christian, it has been necessary to portray Sarpi as being committed to a purely spiritual religion, one little concerned with questions of doctrine, but based upon trust in God.[19] Here certainly we begin at last to find ourselves on firm ground, for the idea is stressed by Sarpi at moments when he is most at odds with his own official statements, in the letters to Gillot on sovereignty and in the replies to Casaubon's praise of the early Church. Even the *History of Trent* fits in with this view, both in the distrust it implies for theological speculation and in the emphasis it places upon trust in God.

None of the previous interpretations can give a satisfactory explanation of Sarpi's writings even if one chooses to leave the *Pensieri* out of account. This last interpretation is compatible with almost all the evidence, other than that of the *Pensieri*. However, it cannot explain how Sarpi came to hold this religious position, in what terms he would have defended it, or even what precisely it consisted in. Nor can it adequately explain why Sarpi's belief in a spiritual religion was not associated with a fideistic acceptance of the doctrines and institutions of the Catholic Church. One cannot dismiss the *Pensieri* as a mere intellectual exercise or an 'early text' precisely because they make it possible to answer these questions. What they show is that Sarpi did not, strictly speaking, believe in a spiritual, non-doctrinal religion, but that he advocated it as the best sort of religion. They show that he had reached this position from a starting point in a materialist agnosticism and a conviction that religion was to be understood in psychological and social, not supernatural terms. Thus they show that Sarpi's preoccupation with questions of religion arises from a set of philosophical rather than political preoccupations. But they also serve to explain why the sceptical philosopher, the advocate of a spiritual religion, could have immersed himself in the writing of political propaganda and the study of history: they give us, I shall argue, a sketch of the principles which guided Sarpi's life.

No interpretation of Sarpi can hope to make him consistent with himself. It is all too evident that he claimed to be a Catholic yet supported Protestantism; that he served Venice yet wrote the *History of Trent* for his own purposes; that he praised the early Church yet had no desire to imitate it. The only hope of making sense of Sarpi lies in starting with the fact of his inconsistency, with the fact that he described himself as a chameleon, taking on the colour of his surroundings, and that he had expressly recommended hypocrisy in the *Pensieri medico-morali*. There Sarpi had insisted that the wise man must act the hypocrite because he cannot openly acknowledge the truths of philosophy. Outwardly he must appear to share the views of others, or, under circumstances where there is a pressing need to correct their errors, he must lay claim to views which merely counterbalance theirs, and at the same time employ arguments to undermine their convictions. Here, surely, we have the clue to Sarpi's inconsistency and his hypocrisy, in the fact that he could not admit to the philosophical truths expressed in the *Pensieri*. The real Sarpi must be presumed to be the Sarpi of the *Pensieri* because no other hypothesis can satisfactorily explain the contradictions running through his life. Either Sarpi was a man with no consistent principle or purpose, or else his principles and purposes derive from the *Pensieri*.

History of the Inquisition

Before I present, however, what seems to me the correct account of Sarpi's motives and principles, we must consider two final pieces of evidence: one, Sarpi's *History of the Inquisition*, which might at first glance seem to tell against my interpretation, and one, Sarpi's letter to Giacomo Badoer, which seems to me to be inexplicable except as evidence of Sarpi's continued attachment to the views he had expressed in the *Pensieri*.

The *History of the Inquisition* was written in 1613 at the request of the senate. Sarpi's *Consulto sopra l'officio dell'inquisizione* was intended to provide guidance for Venetian officials in their dealings with the Inquisition, both in Venice and in the cities of the Terraferma. The work, however, was, by reason of its subject matter, of general interest: it was first published in Italy in 1638, and three English translations appeared in the space of the next forty years.[20]

Sarpi's account of the Inquisition's history need not concern us. The *History of the Inquisition* must, however, constitute an acid test for the interpretation of Sarpi I have sought to present in this book because it appears to contain a direct denial of the *Pensieri*'s argument that the state can maintain itself without the support of providential religion. Had Sarpi indeed changed his mind? We cannot proceed until we have weighed the evidence of this text.

The heart of Sarpi's treatment of the Inquisition is his claim to be presenting a defence of the Republic's existing practice. Consequently Sarpi is keen to insist that the Republic by its very nature favours tradition and is hostile to innovation. The Catholic Church on the other hand is presented as being eager to innovate in matters where it sees some prospect of extending the authority of the curia. It is, Sarpi implies, the papacy's efforts to lay claim to a greater authority than properly belongs to it which have been, throughout history, the main cause of heresy.[21] In face of papal innovation the Republic must defend its traditional faith: everyone knows that alteration in religion leads to political upheaval. Consequently the prince must, in his own interest, exercise control over the teachings of the Church. Moreover the Scriptures promise tranquillity and prosperity to those states where piety is favoured, and threaten with destruction those which show no concern for religious affairs. It is thus the ruler's religious duty to exercise supervision over the Church, lest he provoke God's anger.[22]

Sarpi balances his evident hostility to the modern papacy with a rejection of Protestantism, which seeks to undermine the legitimate authority of the

Church, and is as great a threat to political stability as the Counter-Reformation.[23] It seems unlikely that this should be taken as Sarpi's considered assessment of Protestantism, for Sarpi's activities from 1606 on clearly show that he did not regard Rome and Geneva as a Scylla and a Charybdis, between which the ship of state must seek to steer. His constant argument, after all, is that the Church has no legitimate authority, aside from that – recognised by Protestants – which is exercised through persuasion and admonition. Sarpi's passing swipe at Protestantism is intended merely to render credible his claim to be defending tradition against innovation.

The passage of interest to us comes when Sarpi goes on from a discussion of the state's jurisdiction over cases of heresy to insist on the right of the secular authority to prevent the publication of any Index of prohibited books which does not meet with its approval. In addition the Republic has the right to permit the publication of books which defend secular authority against clerical encroachment, and to forbid the publication of those which deny the divine right of kings and argue that there are cases when the subject may in good conscience disobey his ruler. To allow the papacy to have a monopoly of arguments from conscience would dangerously weaken secular authority:

There are few people in the world who act out of love of what is right; most men fall into two groups: those who act morally for fear of divine punishment [*pene spirituali*], and those who do so for fear of punishment in this world [*pene temporali*]. If one takes away the fear of divine punishment, one loses the obedience of all those who hope to conceal their wrong-doing successfully, or to avoid punishment through influence or other means, along with those who do not expect to (but have no fear of punishment in this world); which taken together amounts to a large number. On the other hand we see how easily some people are persuaded to obey [the secular authority] for fear of divine punishment. Since God has given the secular ruler these two ways of ensuring that he is obeyed, out of fear of this-wordly punishment and out of conscience, as St Paul teaches, it would be a great failing to let slip the second of these means, which is not the least important, by allowing the true Catholic doctrine to be attacked.[24]

There can be no doubt that Sarpi is here maintaining that fear of divine punishment is essential to the maintenance of Venetian political order. But it needs to be remembered that he is considering a situation where two competing authorities are both claiming that they should be obeyed for reasons of conscience: if one abandons its claim then the other will be able to turn those who act out of fear of divine punishment against it. The argument of the *Pensieri* was that the state could survive even if people did not fear hell – that moral atheists could be sociable. The argument of the *History of the Inquisition* is that Christians are potentially unsociable – that where people *do* fear hell, it is important that they should have the right ideas about which actions will incur divine punishment and which will not.

The two arguments can thus be presented as being formally compatible. Sarpi had argued that 'The *tora* is thus not as useful as some people think, for it works because two things are more effective than one': political authority alone would suffice. The situation Sarpi is now considering, however, is one in which the two means of securing obedience are acting against each other, not together. In the *Pensieri* he had recognised the existence of a conflict between the state and the Church, but had felt that the Republic had emerged stronger for that conflict. Now he is admitting that that conflict could lead to the destruction of the state and the victory of the Church.

Thus although the two arguments – that of the *Pensieri* and that of the *History of the Inquisition* – could be presented as being formally compatible, there has clearly been a shift in Sarpi's point of view between the one and the other. And indeed Sarpi actually presents his argument in the *History of the Inquisition* in a way which is incompatible with his argument in the *Pensieri*, for in the *Pensieri* he had denied the validity of Pomponazzi's division of the world into those who do good for its own sake, those who fear punishment in this world, and those who fear it only in the next. There he had insisted that it is the same people who fear punishment in this world and the next, and that those who are bold enough not to fear one sort of punishment are bold enough not to fear the other. By accepting Pomponazzi's categories in the *History of the Inquisition*, Sarpi implicitly commits himself to the view that, since many people who now act morally would not do so but for the fear of divine punishment, 'atheists' would, by and large, be unsociable.

Should we regard this as representing a decisive shift in Sarpi's view of the political role of religion? I do not think so. In the first place we must bear in mind that Sarpi's purpose is to persuade the senate to ban defences of papal authority which deny the divine right of kings: his argument is a purely conventional one which serves his purposes well. The same may be said of his argument that princes are obliged to supervise the Church for fear of divine retribution: such an argument can be no more than an *ad hominem* expedient, coming from a man whose historical writing betrays a conviction that God intervenes in the affairs of neither Church nor state, a conviction which coincides perfectly with the picture of an unbroken chain of natural causation drawn in the *Pensieri*.

Nor is it difficult to find other examples of Sarpi employing arguments that run counter to his convictions. The *Pensieri*, for example, insist that lying may be justified and that wise men should be hypocrites, and it is difficult, on any account of Sarpi's life, to deny that his own behaviour could be devious, or that he was not, on occasion, mendacious. Nevertheless he writes of the Jesuits – whom he hated next only to the papacy – :

their doctrine regarding regicide is abominable, I agree, for its consequence must be the ruin of the state, but their teaching that it is permissible and involves no sin to employ verbal ambiguities and mental reservations – this is a doctrine which must destroy all human relationships [for it permits]...the art of deception, the most pernicious of all with regard to the virtues. I would go so far as to say, I repeat, that this doctrine is worse than that regarding regicide.[25]

What Sarpi is evidently opposed to is the public teaching of a doctrine which should represent the private conviction of philosophers and rulers, but there can be no question that he is here making unscrupulous use of a commonplace argument which is in direct conflict with his own views.

Sarpi's insistence in the *History of the Inquisition* on the importance of fear of divine punishment in ensuring political obedience could thus be dismissed as irrelevant to an assessment of Sarpi's personal convictions. Nevertheless I think it is an indication that Sarpi's views had changed in certain respects since the writing of the *Pensieri*. The Interdict had demonstrated that the Church's authority over Venice's subjects was much greater than Sarpi and his associates had suspected: Sarpi turned towards Protestantism because he became convinced of the need to employ the same weapons as the enemy, to fight religion with religion.[26] In the light of the events of the Interdict, therefore, Sarpi would have felt the need to stress the importance of the state's preserving an effective control over people's consciences. But there was no reason why this change in strategy should be accompanied by the abandonment of the ideal sketched in the *Pensieri*, the ideal of a purely spiritual religion, which stressed neither doctrine nor damnation, which was not, in fact, a *tora*, a law governing men's actions through fear. What it did involve was a recognition that this ideal could not be realised as long as the Church survived as an institution capable of appealing to men's credulity and mobilising opposition to the state: it means that the prospects for the spiritualisation of religion in Venice must be seen as being inseparable from the fate of Catholicism and clerical authority in Europe as a whole. Consequently, after the failure of the Interdict crisis to transform the relationship between Church and state in Venice, Sarpi was forced to look to the international struggle against Catholicism, to give his support to Calvinism, and to cherish the hope that it would destroy clerical authority not just in Venice but in Europe as a whole.

In support of this view stands all the evidence of a substantial continuity in Sarpi's thought between the *Pensieri* and the *History of Trent*. We have seen that Sarpi, even when defending the divine right of kings, saw the state as a purely this-worldly authority; that when confronted with the ideal institutions of the early Church he appealed to the principles of a spiritual religion; that although he supported Protestantism he had no desire to become a member of a Protestant Church or to defend the authority even of a Protestant clergy; that the principles of explanation in the *History of Trent* are purely secular and institutional. Above all, we have seen that in the *Scrittura su Vorstio* Sarpi shows himself unwilling to defend any theological principles whatsoever. All the evidence, then, suggests that Sarpi's views in later life conformed to those expressed in the *Pensieri*. Holding the same convictions, there was no need for him to abandon all hope of creating a society in which those convictions could be more adequately expressed. A more realistic sense of the difficulties of the enterprise need not involve the abandonment of hope. If one thing is evident, it is that Sarpi continued until the end of his life to struggle against clerical authority and to seek to convey a conception of Christianity as a spiritual religion, and of the Church as a worldly institution. These struggles make sense, I would suggest, only in the context of the philosophical ideals expressed in the *Pensieri*, only in the context of the conviction that the state was not dependent upon the subject's fear of God.

On this interpretation then Sarpi did not believe, when he wrote the *History of the Inquisition*, that moral 'atheists' are necessarily unsociable.[27] His argument is partly polemical, but partly also an expression of his recognition that religion is in fact a powerful force within his own society: more powerful than he had taken it to be. Sarpi had not reconciled himself to a world in which the best religion, a spiritual religion, could never be the religion of society as a whole. He may have worked with the Protestants for the destruction of the papacy, but he remained convinced that the abolition of papal authority and clerical privilege would put an end to doctrinal disagreements of all sorts, for these had no basis outside material self-interest and political conflict.[28] Thus a Christianity would be established which would be like that of the early Church in that it would have no creed, but unlike that of the early Church in that it would not proclaim the imminence of the kingdom of God, and in so doing turn men away from the pursuit of virtue in society. In Sarpi's imagination the destruction of the papacy was to lead not just to the spiritualisation of religion, but also to the secularisation of political authority: take away the threat posed by the Church, and the state would have no need to exercise authority over men's consciences. None of this could find expression in the *History of the Inquisition*, for Sarpi had to present himself there as a model of conservative good sense. As he had himself recommended in the *Pensieri medico-morali*: 'Al di dentro vivi e guidica secondo la ragione, al di fuori secondo la comune opinione vivi e parla' ('Your innermost thoughts should be guided by reason, but you should act and speak only as others do').[29]

The letter to Badoer

If the *History of the Inquisition* represents the most telling evidence against the interpretation of Sarpi I have sought to put forward, then that interpretation may claim, at the least, to be plausible. We must turn now to Sarpi's letter to Giacomo Badoer of 30 March 1609 – the only letter to Badoer which survives – for it provides, I believe, evidence which makes my interpretation convincing, and evidence, moreover, which helps to carry us over the inevitable gap between Sarpi's thoughts, as recorded in the *Pensieri*, and his innermost feelings and beliefs.[30]

Giacomo Badoer was the son of a Parisian merchant of Venetian origin. He was brought up a Huguenot, but was converted to Catholicism by the Jesuit

Father Coton. Sarpi had known him for many years, both before and after his conversion. In September 1609, for example, he wrote: 'Mr Badoer is my friend and I know him very well.' He was happy to recommend him to others as being a man *di valore*, despite his conversion and his association with the Jesuits. Sometime between December 1609 and October 1610, however, Sarpi ceased to regard Badoer as a friend. Henceforth he regarded him as someone who had committed himself to the opposing party.[31]

The interesting fact about Badoer, however, is that Sarpi consistently described him as an 'atheist'. In September 1609 he says that Badoer is, in reality, neither Protestant nor Catholic; in October 1610 he is an 'atheist' in alliance with the Jesuits; in July 1617 he is someone who had been converted to Catholicism by atheistical arguments.[32] Moreover Sarpi's opinion on this subject coincided with that of his contemporaries. Castrino, a correspondent of Sarpi's, wrote scurrilous and obscene poems about this *anima impia*. L'Estoile, recording them in his journal in January 1610, commented on Badoer's knowledge and wit, but he too had no hesitation in labelling him an 'atheist'.[33]

Sarpi's letter to Badoer is his only known correspondence with someone with a reputation for unbelief. But it is more than a letter to an 'atheist': it is a letter to an old friend, someone to whom Sarpi might feel free to express his innermost feelings without reserve. The first thing we gather from the letter, however, is that this is an old and outmoded friendship. Sarpi and Badoer are accustomed to discussing scientific questions together, but Sarpi writes to say that he has almost abandoned his interest in the natural sciences and in mathematics. He is too involved in political questions which have dulled his wits and taken a severe toll on his physical and mental health. Even so Sarpi cannot resist entering into an argument about the nature of human action, an argument which refers back to the denial of Aristotelian essences, and, implicitly, of a human 'soul', in the *Pensieri*: 'up to now I have [always] believed that anything we do we do with the whole of ourselves; nor does it seem to me right to say that this hand of mine is writing, but rather that all of me, including my legs, is engaged in this activity. We distinguish between our senses [our bodies, our physical activities] and our reason only in order to be able to disclaim responsibility [for our acts].' Human beings are, consequently, to be identified with their bodies, not to be distinguished from them.

One gets a sense from Sarpi's letter that his old intellectual intimacy with Badoer is threatened not just by the decline in his scientific research, but also by the contrast between his and Badoer's political commitments. Certainly he is not willing to transmit to Badoer the political information he has requested. But he is willing to reveal his feelings, and in doing so he makes clear that he expects no life after death; he talks in classical terms of the Gods, not God; he mockingly misuses a quotation from St Paul, his favourite Biblical author.

Writing of the mental and physical price he has paid for his involvement in politics, he says, 'But, in the end, our very existence is of no importance [*una leggierezza*], and we should laugh at the prospect of losing it.' Then, at the end of the letter, he returns to the same theme:

To give you some news of myself, before I put an end to this letter, [all I can say is that] I find myself so tired of life, that I think it must be time to give up living. I have in fact given up all my hopes, and I have learnt from experience that it is hope alone which sustains life, and that old saying is true, *Iustus ex fide sua vivet*. Hope is the camouflage behind which the Gods conceal the happiness which is to be found in death. I would willingly have news of Monsignor Philip of Neuburg, and hear who you spend your time with; and if you want to know the same about me, I will have to tell you, that it is with no one. I am so solitary, that I fear that if I live longer I will become melancholic, if not worse, and so I meditate on the discourses of Socrates, where he says that it is great good fortune to die in time.
I do not want to trouble you anymore, but kiss your hand in farewell.[34]

Ulianich, publishing this letter, admits himself to be perplexed.[35] The evidence for its authenticity is clear enough, yet it corresponds to none of the received views of Sarpi: this is not Sarpi the Catholic; nor Sarpi the Protestant; nor Sarpi the eirenicist; nor Sarpi the Venetian politician. At the least one must say that it is Sarpi the chameleon: a pagan and an atheist when writing to an atheist. But I think, in fact, that the letter, far from complicating the task of locating Sarpi's true beliefs, simplifies it. What strikes one reading Sarpi is, in general, the dryness of his prose, its detachment, its lack of personal warmth. It is hard to identify a strong feeling, or to find a statement which is not calculated to serve some ulterior purpose. In the letter to Badoer, and there alone, we come face to face with an expression of genuine feeling, an expression which serves no purpose other than that of overcoming an oppressive loneliness, in confiding in a distant friend and former companion.

Where the letter to Badoer makes no sense in terms of the received accounts of Sarpi's beliefs and values it makes every sense in terms of the account given of Sarpi in this book. Here is Sarpi, looking to death not as a gateway to another life, but as release from this world; mocking not only his own hopes, but those of the Christian faith. And here, too, we find emotions which correspond naturally to the life which I have portrayed Sarpi as living: unable to express himself freely, not only in his work as a state theologian, but even in his historical writing, pursuing objectives unknown to his political associates, objectives which could never be avowed and which were increasingly evidently unrealisable. It is hardly surprising that he should have felt himself lonely, his private isolation exacerbated by his constant need to preserve friendships and alliances which might serve his political objectives. In his letter to Badoer Sarpi appears as what he truly was: an alienated intellectual, struggling to find some purchase on a world which refused to recognise his values or his ideals, alone and with no prospect of success. A man too, it must be said, given over entirely to the life of the mind, ill at ease in his body, hypochondriac, hiding from drafts behind castles of paper.[36] There is nothing in Sarpi's writing at least to suggest that he was able to find solace in the beauties of nature, in good food, in the pleasures of the flesh.[37] As a young man he had been serious, studious, withdrawn.[38] As an old man he had continually to take precautions against assassination, to worry that what he wrote might fall into the wrong hands, to fear that what he said might be overheard. Who can doubt that he looked back with regret to the days when he was writing the *Pensieri*, when he could communicate freely with a Badoer, an Acquapendente, a Galileo? Who can be surprised that he had difficulty preserving the *compositione dell'animo* by which he set such store, that his thoughts turned to Socrates, whose compatriots had not understood him, but who had preferred death to exile? It is, in short, because Sarpi's *Pensieri* expressed his private convictions that he became the man he portrays in his letter to Badoer.

Sarpi's objectives

These then were the principles and purposes governing Sarpi's actions. If he was in principle an agnostic, yet he was not, as we have seen, opposed to faith as such. What he was opposed to was any religion which established the Church as an institution with interests in conflict with those of the state: he was consistent in his absolutism and his anti-clericalism. He was opposed too to any religion which inculcated values which were not socially useful.

In Sarpi's view men are led naturally to belief in God by their own intellectual and psychological inadequacies. There is thus, in a certain sense, a natural religion, for religion itself is natural. But there is no reason why this natural religion should be a providential one. Sarpi himself did not believe in a providential order: he denied the immortality of the soul, and so can have had no faith in rewards and punishments in the next life. Moreover he would not even have accepted the philosophical providentialism of Pomponazzi, who had argued that virtue is its own reward and vice its own punishment, and had therefore held that there is a natural moral order which men are rewarded for obeying and punished for disobeying. According to Sarpi the variation between the moral systems of different times and places is sufficient to show that they have no foundation aside from opinion and social utility.[39] Nor does the pursuit of philosophical truth regarding the nature of pleasure and pain lead to the discovery that pleasure is to be obtained from moral activity. Rather the philosopher learns to despise both pain and pleasure as illusory, and he has cause to regret that he has to make do with stoic indifference in place of both the hope and the illusion of happiness.[40]

In Sarpi's ideal of a spiritual religion anti-clericalism passes over into anti-providentialism, into moral atheism. In Sarpi's view belief in providence is neither socially necessary nor psychologically beneficial: the fear of hell is not the only guarantor of good behaviour, while such a fear is unlikely to make a man's soul tranquil and render him generous and humane. The best religion would encourage men to admire God, but not to regard him with hope or fear: it would correspond to the 'pious atheism' of Epicurus as portrayed by Bayle in his *Pensées diverses.*[41]

It is true that there would be little harm in a sense of sin if it encouraged socially useful behaviour and if it was made easy for men to redeem themselves. It would thus be overstating the case to say that Sarpi was out to destroy providential religion. It would be more accurate to say that his attack on clerical authority was not checked by fear that belief in providence might be undermined. It was this alone which made it possible for him to present the claims of secular authority in stark and uncompromising terms and to portray the Church as a purely worldly institution. The implication of Sarpi's attack on clerical authority and doctrinal religion was that men should be free to believe what they liked as long as they did not undermine the state's authority. As long as the Church existed as a threat, the state had good reason to urge acceptance of a particular religious viewpoint, but without the opposition of the *tora* it would cease to have any need to command people's consciences. Thus although Sarpi was not concerned to attack all forms of providential religion, he had in mind a society in which the 'pious atheist' would no longer be required to practise hypocrisy.

Sarpi had an immediate objective: the abolition of a papal authority which he believed threatened all secular rulers. This objective was to be attained by military means, by war in Italy. But he had a further objective: the transformation of Christianity to suit the needs of secular society. This objective was to be attained partly by counterbalancing the poison of Catholic doctrine with the medicine of Calvinist doctrine; partly by directly defending the legitimate interests of secular rulers; and partly by undermining belief by portraying the history of the Church in its true light. Both of these objectives were revolutionary ones, and they were pursued, with *fredda prudenza* but with courage, determination and energy, throughout the last third of Sarpi's life.

If this account of Sarpi's principles and politics is correct he was an accomplished dissimulator, a cynic, a man whose achievements, however great, were bound to fall short of his aspirations. But what is most remarkable about him is the aspiration to free society from the bonds of Christian doctrine, to establish a religion which did not serve the interests of a particular faction, nor encourage a withdrawal from this world, but served to give men confidence and hope. In a sense, of course, an achievement is worth more than an aspiration, and from this point of view Sarpi must always be most notable for his *History of Trent*. But from another point of view Sarpi's greatest achievement was his life itself, a life lived in defiance of the cherished assumptions and unquestioned doctrines of his age, and the most notable thing about that life was the *Pensieri*, the few pages of notes in which he expressed the ideas and arguments which gave coherence to his actions.

Looked at from the outside, the turning point in Sarpi's life was the Interdict crisis, for it was this which drew him on to the public stage and caused him to be recognised as one of the leading intellectuals of the day. Looked at from the inside, though, the turning point must surely have been the *Pensieri* on the *tora*: out of the idea of the sociability of 'atheists' came his implacable attack on the Church, his uncompromising defence of secular authority, and the first beginnings of philosophical history. It was because Sarpi had no reason to defend religion that he could manipulate the existing traditions of political philosophy and of historiography as he did.

Sarpi's purpose in writing was to open up new intellectual possibilities to his contemporaries, not to expose to them his real beliefs. Without the evidence of the *Pensieri* it would be impossible to guess his true motives, for the views expressed in the *Pensieri* are extraordinarily original. They are not only quite unlike the views Sarpi's contemporaries expressed in print as their own, they are even unlike the views they attributed to each other. Unable to imagine a rational refutation of the arguments for belief in God, let alone conceive of a society of 'atheists', Sarpi's contemporaries would, had they known his thoughts, have had difficulty in recognising him as one of themselves. Despite this Sarpi's beliefs were not eccentric: they were grounded in the philosophical debates of the day, and provided a basis for political action and propaganda. Sarpi was able to give practical expression to his convictions because, in imagining a state without a Church, he was giving theoretical expression to the anti-clericalism and the absolutism of the *giovani* and of the Gallicans. It is because his *Pensieri* are so closely related to the politics and the propaganda of his day that they serve to throw new light upon them, drawing attention on the one hand to the decline of republican values and the intellectual limitations of Tacitist history, and on the other to the strength and the variety of the attack upon doctrinal religion which could be, and was, mounted by appeal to the traditions of Gallicanism, stoicism, Ockhamism and Averroism.

The *Pensieri* thus provide, in my view, the key to what Sarpi wrote and did in the years after 1606. But even were it to be shewn that this interpretation of Sarpi was mistaken, and that in later life he turned his back upon the arguments of the *Pensieri*, they would still remain a source of unparalleled importance for the study of early modern irreligion simply because they contain a rejection of fideism. In the case of men like Pomponazzi and Cremonini one can always choose to believe that they were sincere in their protestations, however reluctantly expressed, that philosophy must give way to theology. Sarpi's case is different, for the *Pensieri* present us with the authentic views of an unbeliever, and thus give us the right to suspect that others too had secretly abandoned belief.

Looked at in the context of contemporary discussions of irreligion, the second remarkable aspect of the *Pensieri* is their suggestion that society could be held together without the fear of hell. It was this, I have suggested, which made Sarpi the first unbeliever who was in a position to seek to undermine the authority of doctrinal religion within society. Lucien Febvre described the sixteenth century as a century which wished to believe. In my view there were many who did not believe. What nearly everyone was agreed on, however, was that fear of hell was as important as fear of the hangman in making social life possible: those that did not believe wished that other men might believe. According to a possibly apocryphal story the philosopher Cremonini, despite being an 'atheist', insisted that his servants should be pious Christians, for otherwise he would not be safe in his own house.[42] The attitude attributed to Cremonini is one his contemporaries would have taken for the merest good sense. People in the sixteenth and seventeenth centuries found the idea of a law-abiding society in which people did not believe in a providential God harder to grasp than the idea of a law-abiding universe which was not created and regulated by God. Sarpi, we may be confident, was not the first intellectual to deny the existence of a providential God, although the evidence for his unbelief is better than that for his predecessors. Sarpi's true originality, however, lies not in his rejection of Christianity, nor even in his willingness to conceive of a natural order without God. It lies in his conviction that a society of moral atheists need be no worse than a society of Christians. It was this conviction which made it possible, for the first time, for an unbeliever to pursue different social and political objectives from those pursued by believers.

Sarpi, though a great master of deception, longed for a society in which deception would be unnecessary, in which men could feed upon the truth. It is thus appropriate that, despite his lack of concern for political freedom, he should have been an inspiration to Milton in his defence of freedom of the press, for it was a longing for intellectual freedom which underlay Sarpi's defence of the absolutist state. Milton, reading Sarpi's *History of the Inquisition*, was particularly struck by the following passage:

The matter of books seems to be a thing of small moment, because it treats of words, but through these words come opinions into the world, which cause partialities, seditions, and finally wars. They are words, it is true, but such as in consequence draw after them hosts of armed men.[43]

It was Sarpi's hope that his words would draw hosts of armed men into Italy to destroy the papacy, and with it clerical authority in general. His dream was not to be realised. His words remained mere words, and as a consequence his irreligious convictions failed to give rise, as he had hoped they might, to a new form of political action. Sarpi, as a figure in history, appears in the different disguises he adopted the better to manipulate others. But the man himself was something more than the masks he wore, for he was the first to face unflinchingly the implications, for philosophy, for science, and above all for politics, of unbelief. For Sarpi man was an independent being, with 'no law but his own will, no end but himself'. It is this conception of man as answerable only to himself which makes Sarpi an isolated figure, between Renaissance and Enlightenment.

A dependent intelligent being is under the power and direction and dominion of him on whom he depends and must be for the ends appointed him by that superior being [i.e. God]. If man were independent he could have no law but his own will, no end but himself. He would be a god to himself and the satisfaction of his own will the sole measure and end of all his actions. (J. Locke, *Ethica B*)[44]

The testimony of brother Giovanni Francesco Graziani (1610)

British Library Additional MS 6877 is a report by Giovanni Francesco Graziani, a Servite friar of Perugia, on his activities as a papal spy. It was written after his release from prison in Venice, and was evidently intended to be read by the pope himself.

Giovanni Francesco had been commissioned by Rome to contact Sarpi's secretary, brother Antonio Bonfini of Viterbo, who was an old friend of his, with a view to persuading him to defect to Rome, and also in the hope of obtaining information about Sarpi's activities and copies of his work in progress. Giovanni Francesco, who was studying at Padua, visited Antonio in Venice and found a number of heretical manuscripts in his room. Antonio explained to him:

che M.ʳᵒ Paolo in quelle sue scritture ragionava et trattava di molte cose, ma che in particolare il suo scopo principalé era di dare adosso alli pontefici Romani, et che dimostra che tutti li inconvenienti et danni che son nati nella Chiesa son venturi per causa loro. (f. 1v)

(that Sarpi, in these writings of his, dealt with many subjects, but that his main objective was to attack the papacy, and that he demonstrated that all the faults and errors which have developed in the Church have been brought about by the popes.)

Shortly afterwards Giovanni Francesco was visited in Padua by Antonio. He took the opportunity to promise Antonio payment if he would copy or steal some of Sarpi's texts. Antonio agreed, and offered to go further and poison Sarpi, saying he had already turned down a request to stab him, but that he would be willing to use poison. Giovanni Francesco reported this offer to Rome, sending a letter from Antonio himself, but he received in reply orders to confine himself to his previous instructions.

Despite several visits by Giovanni Francesco to Venice, Antonio failed to deliver the manuscripts he had promised. Giovanni Francesco made a final visit to Venice to arrange for Antonio to make a copy of the key to Sarpi's room. There he was betrayed by Antonio (who hoped to obtain the reward offered by the senate for the capture of anyone plotting against Sarpi's life), arrested by the Council of Ten, and charged with conspiring to murder Sarpi.

Under interrogation Giovanni Francesco maintained that he had been commissioned to obtain copies of heretical works circulating in Venice, and that

Antonio, with whom he was confronted, was lying in saying that his activities had been directed against Sarpi. His answers being unsatisfactory he was handed over for judicial torture, but was discovered to be medically unfit. Nevertheless, on the basis of Antonio's testimony and some letters in Antonio's possession, he was condemned to death by drowning.

Faced with the prospect of the imminent execution of his sentence, Giovanni Francesco's memory improved remarkably. He now told his inquisitors of a number of letters he had left behind in Padua, including a draft of Antonio's offer to kill Sarpi, and the letter from Rome telling him to confine himself to stealing Sarpi's papers. Giovanni Francesco had thus implicated the curia in spying on Sarpi: in his defence, he claims that this was preferable to having the Venetians believe that Rome had sought to assassinate Sarpi. Since his new story was supported by irrefutable documentary evidence Giovanni Francesco's sentence was altered to one of a year's imprisonment, and Antonio was also imprisoned. While Giovanni Francesco languished in prison, however – in a damp underground cell, without proper food or bedding because the members of his order refused to come to his assistance – Antonio was released at Sarpi's request and banished for two years. At the end of his term Giovanni Francesco too was released and banished for life.

This, in substance, is the narrative which takes up the first half of Giovanni Francesco's report. From it we learn that he was, by his own account, a skilful liar, who recognised that the best lies have some foundation in truth. In his life of Sarpi, Fulgenzio Micanzio gives us a narrative of the same events.[1] His account differs significantly from Giovanni Francesco's, for he maintains that Giovanni Francesco and Antonio had jointly plotted against Sarpi's life, and he makes no mention of Antonio's betrayal of his associate, claiming that the conspiracy was discovered independently, and implying that Antonio's arrest preceded Giovanni Francesco's confession. According to Micanzio, Giovanni Francesco was offered by his judges the choice of death, or, should he confess the details of the plot, a year's imprisonment. His confession, Micanzio confirms, led to the discovery of his correspondence, but this, he claims, merely demonstrated his guilt and the involvement of the curia.

These two narratives can be checked against the records of the Council of Ten.[2] These confirm Micanzio's claim that Giovanni Francesco was given an inducement to confess, and that his 'innocence' was never formally established. But in other respects they tell in favour of Giovanni Francesco's narrative. They state that Giovanni Francesco accused Antonio of being 'auttore e complice' of the assassination plot, and that it was only after Giovanni Francesco had made his accusation that Antonio was arrested: a fact which is hard to explain unless Antonio had both cooperated with Giovanni Francesco's accusers and lied to them. Giovanni Francesco had every reason to believe that the Council of Ten would drown him secretly, as they had resolved, if he was less than honest with them. It is hard too to see that there would have been any point in his making false protestations of innocence to the curia, where his instructions had originated. While Giovanni Francesco certainly appears to have placed his confession in as favourable a light as possible, Micanzio appears to have overstated the papacy's involvement in the assassination plot, if there was one, and to have sought to conceal the evidence that Antonio had acted as an *agent provocateur*. The balance of probability appears to be that Giovanni Francesco's account is substantially accurate.

Giovanni Francesco's narrative of events is followed by four further reports: on Sarpi, on Micanzio, on Antonio, and on the Venetian and Terraferma nobility. The last of these (ff. 29–35) is essentially a report on Giovanni Francesco's fellow inmates in prison. He maintains that the young Venetian nobles there were blasphemers, infidels, and deeply hostile to the papacy, and that they told endless stories about incest, promiscuity and prostitution amongst the nobility. There is little reason to question this account of the unsavoury character of Giovanni Francesco's fellow inmates, but he has a number of more serious claims to make, based largely on the assumption that his acquaintances in prison has given him an insight into Venetian society at large.

The first is that the nobles, and particularly the *giovani*, the young nobles, were exercising an increasingly vicious, and deeply resented, tyranny over their subjects, particularly those of the Terraferma, and that their victims were consistently unable to obtain adequate protection from the law. Accusations of this sort were widespread at this time, although Giovanni Francesco is exceptional in describing rapes and other atrocities in some detail.[3]

The second is that it was these same young nobles who were particularly anti-papal. In the words of one of his fellow inmates 'al tempo d'adesso nel Papa non vi credono se non gli menchioni, gli Galantihuomini non vi credono' (f. 30v) ('Nowadays only wets believe in the pope. Our sort of chap doesn't').[4]

The third is that the nobility of the Terraferma, who were also to be found in the prison, had recently, and especially during the Interdict, become increasingly hostile to Venice and favourable to the papacy, partly because of resentment at Venice's economic expansion into the Padovano. On this subject Giovanni Francesco had merely reached the same conclusion as many of Venice's political leaders.[5]

The third of Giovanni Francesco's reports is on brother Antonio of Viterbo (ff. 25v–29r). In reading this one is obliged to bear in mind that Giovanni Francesco is testifying against a man who, by his own account, had sought to betray him to his death. Giovanni Francesco claims that Antonio had once been truly religious, but that under the influence of Sarpi he had become an unbeliever: he had denied the immortality of the soul, eaten meat on Fridays, and visited prostitutes before and after saying Mass. On his release from prison he had cast aside his habit and turned openly to dissolute living. Now, Giovanni

Francesco is pleased to report, he is once more in prison, although his latest crime is unspecified. In support of these reports we are given the names of witnesses and details of their testimony.

The accuracy of Giovanni Francesco's accusations against Antonio would be hard to establish. Impossible to confirm is the second of the two main charges that Giovanni Francesco levies against Sarpi and Micanzio (ff. 20r–22v; 22v–25r), which is that they are homosexuals, Micanzio almost openly and Sarpi in secret. These accusations are supported by the names of their lovers and details of their sexual preferences. Are they plausible? There have been too many examples of men of the highest public reputation having sexual tastes at odds with their professed convictions for it to be possible to simply dismiss Giovanni Francesco's accusations out of hand, as Ulianich does in citing this manuscript.[6] If the accusations could be confirmed they would place Sarpi's character in a new light: his youthful unease in the company of his peers, who called him La Sposa, The Bride; his friendship with Badoer, a reputed homosexual; the abstraction of his prose, carefully purged of any hint of sensuality.[7] But Giovanni Francesco's accusations cannot, of course, be substantiated, any more than they can be disproved simply by appealing to Sarpi's public reputation for ascetic living – a reputation that Giovanni Francesco himself refers to. As a consequence Giovanni Francesco's accusations are best ignored. But they do not in themselves serve to discredit his testimony: the reliability of a witness cannot be judged on the basis of whether one likes or dislikes the evidence he offers.

The main accusation Giovanni Francesco makes against Sarpi and Micanzio is, of course, that they were atheists, and it is his evidence on this point which we must consider in detail. He first discusses the matter in his account of the papers which he had told the authorities to obtain from Padua:

V'era anco un foglio pur di mia mano dove erano notate molte cose che fra Antonio me haveva conferite in Padova, et io per raccordarmele l'havevo notate per essere tutte cose diaboliche et contro la fede. diro quello che mi raccordaro.

La prima notatione era questa. Dimando io a fra Antonio in Padova che cosa diceva M.ro Paolo et quelli Gentilhomini suoi interni del Giubileo c'haveva mandato il sommo Pontefice. Me respose che loro se ne burlavano di queste cose, et che il papa non poteva fare queste cose; lo gli raggionsi ho pur saputo, che alle processioni in Venetia v'era della Nobiltà. Me respose che ve erano delli ignoranti ma gli huomini dotti et intelligenti intrinsichi di M.ro Paolo se ne burlavano.

V'era annotato, che dimandando pur io a fra Antonio che cosa dicevano M.ro Paolo et li suoi Nobili intrinsici della sacra scrittura et di Mose che era stato cosi caro a Dio benedetto me respose che non era vera la scrittura sacra, ma che Mose era un huomo astutissimo et desideroso di dominare, et che quelli popoli erano semplici et idioti et Mose gli dava di intendere tutto quello che voleva lui con dargli da intendere mille fandone con dire c'haveva parlato con Dio, et che quando ando sul monte per la legge fu un suo inganno perche prima si haveva provisto in quel luogo dove voleva stare nascosto da mangiare, et che poi dette ad intendere di haver hauto la legge da Dio erano tutte sue inventioni per farsi obedire et temere, et cosi in questa maniera gli dava da intendere mille baie et chimiere; in tutta somma concludeva, che la scrittura sacra erano fandonie et chimchiere et cose da ridersi; che la creatione del mondo che dice Mose non era vera, et M.ro Paolo trovava l'historie delli Egitii di quatordici milla anni.

Me dice di piu dell'Apocalisse di S. Giovanni che quelle cose che lui diceva in quella Apocalisse erano tutti suoi sogni et inventioni et chimere, et che erano cose da ridersi, soggionse anco vedete, che quando comincia a scrivere il Vangelio, che dice In principio erat verbum et verbum erat, che non sa ne anco lui da se stesso, che cosa si voglia dire, et questo anco era notato come di sopra nel foglio, et che fra Antonio l'haveva sentito dire nelli ragionamenti che faceva M.ro Paolo et alcuni suoi intrinsichi et familiari.

Dimandoli io che cosa diceva M.ro Paolo et quelli suoi Amici et familiari delli santi, et in particolare di san Francesco che era stato cosi grande imitatore delle vestige di Giesu Christo, fra Antonio subbito me respose, che loro dicevano che S. Francesco era stato un gran furbo et sciagurato; Io resposi ò Giesu come un gran furbo che e stato una imagine della vita di Christo et che hebbe li stimate nella sua persona, lui subbito respose (che veramente si cognosceva che possedeva questa diabolica dottrina) che non era vero, che lui havesse haute le stimate, e chi lo dice che sia vero, la cosa di san Francesco sta in questa maniera come vedrò io adesso disse fra Antonio. Il Papa di quelli tempi per volere tenere in credito la Chiesa si accordo con san Francesco, che lui cioe il papa haverebbe testificato che lui havesse le stimate nel suo corpo, ma che non era vero, et che non vi era altro che quel papa che dichi di haverle viste, et questo per tenere per questa strada in credito la Chiesa.

V'era annotato in quel foglio che M.ro Paolo riceveva lettere et libri d'Inghilterra di Germania et di Francia, et che Re et Duchi gli scrivevano.

V'erano molte altre cose importante annotate quali tutte non mi ponno tornare à memoria.

L'ultima annotatione era questa, et mi raccordo le formali parole; Maestro Fulgentio impara la lingua Inglese da quel che predica alla Calvinista all'Ambasciatore del Re d'Inghilterra con pensiero. Leonardo Mocenigo me dimando che cosa voleva dire quello con pensiero; Io resposi che fra Antonio mi haveva detto che se le cose di Venetia un giorno fossero andate in altro termine di quello che vanno al'presente, et c'havesse qualche sospetto di non essere sicuro, che se ne voleva andare in Inghilterra à predicare; Il Mocenigo respose ò buono questo foglio dava da cognoscere che M.ro Paolo non crede cosa alcuna il simele de molti Nobili et gli fu un spegio nella faccia in loro mala disgratia, et Dio benedetto permisse che ci fosse anco questo foglio fra quelle lettere per loro vergogna et dishonore. (ff. 16v–18r)

(Amongst them there was also a piece of paper in my handwriting on which I had made a note of many things which brother Antonio had told me in Padua, and which I had noted down in order to have a record of them, for they were all diabolical and against the Christian faith. I will put down those I remember.

The first note was this. I asked brother Antonio in Padua what Sarpi and those gentlemen who are associated with him were saying about the Jubilee that the pope had declared. He replied that they laughed at such things, and that the pope didn't have the authority to do such things. I added, but I have been told that some members of the nobility participated in the processions in Venice. He replied that there were some people who were stupid, but that the educated and intelligent people associated with Sarpi laughed at it.

There was a note to the effect that I had asked brother Antonio what Sarpi and the nobles associated with him said about the Bible and about Moses, who had been so particularly favoured by God. He replied that the Bible was untrue, but that Moses had been a very cunning man with a love of power, and that the Israelites were simple-minded and dumb. Moses had managed to make them think anything he wanted them to, convincing them of innumerable tall stories by telling them he had spoken with God. When he went up the mountain to obtain the law, it was a trick because earlier on he had chosen a place to lie hidden and had laid in a store of food there. When he claimed to have had the tables of the law from God it was just an invention to make him feared and obeyed. So in this way he persuaded them of many foolish and ridiculous things. In sum, he concluded that the Bible consisted of tall stories, fanciful inventions, and things one should laugh at. Moses' account of the creation of the world was untrue, for Sarpi knew that the history of the Egyptians went back for fourteen thousand years.

He told me moreover that the Revelation of St John was made up of John's dreams and inventions and fancies, and that one couldn't help laughing at it. He added, 'Look, when he began to write the Gospel and wrote "In the beginning was the word and the word was with God" even he didn't know what it meant.' This too was noted down in the piece of paper as something brother Antonio had heard said in the discussions between Sarpi and some of his close associates and friends.

I asked him what Sarpi and his friends and associates had to say about the saints, and in particular about St Francis, who followed so closely in the footsteps of Christ. Without hesitation brother Antonio replied that they said that St Francis had been a con man and a wretch. I replied, 'Oh Lord, how can he have been a con man when he so faithfully lived the life of Christ, and when he had the stigmata?' He replied – proving that he agreed with this diabolical theory – that it wasn't true that he had had the stigmata, and who said it was? 'I'll explain to you about St Francis', said brother Antonio. 'The pope at the time, who wanted to keep up faith in the Church, made an agreement with St Francis that he – the pope – would give witness that he had had the stigmata, but it wasn't true, and there was only the pope who claimed to have seen them, which he did in order to make people believe in the Church'.

There was a note on that piece of paper to the effect that Sarpi received letters and books from England, Germany and France, and that kings and dukes wrote to him.

There were many other important things noted down which I can no longer remember.

The last note was this, and I remember the exact words: 'Micanzio is learning the English language from the Calvinist chaplain of the English ambassador with the intention.' Leonardo Mocenigo [one of the *Inquisitori di stato*] asked me what 'with the intention' meant. I replied that brother Antonio had told me that it was Micanzio's intention if things in Venice changed for the worse, and if he began to fear for his safety, to go and preach in England. Mocenigo replied: 'Isn't it marvellous, this bit of paper shows that Sarpi doesn't believe anything at all, and nor do many of the nobility'. This was a real slap in the face for them, and God be thanked that this paper was amongst those they read, to bring home to them their disgrace and shame.)

Giovanni Francesco returns to the same theme in his 'Vita et costumi di fra Paolo de servi da Venetia':

Beatissimo Padre fra Paolo non ha ingannato mai la nostra Religione del concetto che di lui haveva, si di non credere, et essere Atheista, come anco, dedito al vitio nefando.

Il Cardinale di S.ta Severina di bon.a memoria prottetore di questa Religione, che sapeva li secreti della Religione, et sapeva in particolare la vita di fra Paolo quando intese che al tempo di Papa Clemente veniva proposto dalla Repubblica ad un Vescovato disse non voglio, che lui sia, perche non crede cosa alcuna, et soggionse di piu so ben io che molti tramontani che vanno à Venetia dimandano di lui.

E fama publica per la Religione che sono moltissimi anni che fra Paolo frequenti alcune radunate secrete in Venetia.

Fra Antonio me disse, che venivano persone a posta d'Inghilterra di Germania et di Francia solamente per ragionar con lui, et che in quelli paesi era stimatissimo et tenuto per il maggior huomo c'habbi hoggidi il mondo; Che le Genti dell'Ambasciatore de Inghilterra venivano spesso à trattar con lui alla stretta.

Perche M.ʳᵒ Paolo vede, che essendo lui Atheista, et che con questa opinione non puol'fare molto danno alla Chiesa, favorisse per sdegno che tiene con la Chiesa et mette inanzi la sette di Calvino.

Me disse à me in Venetia un Hebreo, che me dimando, che giuditio facesiamo delli Hebrei fatti Christiani, io gli resposi che noi ne facevamo bonissimo giuditio; Mi soggionse l'hebreo c'haveva ragionato con M.ʳᵒ Paolo sopra di questo particolare, et che gli haveva detto che tutte le legge sono buone pur che se viva da huomo da bene.

Lui ha hauto nome di non dir mai offitio, et me l'ha confirmato fra Antonio.

Me disse fra Antonio alcuni anni sono che M.ʳᵒ Paolo ragionando del' Arca di Noe, she se ne rideva et burlasca. (f. 20rv)

(Holy Father brother Paolo has never taken in the members of our order, who have always known that he was an unbeliever, an atheist, and a practising homosexual.

The late Cardinal of St Severina, cardinal protector of the order, who knew our secrets, and who knew in particular about brother Paolo, heard, when Clement VIII was pope, that he had been put forward by the Republic for a bishopric. He vetoed it, saying he believed nothing at all, and added moreover that he knew very well that many Protestants that came to Venice asked to see him.

It is commonly known in the order that for many years now brother Paolo has attended the meetings of certain secret societies in Venice.

Brother Antonio told me that people come from England, Germany and France just to discuss things with him, and that in those countries he was held in very high regard, and thought to be the greatest man alive today. He also said that people from the English embassy came regularly to meet with him in private.

Sarpi sees that as an atheist he cannot do much harm to the Church. So, because he hates the Church, he encourages Calvinism, which is a much more real threat.[8]

A Jew asked me, when I was in Venice, what we Christians thought of Jews who converted to Christianity. I told him that we had a very favourable opinion of them. The Jew then told me that he had discussed this question with Sarpi, who had told him that all religions are equally good, providing one lives a good life.

Sarpi has a reputation for never saying Mass, and brother Antonio confirmed this to me.

A few years ago brother Antonio told me that Sarpi, discussing Noah's ark, laughed at it and made a joke of it.)

Against Micanzio, Giovanni Francesco alleges that he mocked the sacrament of confession, that he denied that the words used in the consecration of the Host had any meaning, and that he denied the veracity of accounts of miracles associated with the holy sacraments. Moreover,

Ho sentito dir io da M.ʳᵒ Fulgentio che nella scrittura sacra vi sonno alcune cose che non possono stare, et che vi sonno tante contradictioni che non si possono salvare et acordare. (f. 25r)

(I have heard Micanzio say that in the Bible there are some things that cannot be true, and that there are numerous contradictions that cannot be resolved.)

What is one to make of these charges? Taken as a whole Giovanni Francesco's account is generally convincing. Campbell evidently accepted much of his account of his relations with Antonio. Ulianich, for his part, was convinced by Giovanni Francesco's account of Micanzio's activities in 1606 and was willing to give credence to Giovanni Francesco's charge that Sarpi was a close friend of the General of the Servite order, and enjoyed protection from him and other members of the order.[9] As for his account of Sarpi's and Micanzio's beliefs, we can corroborate it at numerous points: Sarpi *had* been refused a bishopric on grounds of infidelity; Micanzio *did* learn English and he and Sarpi *were* in close contact with the English embassy; foreigners *did* come to Venice just to meet with Sarpi. Nevertheless, what we are dealing with is the testimony of a spy, and his evidence is largely based upon the reports of the reprobate Antonio. It might be wise therefore to conclude that Giovanni Francesco's testimony with regard to Sarpi's atheism should be ignored.[10] It is not this aspect of this testimony, after all, which can be most easily corroborated. This was presumably the conclusion of Campbell and Ulianich, neither of whom mention the central argument of Giovanni Francesco's report.

If it is approached in this way, the interest of this text for the history of irreligion would lie simply in the fact that it constitutes a typical accusation of infidelity. One could compare it with the accusations made against Marlowe or Raleigh; or with the lesser known, but extremely interesting, case of Thomas Aikenhead, tried and executed in Scotland in 1696, while not yet of age, for blasphemy.[11] The various elements which make up Giovanni Francesco's charges – the denial of the immortality of the soul, the rejection of miracles, the identification of inconsistencies in the Bible, the treatment of religion as a device of government and religious leaders as imposters – these are the commonplaces of delations for infidelity in the sixteenth and seventeenth centuries, just as they were to become the commonplaces of eighteenth-century attacks upon Christianity.[12] In Giovanni Francesco's case, too, these accusations are supplemented by an unspoken charge of practical atheism: it is unbelief which permits homosexuality. Precisely the commonplace nature of Giovanni Francesco's charges might lead one to suspect that he had simply embroidered a common suspicion that Sarpi and his associates were atheists by inventing suitable details. Particularly interesting in this regard is the theme of Moses the imposter, a theme which seeks to link Sarpi to Machiavellism (by reason of Machiavelli's discussion of religion in *The Prince*, chapter 6) and perhaps even to *The Book of the Three Imposters*, which was often described, despite the fact that it was perhaps still to be written.[13] On this view then what we would be seeing in Giovanni Francesco's account is not the historical truth regarding Sarpi and his associates, but rather the mythical image of the early modern atheist.

This approach, however, seems to me unduly sceptical. In the first place we do have other sources to which we can turn to substantiate the charge of atheism – the *Pensieri* above all. It is true that in Sarpi's writings we find no trace of the mockery of the Bible described by Giovanni Francesco. But a similar disjuncture between blasphemous private conversation and sober philosophical argument can be found in the case of Aikenhead: convicted for the first, he engaged in the latter upon the very steps of the scaffold. Most importantly though there are three seemingly insignificant details which make me believe that in Giovanni Francesco's report we have a substantially accurate account of Sarpi and his associates.

In his final report on the nobility Giovanni Francesco writes:

Un libraro perugiono in Venetia me disse che un Nipote ò figliolo del Procurator Molino gli porto a ligare alcune lettioni di Pre. Marsilio sopra la Politica di Aristotele et che lesse un poco et che vi trovo che diceva che le Religionè erono inventione degli hominè, et che erono state retrovate per tenere in freno li Popoli. (f. 34v)

(A Perugian bookseller in Venice told me that a nephew or grandson of Procurator Molino brought him some comments by Father Marsilio on Aristotle's *Politics* to bind, and he read a bit of it and discovered that it said that religion is the invention of man, and that it was invented to keep the people in subjection.)

Quite probably the manuscript the bookseller read was in the hand of Giovanni Marsilio, a colleague of Sarpi's during the Interdict, executed in Rome in 1612. But none except the most foolish of individuals would compose a text of the sort described and then allow it to fall into the hands of an outsider. What the bookseller read was surely not a work by Marsilio but one of the texts – possession of which was perfectly legal – which we know was of the foremost importance to Sarpi: the discussion of religion in Averroes' commentary on Aristotle's *Physics*, a text which at first sight would seem to come from a commentary on a work of politics. If this is so what we have here is an account which has become garbled in just the way one would expect, but an account which makes perfect sense when set alongside the texts employed by Sarpi in writing the *Pensieri*.

Secondly, Giovanni Francesco attributes to Sarpi the view that 'Moses' account of the creation was untrue, for he knew that the history of the Egyptians went back for fourteen thousand years.' It so happens that one of the books we know that Sarpi owned was Garimberto's *Problemi naturali e morali*, and we can be sure that he read it with care and pleasure for in it are to be found a number of the themes Sarpi was to take up in the *Pensieri filosofici*: an attack on miracles, an Averroist account of religion, a discussion of the pagan view of immortality.[14] Problem 70 (pp. 113–16) discusses why the religion and customs of the inhabitants of the Americas are similar to ours. Problems of this sort were of interest to Sarpi, who discusses for example why women everywhere hold their babies in the same way.[15] Above all though Sarpi would have been interested in Garimberto's account of the origins of religion in universal characteristics of human nature and psychology. Garimberto's discussion centres around three possible explanations for cultural similarities: reason, instinct and diffusion. With regard to the third, he argues that the societies of Europe and the Americas may have a common cultural forebear on the basis of the account of Atlantis in Plato's *Timaeus* (21–5).[16]

Atlantis was a truly ancient civilisation, and its existence posed problems of chronology. In recognition of this fact Garimberto quotes Plato to the effect that: 'alcuni sacerdoti Egittii volendo mostrare à Solone con molte ragioni quanto di gran lunga l'Egitto avanzasse d'antiquità il resto del mondo; tra l'altre affermavano haver appreso di loro l'historie di 9,000 anni passati' (p. 115). Thus in Plato's time nine thousand years of Egyptian history were known. It was Sarpi's belief that chronology was of foremost importance, and here was a chronological fact which could not be reconciled with chronologies of world history derived from the Bible: the world must be older than the Old Testament allowed.[17] Here, I submit, we have the origin of the remark attributed to Sarpi by Giovanni Francesco, who has made only the slightest of numerical errors, substituting fourteen for the eleven thousand years which on Plato's dating have elapsed since the foundation of Egypt.

More tentatively, I would suggest that Garimberto makes it possible for us to identify one of the sources of Sarpi's willingness to, on Giovanni Francesco's account, mock the Biblical story of the Flood. For Plato in his account of Atlantis, drowned in floods and destroyed by earthquakes, insists that there has been more than one great flood. The same argument is to be found in a remarkable work which Sarpi had upon his shelves, the *Dialogus de montium origine* of Valerio Faenzi (Venice, 1561).[18] Faenzi, although accepting that the world is only six thousand years old, maintains that it has been continuously subject to geological change: the mountains that exist now are not necessarily those which were originally created (for there are often fossil seashells at their summits). Floods are amongst the causes of change, and Faenzi identifies no less than six great deluges. This assimilation of the Flood to more limited natural catastrophes which is to be found in Plato and Faenzi goes some way towards explaining Sarpi's willingness to mock the Biblical account.

The testimony of the Perugian bookseller and of Antonio, as reported by Giovanni Francesco, thus matches very neatly against the reading we know Sarpi did. Could one expect so close a match if Giovanni Francesco's testimony was a mere fabrication? Certainly no jury would convict on the evidence of Giovanni Francesco alone, even supplemented by a catalogue of Sarpi's library – unless of course the accused was denied counsel, as was poor Thomas Aikenhead. But faced with such evidence a detective would surely be tempted to investigate further, and if he found amongst Sarpi's papers a copy of the *Pensieri sulla religione* would he be left in any real doubt?

The historian, however, is neither detective nor jury: for him no case is ever closed. And the historian of irreligion in particular has good reason to remember the old saying that the more tightly you grip an eel, the more easily it slips through your fingers.[19]

Notes on illustrations

1. Titlepage of Sarpi's *Apologia per le oppositioni fatte dall'...Cardinale Bellarmino*. This titlepage led Bellarmine to accuse Sarpi of being irreligious: 'Father Paul says that many provinces and kingdoms have left the Roman Church simply and solely because the popes have sought to infringe upon temporal sovereignty. What these words mean, and what this sovereignty entails, we can learn from what those countries which have left the Roman Church have done. For they have in practice abolished all ecclesiastical authority, leaving to the Church only preaching and the administration of the sacraments, and their rulers have taken control of the Church's property and made themselves the final authority on questions of faith: behaviour unparalleled in previous history. To this state Father Paul would like to reduce the clergy of Venice, and perhaps it is to indicate this that he has placed at the beginning of his book an illustration of Christ, who is showing by his gesture that he does not want the world, and saying, "My kingdom is not of this world." By this Father Paul shows that he and his associates want to belong to this world, and because Christ's kingdom is not of this world they wish to have nothing to do with Him, nor with His vicar' (*Risposta alle oppositioni di Fra Paulo Servita*, Rome, 1607, p. 123).

2. Titlepage of Sarpi's *Considerationi sopra le censure della santità di Papa Paulo V*.

3. Titlepage of Micanzio's *Confirmationi delle considerationi del padre Paulo*. The titlepage of Sarpi's *Considerationi* portrays the lagoonal world of Venice: it was to Venice's geographical situation that her survival as a free state was often attributed. Micanzio's *Confirmationi delle considerationi* on the other hand convey by their titlepage the same message as Sarpi's *Apologia*: the Church should reject worldly authority as Christ had rejected the temptations of the devil. But Micanzio's titlepage also employs, as an image of worldly despotism, the landscape of the mainland, associated as it was with military conflict and princely authority.

It is the juxtaposition of these two images of the *Dominante* (Venice herself) and the Terraferma which Boccalini employs, in the epigraph to chapter 2, to suggest that Venice's republican institutions are threatened as never before. The shift in Venice's economic interests from seaborne trade to landholding had tied Venice ever more closely to the mainland, and had made the Venetian nobility more and more like the nobility of other states. Thus the terrestrial empire rejected by Christ was at the same time an image of the authority the Venetian state increasingly sought to exercise in the Terraferma. The world of Venice was no longer isolated from that of the mainland.

(On the publisher of these three works see P. F. Grendler, 'Books for Sarpi: the smuggling of prohibited books into Venice during the Interdict of 1606–7', in S. Bertelli and G. Ramckus, eds., *Essays Presented to Myron P. Gilmore* (2 vols., Florence, 1978), vol. I, pp. 105–14, where Meietti's long-term association with prohibited books is traced.)

Notes

A note on the text. I have modernised the spelling and punctuation of all quotations taken from texts in sixteenth- or seventeenth-century English. I have retained the original spelling and punctuation in quotations given in other languages.

Introduction

1 F. A. Yates, 'Paolo Sarpi's *History of the Council of Trent*', *The Journal of the Warburg and Courtauld Institutes*, VII (1944), 123–43; H. R. Trevor-Roper, 'The religious origins of the Enlightenment', pp. 193–236 of his volume of essays, *Religion, the Reformation and Social Change* (London, 1967).

2 [F. Micanzio], *Vita del padre Paolo* (Leiden, 1646) (edn cit. in P. Sarpi, *Istoria del Concilio Tridentino*, ed. C. Vivanti (2 vols., Turin, 1974), vol. II, pp. 1273–413), pp. 1291–5. For a discussion of Sarpi's priority in this and other discoveries, see C. Bertone, 'Fra Paolo Sarpi nelle scienze esatte e naturali', in *Paolo Sarpi e i suoi tempi* (Città di Castello, 1923), pp. 87–99.

3 The best introductions to Sarpi's scientific work are now G. Cozzi, 'Galileo Galilei, Paolo Sarpi e la società veneziana', pp. 135–234 of his volume of essays *Paolo Sarpi tra Venezia e l'Europa* (Turin, 1979), and L. Sosio, 'I *Pensieri* di Paolo Sarpi sul moto', *Studi veneziani*, XIII (1971), 315–92. Cozzi's volume contains a valuable bibliography of works on Sarpi.

4 Micanzio, *Vita*, p. 1321.

5 On Sarpi's place in Venetian political life the fundamental work is G. Cozzi, *Il doge Nicolò Contarini: ricerche sul patriziato Veneziano agli inizi del seicento* (Venice, 1958). See also W. J. Bouwsma, *Venice and the Defence of Republican Liberty: Renaissance values in the age of Counter-Reformation* (Berkeley, 1968), which contains a useful bibliography. For Sarpi's place in the history of political thought, see, for example, J. N. Figgis, 'Political thought in the sixteenth century', *The Cambridge Modern History of Europe*, vol. III (Cambridge, 1904), pp. 736–69.

6 Selections from the *Pensieri filosofici e scientifici*, along with the *Pensieri medico-morali* and the *Pensieri sulla religione* are to be found in P. Sarpi, *Opere*, ed. G. and L. Cozzi (Milan, 1969, pp. 39–110; printed separately, with different pagination, as P. Sarpi, *Pensieri*, Turin, 1976). R. Amerio published all the philosophical *Pensieri filosofici e scientifici* in P. Sarpi, *Scritti filosofici e teologici editi e inediti* (Bari, 1951), although this edition is not entirely satisfactory (see G. da Pozzo, 'Per il testo dei *Pensieri* del Sarpi', *Bollettino dell'Istituto di Storia della Società e dello Stato Veneziano*, III (1961), 139–76). A complete edition of all the *Pensieri filosofici e scientifici*, edited by L. Cozzi and L. Sosio, is awaited.

7 On the authenticity of the *Pensieri*, see below, p. 14.

8 C. Ginzburg, *Il formaggio e i vermi: il cosmo di un mugnaio del '500* (Turin, 1976; English translation, London, 1980). Of Hill's many works see in particular C. Hill, 'Plebeian irreligion in seventeenth century England', in *Studien über die Revolution*, ed. M. Kossok (1969, rev. edn, Berlin, 1971), pp. 46–61, and *Irreligion in the 'Puritan' Revolution* (Barnett Shine Foundation Lecture, London, 1974).

9 See for example the terms in which Pufendorf rejects atheism as irrational. In his view the insuperable problem for an atheist is that he cannot hope to demonstrate 'that the interests of mankind are better advanced by atheism than by continuing the worship of God... since this is clearly impossible, atheists must be held to offend not only against God, but against all mankind as well' (S. Pufendorf, *de Iure Naturae et Gentium Libri Octo* (1688; reprinted Oxford, 1934, in 2 vols., with translation by C. H. and W. A. Oldfather), p. 260).

10 J. C. A. Gaskin, 'Hume, atheism, and the "interested obligation of morality"', in *McGill Hume Studies*, ed. D. F. Norton and N. Capaldi (San Diego, 1979), pp. 147–60; p. 151. Other scholars who have sought to follow the logic of early modern discussions of 'atheism' have been forced to use the word in its early modern rather than its modern sense: e.g. D. P. Walker, *The Ancient Theology: Studies in Christian Platonism from the Fifteenth to the Eighteenth Century* (London, 1972), ch. 4: 'Atheism, the ancient theology and Sidney's Arcadia'; M. Hunter, *Science and Society in Restoration England* (Cambridge, 1981), ch. 7: 'Atheism and orthodoxy'.

11 For a general survey see S. J. Woolf, 'Venice and the Terraferma: problems of the change from commercial to landed activities' (1962); reprinted in B. S. Pullan, ed., *Crisis and Change in the Venetian Economy* (London, 1968), pp. 175–203.

12 B. S. Pullan, 'The occupations and investments of the Venetian nobility in the middle and late sixteenth century', in J. R. Hale, ed., *Renaissance Venice* (London, 1973), pp. 379–408; B. S. Pullan, 'Service to the Venetian state: aspects of myth and reality in the early seventeenth century', *Studi secenteschi*, V (1964), 95–148; Cozzi, *Contarini*, p. 18.

13 For a valuable account of absolutism see P. Anderson, *Lineages of the Absolutist State* (London, 1974), where absolutism is defined as 'a redeployed and recharged apparatus of feudal domination' (p. 18). The great defect of this book, however, is that it contains no sustained account of the income and expenditure of the absolutist states and their nobilities, and so fails to distinguish the differing roles of tax and rent in different absolutist societies and for different sectors of the nobility. It also fails to recognise (e.g. p. 17) the extent to which absolutism was compatible with a free market in land and labour: the fact that rents under absolutism are generally higher than they would be under capitalism can usually be explained in terms of economic mechanisms, rather than in terms of extra-economic coercion: see K. Marx, *Capital*, vol. III (1st [German] edn, 1894), ch. 47, pt IV; A. V. Chayanov, *The Theory of Peasant Economy* (1st [Russian] edn, 1925; English translation, Homewood, 1966). As a result it is doubtful whether absolutist society should properly be called feudal.

14 Bouwsma, *Republican Liberty*, passim.

15 See C. Vivanti's suggestive remarks in his introduction to Sarpi, *Concilio Tridentino*, edn cit., pp. xxxvii–viii, and P. F. Grendler, *The Roman Inquisition and the Venetian Press 1540–1605* (Princeton, 1977), pp. 207–8.

16 G. Contarini, *de Magistratibus et Republica Venetorum Libri Quinque* (Paris, 1543); P. Paruta, *Della perfettione della vita politica* (Venice, 1579); Bouwsma, *Republican Liberty*, pp. 144–53, 200–23; M. P. Gilmore, 'Myth and reality in Venetian political theory', in J. R. Hale, ed., *Renaissance Venice* (London, 1973, pp. 431–44), pp. 431–4.

17 See Sir Dudley Carleton, 'Particular Notes of the Government and State of Venice', Public Record Office, State Papers 99, file 8, ff. 340–4; *Opinions et raisons d'Estat proposées en un discours tenu au Grand Conseil de Venise par le clarissime L.B.* (n. l, 1606); Angelo Badoer, speech to the senate, recorded in E. Cornet, ed., *Paolo V e la Repubblica Veneta: giornale dal 22 Ottobre 1605–9 Giugno 1607* (Vienna, 1859), appendix 16, pp. 307–15. For a portrait of the Venetian nobleman as courtier (although dating from the 1630s), see H. Potterton, *Venetian Seventeenth Century Painting* (catalogue of an exhibition at the National Gallery, London, 1979), pp. 100–1.

18 E. E. Evans-Pritchard, *Witchcraft, Oracles and Magic among the Azande* (Oxford, 1937).

19 *The Autobiography of Charles Darwin* (London, 1958), pp. 85–96; D. Ospovat, 'God and natural selection: the Darwinian idea of design', *Journal of the History of Biology*, XIII (1980), pp. 169–94.

20 A. Koyré, *La révolution astronomique* (Paris, 1961; English translation, Paris, 1973), pt I, ch. 3.

Sarpi's life: a brief survey

1 The two most useful accounts of Sarpi's life are Micanzio's *Vita* and the introductory notes to G. and L. Cozzi's edition of the *Opere* (on which see C. Vivanti, 'L'opera che mancava su Paolo Sarpi', *Rivista storica italiana*, LXXXII (1970), 917–25). In English, see P. Burke's introduction to P. Sarpi, '*History of Benefices' and selections from 'History of the Council of Trent'* (New York, 1967), pp. ix–xli. What follows is based on them, and on the next chapter, except where indicated.

2 On the confession-box see J. Bossy, 'The social history of the confessional', *Transactions of the Royal Historical Society*, ser. V, vol. XXV (1975), 21–38; pp. 29–30; on sexual segregation see Bossy, 'editor's postscript' to H. O. Evenett, *The Spirit of the Counter-Reformation* (Cambridge, 1968, pp. 126–45), p. 138. On Borromeo's influence in general see G. Alberigo, 'Carlo Borromeo come modello di vescovo nella chiesa post-tridentina', *Rivista storica italiana*, LXXIX (1967), 1031–52.

3 According to Pallavicino, du Ferrier read Lucian during Mass (Yates, 'Sarpi's History', p. 139). Sarpi himself owned an expurgated copy of Lucian: G. L. Masetti Zannini, 'Libri di fra Paolo Sarpi e notizie di altre biblioteche dei Servi (1599–1600)', *Studi storici dell'ordine dei servi di Maria*, XX (1970), 174–202, appendix (pp. 192–200), no. 244.

4 For a discussion of Montaigne's neo-stoicism see Q. Skinner, *The Foundations of Modern Political Thought* (2 vols., Cambridge, 1978), vol. II, pp. 276–9.

5 J. Brodrick, *The Life and Work of Blessed Robert Francis Cardinal Bellarmine, S.J., 1542–1621* (2 vols., London, 1928), vol. I, ch. 13.

6 G. and L. Cozzi, eds., *Opere*, p. 19. Amongst the books Sarpi owned was A. Pellegrini, *I segni de la natura ne l'huomo* (Venice, 1546: Masetti Zannini, 'Libri di fra Paolo', appendix, no. 266), an account of how men's characters can be known from their physical characteristics. Pellegrini discusses the implications of materialism for psychology and moral philosophy, and employs as one of his interlocutors an Epicurean (ff. 49v–52r; 54v–55r; 57rv; 73rv).

7 Canaye de Fresnes lists 145 publications relating to the Interdict: see the appendix to P. Canaye, seigneur de Fresnes, *Lettres et ambassades* (3 vols., Paris, 1635–6), vol. III.

8 See G. Cozzi, 'Paolo Sarpi tra il cattolico Philippe Canaye de Fresnes e il calvinista Isaac Casaubon' (1958), in his *Sarpi tra Venezia e l'Europa*, pp. 3–133, pp. 102–3; P. R. Taucci, *Intorno alle lettere di Fra Paolo ad Antonio Foscarini* (Florence, 1939), pp. 31, 148–9; La Broderie's letter of 24 Oct. 1606, in *Les ambassades et negotiations de l'Illustrissime et Reverendissime Cardinal du Perron* (1623; edn cit. 3rd rev. edn. Paris, 1629).

9 For the impact of the Interdict in France see C. Vivanti, *Lotta politica e pace religiosa in Francia tra cinque e seicento* (Turin, 1963), pp. 364–7; W. J. Bouwsma, 'Venice and the political education of Europe', in Hale, ed., *Renaissance Venice*, pp. 445–66; p. 452. For England see J. L. Livesay, *Venetian Phoenix: Paolo Sarpi and some of his English friends* (Lawrence, 1973), pp. 19–25; E. de Mas, *Sovranità politica e unità cristiana nel seicento anglo-veneto* (Ravenna, 1975).

10 G. Cozzi, *Contarini*, chs. 1, 3, 4; S. Secchi, *Antonio Foscarini: un patrizio veneziano del '600* (Florence, 1969), pp. 29–76.

Chapter 1. The *Pensieri filosofici*

1 L. Cozzi, 'La tradizione settecentesca dei *Pensieri* Sarpiani', *Studi veneziani*, XIII (1971), 393–448.

2 G. and L. Cozzi, eds., *Opere*, pp. 1291–2.

3 Micanzio, *Vita*, p. 1323.

4 The marginal dates in the earlier of the two MSS of the *Pensieri filosofici* are, for the most part, reproduced in G. and L. Cozzi, eds., *Opere*. For a full list, see Amerio, *Scritti filosofici*, p. 159. In what follows I refer to the *Pensieri filosofici* according to their numbering in this MS, which both Amerio and G. and L. Cozzi follow, and which surely will be followed in any complete edition.

5 He does not, of course, use the term, which appears in Italian only in the eighteenth century.

6 Sarpi's materialism is discussed in R. Amerio, *Il Sarpi dei Pensieri filosofici inediti* (Turin, 1950), pp. 19–20. See, for example, *Pensieri filosofici*, nos. 4, 5, 111, 114, 115, 356, 371, 401, 555.

7 Amerio, *Il Sarpi dei Pensieri*, pp. 20–1; *Pensieri*, nos. 5, 131, 133, 138.

8 On Cremonini see M. A. del Torre, *Studi su Cesare Cremonini* (Padua, 1968).

9 Ibid., p. 35. Perhaps this story originates with someone who had been struck by the use of the word *totus* in Cremonini's will: 'Ad philosophiam sum vocatus, in ea totus fui, si aliquid philosophanda peccavi, memento me esse hominem, cui innatum est peccare...' (quoted in A. Favaro's review of L. Mabileau, *Étude historique sur la philosophie de la Renaissance en Italie (Cesare Cremonini)*, *Archivio veneto*, XXV (1883), 430–50, p. 437). If Cremonini was *entirely* an Aristotelian philosopher, was he *at all* a Christian?

10 Quoted by del Torre from the *Naudeana* (1701): *Cremonini*, p. 18. P. O. Kristeller, it must be said, doubts the authenticity of the *Naudeana* ('The myth of Renaissance atheism and the French tradition of free thought' (1953), *Journal of the History of Philosophy*, VI (1968), 233–43). The passage, however, seems right for the time and place: see below, p. 37; C. Hill, *Milton and the English Revolution* (London, 1977), p. 197; and J. S. Spink, *French Free-Thought from Gassendi to Voltaire* (London, 1960), p. 9. On Naudé in general see R. Pintard, *Le libertinage érudit dans la première moitié du XVIIᵉ siècle* (2 vols., Paris, 1943), vol. I, pp. 156–73, 245–67, 442–76; E. Thuau, *Raison d'état et pensée politique à l'époque de Richelieu* (Paris, 1966), pp. 318–34.

11 No. 40; see also no. 7.

12 Sarpi presents the matter as a choice between alternatives. He may have been a Copernican at this time, but his conversion to Copernicanism is difficult to date (Sosio, 'Sarpi sul moto', pp. 328–9, 349–52). Copernicanism would have helped in formulating the idea of an infinite universe, even though Copernicus himself had not taken this step. Equally important were the classical sources: Democritus, Epicurus and above all Lucretius (*On the Nature of Things*, trans. C. Bailey (Oxford, 1910), pp. 62–4, 100–1). These were used, along with Copernicus, by Bruno, whose *La cena de le ceneri* (1583) was the first book to argue in favour of an infinite universe (see A. Koyré, *From Closed Space to the Infinite Universe* (Baltimore, 1957), pp. 5–6, 39–54). In 1600 Sarpi owned copies of Lucretius and Copernicus (Masetti Zannini, 'Libri di fra Paolo', appendix, nos. 106, 215).

13 Nos. 131, 132, 133, 134.

14 Sarpi seems to have a fully developed concept of physical law, something E. Zilsel was unable to discover in any author before Descartes ('The genesis of the concept of physical law', *Philosophical Review*, LI (1942), 245–79). Sarpi's approach to the question of natural law (which may have been influenced by Averroes' account of causation: see E. Renan, *Averroès et l'Averroïsme* (1st edn, 1852; edn cit. 5th edn, Paris, n.d.), pp. 107–22) would seem to put in doubt the claim made by Needham and, following him, by Oakley, that the idea of an omnipotent God was a prerequisite for the development of modern science. Sarpi's view is closer to the modern conception of natural law as a form of statistical regularity than to a Newtonian view of natural law as a manifestation of divine providence. Sarpi's very avoidance of the term law may be taken as an indication of his concern to avoid a voluntarist formulation. (See J. Needham, 'Human law and the laws of nature' (1951), in Needham, *The Grand Titration: Science and Society in East and West* (Toronto, 1969), pp. 299–330; F. Oakley, 'Christian theology and the Newtonian science, the rise of the concept of the laws of nature', *Church History*, XXX (1961), 433–57).

15 J. Bodin, *Colloquium of the Seven about Secrets of the Sublime*, ed. M. L. D. Kuntz (Princeton, 1975), p. 34.

16 On Sarpi's denial of supernatural events, see Amerio, *Il Sarpi dei Pensieri*, pp. 20–1; C. Vivanti, ed., *Concilio Tridentino*, p. xlix. Amongst the books Sarpi owned was G. Garimberto, *Problemi naturali e morali* (Venice, 1549: Masetti Zannini, 'Libri di fra Paolo', appendix, no. 102). In problem 63, 'D'onde viene che l'huomo si maraviglia assai d'una cosa che avvenga di raro per piccola che sia; e d'una grandissima, e che occorra spesso non prende maraviglia alcuna?' (pp. 102–3), Garimberto rejects any idea of the supernatural, as indeed all Averroists were bound to do. Such a rejection could still leave a great deal of scope for credulity as to what was natural. Apart from *Pensiero* no. 239, which betrays the influence of Pomponazzi, Sarpi was never credulous. Lucien Febvre, in 'Sorcellerie, sottise ou révolution mentale?' (1948), in his *Au coeur religieux du XVIe siècle* (Paris, 1957), pp. 301–9, forgot that it was possible in the sixteenth century to deny the existence of supernatural forces. For an attack on those who, following Pomponazzi, denied the existence of angels, demons and other supernatural forces, see F. Fabri, *Adversus Impios Atheos* (Venice, 1627), bk I. There is more justification for Febvre's insistence on popular credulity in 'De l'à peu près à la précision en passant par ouï-dire' (1960), *Au coeur religieux*, pp. 293–300.

17 See Ockham, *Philosophical Writings*, ed. P. Boehmer (Edinburgh, 1957), pp. xliii–xlvi, 114–26; G. Leff, *William of Ockham: the Metamorphosis of Scholastic*

Discourse (Manchester, 1975), pp. 382–98. A similar view was held by Averroes: see Renan, *Averroès*, p. 112.

18 Sarpi's approach to the problem of infinity may be contrasted to that of Campanella, who wrote 'spatium autem et corpora infinitare...non audeo' (see A. Garfunkel, 'Note sul problema dell'infinita nella *Cosmologia* di Tommaso Campanella', in *Tommaso Campanella (1568–1639): Miscellanea di studi nel 4° centenario della sua nascita* (Naples, 1969), pp. 385–91; p. 387). It was presumably the weakness of Ockham's proof, after Bruno had demonstrated that he at least could conceive of an infinite universe, which made it necessary for Fabri to retreat to the earlier arguments of Duns Scotus, who had denied the possibility of a universe infinite in either space or time (*Adversus Impios Atheos*, pp. 249–50). For other aspects of Fabri's use of Scotus see C. B. Schmitt, 'Filippo Fabri and scepticism: a forgotten defence of Scotus', in *Storia e cultura al Santo*, ed. A. Poppi (Vicenza, 1976), pp. 309–12. There were, of course, other contemporary arguments for the existence of God, aside from those from infinity (see L. E. Loemker, *Struggle for Synthesis: the Seventeenth Century Background of Leibniz's Synthesis of Order and Freedom* (Harvard, 1972) pp. 70–4). Sarpi, however, implicitly rejects them all in the *Pensieri*. Particularly important in this context is his rejection of Aristotelian teleology.

19 Sarpi says of Ockham: 'Io l'ho stimato sopra tutti li scolastici': letter to Hotman, 22 July 1608, in P. Sarpi, *Lettere ai Gallicani*, ed. B. Ulianich (Wiesbaden, 1961), p. 173.

20 Sarpi, *Pensieri filosofici*, nos. 111, 265, 308.

21 ibid., nos. 138, 253, 257, 259, 270. The example of Darwin, above p. 7, is relevant here.

22 ibid., nos. 251, 255, 277. See Sextus Empiricus, *Outlines of Pyrrhonism*, ed. R. G. Bury (4 vols., London, 1933–49), bk I, ch. 12.

23 L. Febvre, *La religion de Rabelais: le problème de l'incroyance au seizième siècle* (Paris, 1942), pp. 397–400.

24 Amerio, *Il Sarpi dei Pensieri*, p. 13. It is worth noting that Amerio had no knowledge of the *Pensieri sulla religione*.

25 ibid., pp. 17–19; Amerio, *Scritti filosofici*, pp. 141–2. That Sarpi believed in the immortality of the soul is asserted by G. Bianchi-Giovini, *Biografia di fra Paolo Sarpi* (2 vols., Brussels, 1836), vol. I, pp. 141–4, and by L. Troilo, 'La filosofia di fra Paolo Sarpi', in *Paolo Sarpi e i suoi tempi* (Città di Castello, 1923), pp. 17–85; pp. 33–6. Neither provides any evidence in support of his claim. If *Pensiero* no. 255 is read as presuming the mortality of the soul, its argument coincides with that of Garimberto, *Problemi naturali*, problem 106, 'D'onde si causava che i Gentili si dilettassero tanto di lasciar memoria di loro, se credevano dopo la morte non sentire nuova, ne piacer, ne dispiacer alcuno delle cose di qua?' (pp. 178–9). Both Garimberto and Sarpi are probably replying to L. Valla, *On Pleasure* (1st edn, 1433; English translation, ed. M. de P. Lorch, New York, 1977), pp. 156–9, where it is argued that if the soul is mortal one's reputation after death is as irrelevant as a grave-stone to a dog. Sarpi would also, of course, have been aware of the debate as to whether man's natural desire for immortality was proof of the immortality of the soul: Duns Scotus and Pomponazzi had argued, against Aquinas, that it was not (see B. Nardi, 'Il preteso desiderio naturale dell'immortalità' (1955), in his *Studi su Pietro Pomponazzi* (Florence, 1965), pp. 247–68).

26 1582–3 is often seen as a year of revolution, in which an anti-clerical faction (the *giovani*) took power from a pro-clerical one (the *vecchi*): e.g. Cozzi, *Contarini*, pp.

1–52; Bouwsma, *Republican Liberty*, pp. 232–92. However, M. J. C. Lowry has shown that offices continued to be held by the same men after the supposed revolution as before: 'The reform of the Council of Ten, 1582–3: an unsettled problem', *Studi veneziani*, XIII (1973), 275–310. In the light of this Grendler (*Roman Inquisition*, p. 202) dates the adoption of anti-clerical policies to the 1590s, when new men were coming to power. Changes in policy, however, do not necessarily require changes in office-holders, and 1582 seems to mark, as I will argue elsewhere, a turning point in the development of the anti-clerical faction.

27 B. Nardi, 'Filosofia e religione' (1951), in his *Studi su Pietro Pomponazzi* (Florence, 1965), pp. 122–48; pp. 124–6, 129–39. For Averroes' views on religion see Renan, *Averroès*, pp. 162–72 and L. Gauthier, *La théorie d'Ibn Rochd (Averroès) sur les rapports de la religion et la philosophie* (Paris, 1909).

28 Nardi, 'Filosofia e religione', p. 123; see also G. Spini, *Ricerca dei libertini* (Rome, 1950), pt II, ch. 1, esp. pp. 51–2.

29 Nardi, 'Filosofia e religione', pp. 131–48. But see also P. Pomponazzi, *de Immortalitate Animae* (1516), ch. 14, and the passages quoted by J. H. Randall at pp. 277–8 of his introduction to an English translation of the *de Immortalitate* in E. Cassirer, P. O. Kristeller and J. H. Randall, eds., *The Renaissance Philosophy of Man* (Chicago, 1948), pp. 257–79: both are strangely ignored by Nardi. For a general account of Pomponazzi which portrays him as being most probably irreligious see Randall's introduction, together with Kristeller's introduction to the volume as a whole (pp. 1–20; pp. 12, 18).

30 Bruno arrived in Venice in 1592, after the composition of these *Pensieri*, but he had published Averroist accounts of religion in 1584. Sarpi owned a copy of Aristotle–Averroes (Lyons, 1530: Masetti Zannini, 'Libri di fra Paolo', appendix, no. 179). He would also have been familiar with the Averroist account of religion to be found in Garimberto, *Problemi naturali*, problem 103, 'Qual è la causa che i Gentili biasimando il vitio, e lodando grandamente la vita morale, dipoi fingessero ne lor Dei una vita brutta, e vitiosa' (pp. 172–5), and perhaps with that in Marsilius of Padua: see A. Gewirth, *Marsilius of Padua, the Defender of Peace* (2 vols., New York, 1951–6), vol. II, p. 19. Averroes' commentaries on Aristotle were widely known: see C. B. Schmitt, 'Renaissance Averroism studied through the Venetian editions of Aristotle–Averroes', *Atti dei convegni Lincei*, XL (1979), 121–42. Some editions of Averroes seem to have omitted the crucial prologue to the commentary on bk III of the *Physics* in which Averroes' attitude to religion is most clearly expressed: see Nardi, 'Filosofia e religione', p. 129; Kristeller, in Cassirer et al., *Renaissance Philosophy*, p. 364. In at least one edition it was printed as part of ch. 60 of bk I of the commentary on the *Physics* (*Aristotelis Opera cum Averrois Commentariis* (Venice, 1562–74), vol. IV). I have not been able to inspect a copy of the edition owned by Sarpi.

31 G. and L. Cozzi, eds., *Opere*, pp. 65, 1289; Amerio, ed., *Scritti filosofici*, p. 161.

32 In common speech 'law' was often coupled with 'faith' to mean religion, e.g. above, p. 13. The word *libertine*, similarly, derives from the Latin *libertus*, a freedman, one who is no longer under an obligation of obedience (Loemker, *Struggle for Synthesis*, p. 253).

33 The reading of *tora* as *tortura* (e.g. Troilo, 'Filosofia di Sarpi', p. 66) is thus, as a conjecture, not outrageously wide of the mark, for it is fear of hell that Sarpi is primarily discussing. The MS gloss *legge*, however, leaves no room for doubt (Amerio, ed., *Scritti filosofici*, p. 168).

34 For attacks on 'Judaical' religion see, for example, D. Erasmus, *Enchiridion Militis*

Christianae (Antwerp, 1504), ch. 14, and the opening passage of J. Milton, *Of Reformation in England* (London, 1641).

35 *de Immortalitate Animae*, ch. 14. By 'Plato and Aristotle' Pomponazzi meant Averroes: see Averroes, *On Plato's Republic*, ed. R. Lerner (Ithaca, 1974), pp. 21–4, 76; id., *Tahāfut al-tahāfut*, ed. S. van den Bergh (2 vols., London, 1954), vol. I, pp. 215–6; and (a text unpublished until the nineteenth century) id., *On the Harmony of Religion and Philosophy*, ed. G. F. Hourani (London, 1961), pp. 67–8. Sarpi's use of Pomponazzi, whom I take to be his immediate source, goes some way to justifying H. Busson's preoccupation with him in his *Le rationalisme dans la littérature française de la Renaissance, 1533–1601* (1922; rev. edn, Paris, 1957), which has been dismissed by Walker as a 'King Charles's Head'. Walker thinks contemporaries regarded the sceptics as a greater threat to religion than the Aristotelians (*Ancient Theology*, p. 139), but Mersenne's attack on scepticism is in defence of science not faith (M. Mersenne, *La vérité des sciences, contre les septiques ou Pyrrhoniens* (Paris, 1625)), while Fabri and Campanella both regarded the Aristotelians as the main threat (A. Poppi, 'Un teologo di fronte alla cultura libertina del Rinascimento italiano: l'*Adversus Impios Atheos* di Filippo Fabri', *Quaderni per la storia dell'Università di Padova*, IV (1971), 103–18). The leading representatives of the sceptics, for their part, all insisted that scepticism was easier to reconcile with Christianity than was any other philosophy (see R. H. Popkin, *The History of Scepticism from Erasmus to Descartes* (1969; rev. edn, Assen, 1964), pp. 48, 61–2, 96). They may have been secret unbelievers, and their arguments might properly give cause for concern, but they, unlike the Aristotelians, could hardly be regarded as outright opponents of Christianity.

36 See M. Mersenne, *De l'impiété des déistes, athées et libertins de ce temps* (2 vols., Paris, 1624), a reply to the *Quatrains*.

37 G. and L. Cozzi, eds., *Opere*, pp. 95–101.

38 ibid., p. 100.

39 ibid., p. 100; P. Charron, *De la sagesse* (1601; edn cit. 4 vols., Dijon, 1801), bk II, ch. 5 (vol. III, pp. 13–14); R. Kogel, *Pierre Charron* (Geneva, 1972), p. 91.

40 G. and L. Cozzi, eds., *Opere*, p. 100; Charron, *Sagesse*, vol. III, p. 2.

41 G. and L. Cozzi, eds., *Opere*, p. 1292.

42 See, for example, Randall, in Cassirer et al., *Renaissance Philosophy*, pp. 274, 279; Kogel, *Charron*, ch. 3; Popkin, *Scepticism*, pp. 57–63. Lucretius had stressed ignorance of the true causes of natural events as a source of faith (*On the Nature of Things*, edn cit., pp. 225, 236–7). The natural origins of religion are discussed in Garimberto, *Problemi naturali*, problems 63 and 70 (pp. 102–3, 113–16). This was translated into French (Lyons, 1559), and so may perhaps have been a source for Charron.

43 G. and L. Cozzi, eds., *Opere*, pp. 101–2.

44 Charron, *Sagesse*, vol. III, pp. 18–23.

45 G. and L. Cozzi, eds., *Opere*, p. 102; Charron, *Sagesse*, vol. III, pp. 23–32.

46 e.g. Charron: 'sans grande declaration ou determination d'icelle' (*Sagesse*, vol. III, p. 24); Sarpi: 'senza gran determinazione del suo essere' (G. and L. Cozzi, eds., *Opere*, p. 102).

47 ibid., pp. 99–102; Charron, *Sagesse*, vol. III, pp. 30–1.

48 G. and L. Cozzi, eds., *Opere*, p. 102; Charron, *Sagesse*, vol. III, pp. 12–14.

49 ibid., vol. III, p. 29.

50 ibid., vol. III, p. 11.

51 See P. Charron, *Les trois veritez* (Bordeaux, 1593), pp. 1–2.

52 G. and L. Cozzi, eds., *Opere*, p. 95.

53 ibid., pp. 108–9.
54 See Sextus Empiricus, *Outlines*, bk I, chs. 8, 11.
55 Charron, *Sagesse*, vol. III, p. 26.
56 G. and L. Cozzi, eds., *Opere*, pp. 102–5.
57 ibid., pp. 105–6.
58 Indeed Acton may have mistaken it for an account of Protestantism: see the quotation below, p. 43.
59 G. and L. Cozzi, eds., *Opere*, pp. 107–8.
60 ibid., p. 106.
61 See also, for example, M. de Montaigne, *Essais* (definitive text, 1588), bk I, no. 23. 'La religion Chrestienne a toutes les marques d'extreme justice et utilité; mais nulle plus apparente, que l'exacte recommendation de l'obeissance du Magistrat et manutention des polices. Quel merveilleux example nous en a laissé la sapience divine, qui, pour establir le salut du genre humain et conduire cette sienne glorieuse victoire contre la mort et le peché, ne l'a voulu faire qu'à la mercy de nostre ordre politique' (ed. M. Rat, 3 vols., Paris, 1941–2, vol. I, p. 127).
62 On Machiavelli's view of religion see J. A. Mazzeo, *Renaissance and Revolution, the Remaking of European Thought* (London, 1967), pp. 107–15; on Bruno's see Spini, *Libertini*, pp. 55–60.
63 I have used the copies in the Bibliothèque Nationale (Lb.35.404; Lb.35.744). Both works are discussed in Vivanti, *Lotta politica*, pp. 56–8, 61–3. J. Lecler discusses *De la concorde de l'estat* in *Toleration and the Reformation* (2 vols., New York, 1960), vol. II, pp. 149–51.
64 On the evolution of the term 'state' see Skinner, *Foundations*, vol. II, pp. 352–8.
65 *De la vraye et legitime constitution de l'estat* (n. l, 1591), p. 11.
66 *De la concorde de l'estat par l'observation des edicts de pacification* (n. l, 1599), pp. 18–20. Vivanti misinterprets what is intended as a *reductio ad absurdum* as an expression of Utopian idealism (*Lotta politica*, pp. 62–3).
67 *Constitution de l'estat*, pp. 15–16; *Concorde de l'estat*, pp. 33–6.
68 *Constitution de l'estat*, p. 42.
69 *Concorde de l'estat*, p. 57.
70 ibid., pp. 79–82.
71 *Constitution de l'estat*, ch. 7; also pp. 44–5.
72 ibid., pp. 16–17; *Concorde de l'estat*, pp. 13–14.
73 ibid., pp. 28–9.
74 *Constitution de l'estat*, p. 15.
75 ibid., pp. 32, 42.
76 ibid., pp. 5–6.
77 See Charron, *Trois veritez*, ch. 2: 'Raisons politiques pour la preuve de la religion'.
78 See C. R. Baxter, 'Jean Bodin's daemon and his conversion to Judaism', in *Jean Bodin: Verhandlungen der internationalen Bodin Tagung in München* (Munich, 1973), pp. 1–21; E. Herbert, *de Veritate* (1624; ed. M. H. Carré, Bristol, 1937); G. du Vair, *The Moral Philosophie of the Stoicks* (1585; ed. R. Kirk, New Brunswick, 1951); J. Lipsius, *Two Bookes of Constancie* (1584; ed. R. Kirk, New Brunswick, 1939).
79 Nardi, 'Filosofia e religione', p. 123; Spini, *Libertini*, pp. 107–12.
80 On Bodin see Skinner, *Foundations* vol. II, pp. 284–301; on de Thou see V. Martin, *Le Gallicanisme et la Réforme Catholique: essai historique sur l'introduction en France des décrets du Concile de Trente, 1563–1615* (Paris, 1919), pp. 316–20.

81 C. Dumoulin, *Concile sur le faict du Concile de Trente* (Lyons, 1564). Dumoulin
was arrested by the Parlement for attacking not only papal encroachment on secular
jurisdiction, but also Catholic doctrine: Martin, *Gallicanisme*, p. 73. E. Richer, *A
Treatise of Ecclesiasticall and Politicke Power* (1st [Latin] edn, 1611; English
translation, London, 1612).

82 On Casaubon see below, pp. 86–9. On Hotman see Vivanti, *Lotta politica*, esp.
pp. 273–4.

83 Above, p. 13.

84 This is a rejection, not only of Christianity, but also of stoicism: see Cicero, *de
Finibus*, bk II, ch. 11; bk III, chs. 5–6; bk V, ch. 9.

85 Burke, ed., *History of Benefices*, p. xvi.

86 Pintard, *Libertinage érudit*, p. 261.

87 *Pensieri filosofici*, nos. 260, 468, 471, 531.

88 G. and L. Cozzi, eds., *Opere*, p. 90.

89 ibid., p. 94.

90 ibid., p. 93. See also 'Arte di ben pensare', Amerio, ed., *Scritti filosofici*, pp. 140–1.

91 There seems to be an echo of Charron's *De la sagesse* in 'Non ti maravigliare mai
di azzione o opinione alcuna perchè non vi è cosa cosi absurda, che non sia stata
piantata per legge: e quello ch'oggi e favola, fu già articolo di fede' (G. and L. Cozzi,
eds., *Opere*, p. 92). The Cozzis find this reminiscent of *De la sagesse*, bk II, ch.
3, but, as elsewhere, do not claim that Sarpi had read Charron. As Sarpi had religion
in mind, the passage in question seems more reminiscent of the one quoted above,
p. 25. And as Sarpi did read Charron before writing the *Pensieri sulla religione*, it
seems highly likely that the *Pensieri medico-morali* were also written after reading
Charron, but probably (for the same reasons as with the *Pensieri sulla religione*)
before 1606, although a later date cannot be excluded.

92 G. and L. Cozzi, eds., *Opere*, pp. 73, 77. The inspiration for the *Pensieri medico-morali*
is probably Sextus Empiricus, *Outlines*, bk III, ch. 32, along with the passages of
Averroes cited above, n. 35. For an argument comparable to Sarpi's, but based
on the assumption that the healthy mind is religious, the sick mind atheistical, see
E. A. Strathman, *Sir Walter Ralegh: a Study in Elizabethan Skepticism* (New York,
1951), p. 80.

93 G. and L. Cozzi, eds., *Opere*, p. 76.

94 ibid., pp. 73–5.

95 ibid., p. 77.

96 ibid., p. 92.

97 e.g. letter to Leschassier, 14 Sept. 1610: G. and L. Cozzi, eds., *Opere*, p. 270.

98 Q. Skinner has discussed the problem of correctly interpreting the views of people
who, it can be argued, said one thing while meaning to be understood as saying
something else: he takes as his examples the treatment of religion in Hobbes and
Bayle, and argues that 'contextual' interpretation helps elucidate such cases. In
some circumstances, however, authors do *not* wish to convey their real opinions,
and in such cases it is important to know not only what they mean to be understood
as saying, but also what their real opinions are and why they do not wish to give
expression to them. Such questions can usually be answered in terms which are
of little interest to the historian of ideas: e.g. the desire to win political support.
However, this is not always the case. It is reasonable to assume that one can only
understand why Sarpi's *History of the Council of Trent* takes the form it does if
one knows what his views on religion were, and what views he thought others ought
to hold. But Sarpi ensured that contemporaries would find it almost impossible to

deduce his real views and motives from the text itself. In such a case one needs to study a quite different sort of context from that identified by Skinner in order to discover not only the 'social' meaning of the text, but also its meaning for the author. It is true that such a study will tell one nothing new about the text's significance for the development of the ideas of others. But it may explain how certain ideas came to be formulated, quite apart from showing how an unorthodox thinker might seek to modify, but not fracture, an orthodox mode of discourse, hoping to create the conditions in the long term for the dissemination of his real ideas. See Q. Skinner, 'Meaning and understanding in the History of Ideas', *History and Theory*, VIII (1969), 3–53, esp. pp. 32–5; id., '"Social Meaning" and the interpretation of social action', in *Philosophy, Politics and Society*, ser. IV, ed. P. Laslett, W. G. Runciman and Q. Skinner (Oxford, 1972), pp. 136–57, esp. pp. 147–8.

99   On Sarpi's preoccupation with unmasking see P. Burke's introduction to *History of Benefices*, pp. xvii, xxxiv, xxxv, xl–xli; and id., 'The Great Unmasker: Paolo Sarpi, 1552–1623', *History Today*, XV (1965), 426–32. On Boccalini see below, pp. 70–6. But the theme of hypocrisy is a commonplace of the time, and contemporaries were naturally keen to convict Sarpi on this charge (Micanzio, *Vita*, pp. 1366–71). They had difficulty, however, in identifying Sarpi's motives. See below, pp. 132, 142.

100   Spini, *Libertini*, pp. 12, 14. Sarpi described his own procedure as follows: 'Ego tamen sic soleo. Ubi aliquid dicendum est, integram veritatem prae oculis pono; ex ea eam partem desumo, quae auribus temporis accommodari possit. Iis partibus, quas silentio tego, non tamen aliquid contrario profero, ut semper aperta via maneat, per quam ulterius progredi possim, neque mihi ipsi pugnantia dicam' (Ulianich, ed., *Lettere ai Gallicani*, p. 109).

101   e.g. Kristeller, 'Renaissance atheism', p. 243.

102   For examples of continuity between the *Pensieri* and Sarpi's other writings see pp. 58, 90, 100, 127, 171 (n. 143), 172 (n. 165).

103   Bianchi-Giovini, *Biografia*, vol. I, pp. 141–2.

104   The publication of the *Pensieri sulla religione* did not, however, see the end of this tradition: see, for example, G. and L. Cozzi, eds., *Opere*, pp. 22–3, 28.

105   P. Pirri, 'Come Paolo Sarpi non fu vescovo di Nona', *Civiltà Cattolica*, IV (1936), 196–206.

106   [A. Possevino], *Risposta di Teodoro Eugenio di Famagosta all'aviso mandato fuori dal signore A. Quirino* (Bologna, 1606), p. 5. Possevino's claim implies that if recent historians have been right to claim that there never was a 'school of Padua' consisting of philosophers committed to Averroism, then there were at any rate plans to establish such a school.

107   P. Savio, ed., 'Per l'epistolario di Paolo Sarpi' (*Aevum*, X (1936), 1–104; XI (1937), 13–74, 275–322; XIII (1939), 558–622; XIV (1940), 3–84; XVI (1942), 3–43, 105–38), X, 9–14.

108   W. Hoffmann, *Avvertimento et ammonitione Catolica al Padre A. Possevino* (n. l, 1607), p. 5.

109   Quoted in Lord Acton, 'Fra Paolo Sarpi' (1867), in his *Essays on Church and State* (London, 1952), pp. 251–60; p. 255.

110   V. Siri, *Memorie recondite dell'anno 1601 all'anno 1641* (8 vols., Ronco, 1677–9), vol. I, p. 437.

111   *Lettres de Peiresc aux frères Dupuy*, ed. P. T. de Larroque (7 vols., Paris, 1888–98), vol. 6, p. 96. For Peiresc's admiration for the *Council of Trent* see Yates, 'Sarpi's History', p. 131.

112 'Origine e cause della scomunica fulminata da Papa Paolo V...', British Library, Additional MSS 10786, ff. 6rv, 111r.
113 See L. Pastor, *History of the Popes* (1st [German] edn, 1886–; edn cit. 40 vols., London, 1891–1953), vol. XXIV (1933), p. 215. See also vol. XXIX, p. 41.
114 G. and L. Cozzi, eds., *Opere*, p. 27. According to G. Fontanini Sarpi had already been refused a bishopric in 1593 for consorting with heretics (*Storia arcana della vita di Fra Paolo Sarpi Servita* (Venice, 1807), p. 15).
115 Two further examples may be mentioned: the 'Relatione dello stato, costumi, disordini et rimedii di Venetia' (Biblioteca Correr, Venice, MSS 2989–90; see the excerpts published by F. Odorici in 'Paolo V e le città di Terraferma', *Archivio storico italiano*, new series, XII (1859), 171–80; p. 175); O. de Franceschi (pseud.), *Ducento e più calonnie opposte da G. Marsilio all'Illustrissima Cardinale Bellarmino confutate* (Macerata, 1607), p. 4.
116 Above, p. 19.
117 Pomponazzi, *de Immortalitate Animae*, ch. 4.
118 [Possevino], *Risposta*, p. 5.
119 L. Firpo, 'Appunti Campanelliani XXV: storia di un furto', *Giornale critico della filosofia italiano*, XXXV (1956), 541–9; p. 545. Another denunciation which seems to be independent of that of Dardano and Gagliardi is a reference made by someone in the curia to Sarpi as 'un ateista, un ateista pirroniano' (Taucci, *Intorno alle lettere*, p. 87).
120 Acton, 'Fra Paolo Sarpi', p. 255.
121 Bianchi-Giovini, *Biografia*, vol. II, pp. 462–4; G. Cozzi, 'Una vicenda della Venezia barocca: Marco Trevisan e la sua "eroica amicizia"', *Bollettino dell'Istituto di storia della società e dello stato veneziano*, II (1960), 61–154, pp. 101–2.
122 Acton, 'Fra Paolo Sarpi', p. 255.

Chapter 2. Sarpi and the Venetian Interdict

1 In an unpublished paper, 'Venetian political life and the crisis of the Interdict (1606–7): the reality behind the myth'.
2 P. Sarpi, *Lettere ai Protestanti*, ed. M. D. Busnelli (2 vols., Bari, 1931), vol. II, p. 127.
3 For a comparison between Venetian Church–state conflicts and such conflicts elsewhere in Italy at this time, see A. D. Wright, 'Why the *Venetian* Interdict?', *English Historical Review*, LXXXIX (1974), 534–50, and also Wright, 'The Venetian view of Church and State: Catholic Erastianism?', *Studi secenteschi*, XIX (1978), 75–106.
4 A. Quirino [Querini], *Aviso dalle ragioni della serenissima republica di Venetia* (Venice, 1606, edn cit. of 55 pp.), pp. 9–12. Papal polemicists responded by insisting on the social utility of clerical wealth. The 'Origine e cause della scommunica' (f. 81 *et seqq.*) even claims that the Church, unlike the nobility, was an improving landlord, and so provided food for the population at large.
5 See table 5.1 in R. T. Rapp, *Industry and Economic Decline in Seventeenth Century Venice* (Cambridge, Mass., 1976). In approximate agreement with Rapp's figures is the *Discorso sopra la fragiltà di Venetia* (in L. Amabile, *Fra Tommaso Campanella nei castelli di Napoli, in Roma ed in Parigi* (2 vols., Naples, 1887), vol. II, doc. 198, but not by Campanella), which emphasises, however, that the revenue from the Terraferma would be more important in time of war. According to a Venetian nobleman, however, state revenue in 1603 was much lower than generally believed, while over half was already derived from the Terraferma, as opposed to the city

and port of Venice ('Ravedimento o sia protesto di un clarissimo senatore veneto', Bodleian Library, Rawlinson MSS D. 625/31, f. 720r.).

6 B. S. Pullan, *Rich and Poor in Renaissance Venice* (Oxford, 1971), pp. 138–40.

7 e.g. Possevino, *Risposta di Teodoro Eugenio*, p. 6; *Apologia di Baldassar Nardi Aretino...con due discorsi politici* (Naples, 1607), p. 37; de Franceschi, *Ducento e più calonnie*, p. 15.

8 For the classic statement of Sarpi's views, see the 'Considerazioni sopra le censure', in G. and L. Cozzi, eds., *Opere*, pp. 153–217.

9 e.g. R. Bellarmine, *Risposta al trattato dei sette theologi di Venetia*, followed, on p. 65, by the *Risposta alle oppositioni di fra Paolo Sarpi* (Rome, 1607), p. 123; Nardi, *Apologia*, p. 24; see also Querini, *Aviso*, p. 13.

10 J. M. Pou y Marti, 'La intervencion española en el conflicto entre Paulo V y Venecia (1605–7)', in *Miscellanea Pio Paschini*, vol. II (Rome, 1949), pp. 359–81.

11 Bellarmine, *Risposta*, p. 89.

12 ibid., p. 122. Bellarmine goes on to accuse Sarpi of having said that one cannot achieve salvation within the unreformed Church of Rome. This, however, was something of a misrepresentation of Sarpi's argument: cf. *Apologia per le oppositioni fatte dall'...Cardinale Bellarmino* (Venice, 1606), f. 13v.

13 [P. de Belloy], *Apologie Catholique...par E.D.L.I.C.* (n. l., 1585), pt II, chs. 9, 26.

14 J. F. d'Espesse, *Advertissement sur la réception et publication du Concile de Trente* (1583), reprinted in E. Mignot, *Histoire de la réception du Concile de Trente* (2 vols., Amsterdam, 1756), vol. II, pp. 104–42; pp. 126–7.

15 Bellarmine, *Risposta*, pp. 26, 97–8.

16 e.g. R. Bellarmine, *Scritti politici*, ed. C. Giacon (Bologna, 1950), pp. 233–6.

17 Bellarmine, *Risposta*, p. 19.

18 ibid., pp. 30–1.

19 Despite the efforts of the nuncios to persuade her of it. See, for example, A. Stella, *Chiesa e stato nelle relazioni dei nunzi pontifici a Venezia: Ricerche sul giurisdizionalismo veneziano del XVI al XVIII secolo* (Vatican City, 1964), pp. 26, 58, 62, 236.

20 e.g. letter of 18 July 1606 in *Receuil des lettres missives de Henri IV*, ed. M. Berger de Xivrey and J. Guadet (9 vols., Paris, 1843–76), vol. VI. Venice's stubbornness made some doubt whether her reputation for political wisdom was well deserved: e.g. Nardi, *Apologia*, p. 30; du Perron, *Ambassades*, letter of 9 Jan. 1607; Bodleian Library, Italian MSS c. 5n ('Cause per le quali la Republica Venetia non deve aspettare la scommunica'), f. 235r.

21 e.g. F. Priuli, 'Relazione di Spagna', in N. Barozzi and G. Berchet, eds., *Relazioni degli stati europei lette al senato dagli ambasciatori veneti nel secolo decimosettimo* (10 vols. in 11, Venice, 1856–78), ser. I, *Spagna*, vol. I, pp. 339–430; pp. 397–8; F. Molin, P. Duodo, G. Mocenigo, F. Contarini, 'Relazione di Roma', in ibid., ser. III, *Roma*, vol. I, pp. 51–79; p. 66.

22 See the shrewd comment of Foscarini in Savio, ed., 'Per l'epistolario', *Aevum*, X, 13.

23 S. Tramontin, 'La visita apostolica del 1581 a Venezia', *Studi veneziani*, IX (1967), 453–533, pp. 478, 523–4; Pullan, *Rich and Poor*, pp. 327–71.

24 Tramontin, 'Visita apostollica', pp. 453–98; esp. pp. 480–1.

25 B. S. Pullan, 'Wage earners and the Venetian economy, 1550–1630', in Pullan, ed., *Crisis and Change in the Venetian Economy* (London, 1968), pp. 146–74.

26 Pullan, 'Occupations and investments', pp. 397–8; Stella, *Chiesa e stato*, p. 46; G. and L. Cozzi, eds., *Opere*, p. 266 (letter to Leschassier, 14 Oct. 1609).

27 Tramontin, 'Visita apostolica', pp. 479–80.
28 O. M. T. Logan, 'Studies in the religious life of Venice in the sixteenth and seventeenth centuries' (Ph.D. thesis, Cambridge, 1967), p. 36.
29 P. Burke, *Venice and Amsterdam: a study of seventeenth-century élites* (London, 1974), pp. 29–30.
30 Only 4% of noblemen were clerics in 1615–20; by 1760 the proportion was 12%: Pullan, 'Occupations and investments', p. 399.
31 See for example the 'Relazione di M. Vicenzo Gussoni nel ritorno di Podestà di Vicenza' (15 May 1607; Venetian State Archives).
32 Pullan, *Rich and Poor*, pp. 332–5; 381–2.
33 ibid., pp. 337–8; 588.
34 ibid., pp. 335–9.
35 ibid., pp. 270–7; 593–4.
36 See Pullan, 'Occupations and investments', p. 398. [G. Malatesta], 'Relatione historica e politica delle differenze nate tra Paulo V et i Venetiani' (British Library, Add. MSS 8589), ff. 105rv, 143v.
37 The contemporary lesson was drawn explicitly by Querini, *Aviso*, p. 13.
38 See plate 1.
39 R. Mousnier, *The Assassination of Henry IV: the tyrranicide problem and the consolidation of the French absolute monarchy in the early seventeenth century* (1st [French] edn, 1964; edn cit. London, 1973), pp. 162–3.
40 D. Pithou, *Les libertez de l'Eglise Gallicane* (Paris, 1594), f. 2r.
41 Richer, *Treatise*, chs. 1, 11, 12.
42 de Belloy, *Apologie Catholique*, pt II, ch. 19.
43 F. Romulo (i.e. R. Bellarmine), *Responsio ad Praecipua Capita Apologiae quae Falso Catholica Inscribitur* (Fani, 1591), ch. 24.
44 ibid., p. 5.
45 de Belloy, *Apologie Catholique*, pt. iii, ch. 2.
46 W. J. Bouwsma presents Sarpi's arguments in this guise in 'The Venetian Interdict and the problem of order', *Archiwum historii filozofii i mysli spolecznej*, XII (1966), 127–40. See also L. Emery, 'Religione e politica nella mente di Paolo Sarpi', *Nuova rivista storica*, VIII (1924), 304–29, 443–75, and below, pp. 131–5.
47 Letter to J. Gillot, 29 Sept. 1609, in G. and L. Cozzi, eds., *Opere*, pp. 278–81; *Pensieri sulla religione*, ibid., pp. 103, 106.
48 Letter to Gillot, 15 Sept. 1609, ibid., pp. 275–8.
49 There is a transcript of this text in G. C. Sivos, 'Delle vite dei Dosi di Venetia, Libero Terzo', Biblioteca Nazionale Marciana, Venice, MS 1818 (9436).
50 Nardi, *Apologia*, pp. 35–6.
51 ibid., pp. 34, 38; below, p. 67.
52 ibid., pp. 20–3; L. Firpo, ed., *Il pensiero politico del rinascimento e della controriforma* (Milan, 1966), pp. 691–8.
53 Nardi, *Apologia*, pp. 54, 68; T. Campanella, *Antiveneti* (1st complete edn, Florence, 1945, ed. L. Firpo), bk II, discourse 6; G. Botero, *Della ragion di stato* (1589; ed. F. Chabod, Turin, 1948), pp. 132–41.
54 Campanella, *Antiveneti*, pp. 125–7; 165.
55 ibid., pp. 111–12.
56 ibid., p. 84.
57 ibid., pp. 26–9, 76–81.
58 Below, pp. 107–9.
59 Querini's conclusions are reprinted in appendix to Cornet, ed., *Giornale*.

60 F. Gilbert, 'Venice in the crisis of the League of Cambrai', in Hale, ed., *Renaissance Venice*, pp. 274–92.
61 See Malatesta, 'Relatione historica', f. 34r. According to Sarpi the opponents of the papacy were 'i buoni, e malcontenti, e politici' (Savio, ed., 'Per l'epistolario', *Aevum*, XVI, 106). On the problems posed by the poor nobles see B. S. Pullan, 'Poverty, charity and the reason of state: some Venetian examples', *Bollettino dell'Istituto di storia della società e dello stato veneziano*, II (1960), 17–60, and Cozzi, *Contarini*, ch. 6.
62 For Donà's hostility to Protestantism, see *La corrispondenza da Madrid dell'ambasciatore Leonardo Donà, 1570–3*, ed. M. Brunetti and E. Vitale (2 vols., Venice, 1963), vol. I, p. lviii. Donà is generally presented in the secondary literature as being anti-Spanish. Contemporaries were of a different opinion: e.g. du Perron, *Ambassades*, letter of 25 July 1606; Canaye, *Lettres*, letters to de Commartin, 29 Dec. 1606, and d'Alincourt, 30 Dec. 1606; Malatesta, 'Relatione historica', f. 207rv; 'Discorsi fatti dal Nob. Ho. B.M....l'anno 1606' (Biblioteca Nazionale Marciana, MS It. VII 155 (8159)), ff. 20r, 34r.
63 A. Tenenti, 'Il *de Perfectione Rerum* di Nicolò Contarini', *Bollettino dell'Istituto di storia della società e dello stato veneziano*, I (1959), 155–66.
64 Cozzi, *Contarini*, pp. 99, 132–5.
65 ibid., p. 56.
66 ibid., pp. 78–80. Although in the post-Interdict period Contarini favoured alliances with Protestant states, despite the fact that he had previously sought to preserve Venetian political independence (ibid., pp. 84–5, 206), he continued to be hostile to the Reformation, which he saw as a threat to political order (ibid., p. 211).
67 ibid., pp. 215–18; below, pp. 106–9. It is difficult to know what weight to give to the nuncio's opinion, in 1624, that some of Sarpi's followers, leaders of the anti-clerical faction, 'credono poco' (ibid., p. 237).
68 P. Priuli, 'Relazione di Francia', in Barozzi and Berchet, eds., *Relazioni*, ser. II, *Francia*, vol. I, pp. 175–287; Secchi, *Foscarini*, pp. 76–80.
69 On Foscarini, see in particular the materials collected in Savio, ed., 'Per l'epistolario', and Secchi, *Foscarini, passim*.
70 Cozzi, 'Galilei, Sarpi', esp. p. 224. Giovanni Francesco Graziani reports that Alessandro Malipiero, a friend of Sarpi's, when on his deathbed refused to take any of the sacraments, and would not see any priest, apart from Sarpi ('Ragguaglio del caso occorso intorno alla mia persona in Venetia', British Library, Add. MS 6877, f. 33v).
71 G. Cozzi, 'Sulla morte di fra Paolo Sarpi', in *Miscellanea in Onore di Roberto Cessi* (2 vols., Rome, 1958), vol. II, pp. 387–96.
72 Cozzi, 'Una vicenda della Venezia barocca'.
73 F. Priuli, 'Relazione di Spagna'; Cozzi, *Contarini*, p. 136; Secchi, *Foscarini*, p. 39. Sarpi's correspondence with Priuli is in Sarpi, *Opere* (6 vols. and 2, Helmstadt–Verona, 1761–8), vol. VI, pp. 121–40.
74 Bouwsma, *Republican Liberty, passim*.
75 L. B., *Opinions et raisons d'Estat*; B.M., 'Discorsi'.
76 F. Gaeta, 'Alcune considerazioni sul mito di Venezia', *Bibliothèque d'Humanisme et Renaissance*, XXIII (1961), 58–75.
77 Carleton, 'Particular Notes'.
78 *Squitinio della libertà Venetiana* (Mirandola, 1612).
79 One of them is published as 'Una relazione del Marchese di Bedmar sui Veneziani', ed. I. Raulich, *Nuovo archivio veneto*, XVI (1898), 5–32.

80 Cozzi, 'Una vicenda', pp. 101–5. The tract was published in English as *The Maxims of the Government of Venice* (London, 1707).
81 'Ravedimento, o sia protesto'; Cozzi, *Contarini*, ch. 6.
82 e.g. 'Discorso del senatore Badoer', in Cornet, ed., *Giornale*, pp. 307–15.
83 L. Lollino, *Vita del cavalier Ottaviano Bon* (Venice, 1854), pp. 15–16. See also Cozzi, *Contarini*, pp. 141–4, 231; Secchi, *Foscarini*, p. 36. The latter records that Bon chose to be buried in the habit of a Capuchin, one of the orders expelled from Venice in 1606.
84 Lowry, 'The reform of the Council of Ten'.
85 *Pensieri filosofici*, nos. 379, 420 (which may be a comment on the debate between Socrates and Thrasymachus in Plato's *Republic*), 471.
86 The tension between Sarpi's absolutism and Venice's republican constitution is exploited by de Franceschi, *Ducento e più calonnie*, pp. 37–8.
87 Priuli, 'Relazione di Francia', p. 285. Venetian political discourse was couched almost entirely in terms of reason of state: it was certainly not seen as an inappropriate mode of discourse for a republic, notwithstanding, for example, N. O. Keohane, *Philosophy and the State in France, The Renaissance to the Enlightenment* (Princeton, 1980), p. 169. There was, however, a real tension between argument in terms of reason of state and argument couched in religious terms.
88 See Masetti Zannini, 'Libri di fra Paolo', appendix, nos. 60–75, 77, 80, 82, 101, 278, 292–3.
89 A. Momigliano, 'The first political commentary on Tacitus' (1947), in his *Essays in Ancient and Modern Historiography* (Oxford, 1977), pp. 205–29.
90 On Tacitism in general see G. Toffanin, *Machiavelli e il 'Tacitismo': la 'politica storica' al tempo della controriforma* (Padua, 1921) and P. Burke, 'Tacitism', in T. A. Dorey, ed., *Tacitus* (London, 1969), pp. 149–71.
91 Toffanin, *Tacitismo*, esp. pp. 94–8; G. Spini, 'The art of history in the Italian Counter Reformation' (1st [Italian] edn, 1948), in E. Cochrane, ed., *The Late Italian Renaissance* (London, 1970, pp. 91–133), pp. 114–20.
92 J. Lipsius, *Six Bookes of Politickes or Civil Doctrine* (1594, reprinted, New York, 1970), p. 123.
93 As Toffanin puts it, 'la politica è con la pratica di Tiberio, la morale è con il commento di Tacito': *Tacitismo*, p. 147.
94 Lipsius, *Politickes*, p. 5.
95 For a recent discussion of Lipsius' religious views see L. Forster, 'Lipsius and Renaissance neo-Stoicism', in *Festschrift for Ralph Farrell* (Bern, 1977), pp. 201–20. Forster's conclusion, that Lipsius was a Familist, is supported by B. Rekers, *Benito Arias Montano (1527–98)* (London, 1972), pp. 70–104.
96 S. Ammirato, *Discorsi sopra Cornelio Tacito* (Florence, 1594), bk V, discourse 5. Ammirato presents the Romans as models of piety: see for example the posthumously published chapter, 'Non esser vero che i Romani se servissero della religione per ordinar la città, ma per fine di essa religione', in appendix to R. de Mattei, *Il pensiero politico di Scipione Ammirato* (Milan, 1963), pp. 375–83. Like Lipsius, Ammirato insists on the need to remain faithful to the religion of one's ancestors: see the chapter 'Quanto temerariamente parlan coloro i quali dicono che gli stati si reggono co'paternostri' (ibid., pp. 367–74), where he argues that no one could trust a ruler willing to innovate in matters of religion. It is true that Ammirato argues for the need to obey the law of God even when it conflicts with reason of state (ibid., pp. 126–7), but he seems to have no conception of a specifically Christian divine law.
97 F. Meinecke's account of Boccalini's thought (*Machiavellism: the Doctrine of Raison*

d'Etat and its Place in Modern History, ed. W. Stark (New Haven, 1957), pp. 70–89)
has scarcely been superseded. His account of Boccalini's life, however, should now
be contrasted with that presented by G. Cozzi ('Traiano Boccalini, il Cardinal
Borghese e la Spagna, secondo le riferte di un confidente degli inquisitori di stato',
Rivista storica italiana, LXIII (1956), 230–44). Where Meinecke presents Boccalini
as a correspondent of Sarpi, a victim of Spanish assassins, and as someone who
may have acted as a Venetian spy prior to 1606, Cozzi presents him as someone
who had no known contact with Sarpi, who died a natural death, and who was
employed by Spain as a spy while he was resident in Venice. The first two points
are now well established: the new evidence Cozzi presents regarding Boccalini's
contacts with the Spanish ambassador is, in my view, inconclusive.

98 T. Boccalini, *Ragguagli di Parnaso e scritti minori*, ed. L. Firpo (3 vols., Bari, 1948:
vols. I and II correspond to the *Ragguagli* published in Boccalini's lifetime, in 1612
and 1613), vol. III, no. 31; see also, for example, vol. I, no. 64; vol. III, pp. 275–6,
and *La bilancia politica di tutte le opere di Traiano Boccalini*, ed. L. du May (2 vols.,
Castellana, 1678), vol. I, pp. 99–101; vol. II, p. 167.

99 Boccalini, *Ragguagli*, vol. III, no. 7.

100 ibid., vol. II, no. 13.

101 ibid., vol. II, no. 68.

102 F. A. Yates has suggested that Boccalini may have been influenced by Bruno: see
The Rosicrucian Enlightenment (London, 1972), pp. 135–6.

103 On Erasmianism, see L. Febvre, 'The origins of the French Reformation: a
badly-put question?' (1928), in his *A New Kind of History*, ed. P. Burke (London,
1973), pp. 44–107; H. R. Trevor-Roper, 'Religion, the Reformation and social
change' (1963), in Trevor-Roper, *Religion, the Reformation and Social Change*
(London, 1967), pp. 1–45. Febvre's essay is criticised by D. B. Fenlon in '*Encore
une question*: Lucien Febvre, the Reformation and the School of *Annales*', *Historical
Studies*, IX (Belfast, 1974), pp. 65–81.

104 A classic critique of Tacitism is that of the Jesuit F. Strada, selections from whose
Prolusiones Academicae (1617) are reprinted in *Politici e moralisti del seicento*, ed.
B. Croce and S. Caramella (Bari, 1930), pp. 1–21. Strada complains, amongst other
things, that to openly teach that religion is a device of government is to make the
populace less tractable and the task of rulers more difficult, and he accuses the
Tacitists of turning people away from religious worship.

105 E. A. Cigogna, *Delle inscrizioni veneziane* (6 vols., Venice, 1824–53), vol. IV, pp.
355–72.

106 See above, p. 150, n. 10.

107 Or, as Sarpi put it elsewhere, 'ogn'un confessa che il vero termine di regere il
suddito è mantenerlo senza saputa delle cose publiche et in venerazione di quelle'
('Del confutar scritture malediche' (1620), in G. and L. Cozzi, eds., *Opere*, pp.
1170–80).

108 Boccalini's posthumous work, especially the *ragguagli* printed in 1614 as the *Pietra
del paragone politico*, is even more vituperatively anti-Spanish than the work he
published in his lifetime. But, interestingly enough, it is not uncritical of Venice:
see the caption to plate 2 and the passage cited below, p. 174, n. 2; also *Ragguagli*,
vol. III, nos. 27, 52. No. 49, a comparison between the relative merits of Venice
and the German Republics, was, unfortunately, left unfinished: but see vol. I,
no. 39 on this subject.

109 Boccalini, *Bilancia politica*, vol. I, p. 344.

110 ibid., vol. I, p. 337.

111 ibid., vol. II, p. 22.

112 id., *Ragguagli*, vol. II, no. 6. On ignorance and absolutism see, for example, vol. III, p. 269; *Bilancia politica*, vol. I, p. 181.

113 Boccalini, *Ragguagli*, vol. I, p. 226; *Bilancia politica*, vol. I, p. 181.

114 Boccalini, *Ragguagli*, vol. II, p. 22.

115 ibid., vol. I, no. 67.

116 Sarpi, *Pensieri filosofici*, nos. 403, 470.

117 Bedell, *Letters*, pp. 17, 31; P. Du Plessis-Mornay, *Mémoires et correspondence* (12 vols., Paris, 1824–5), vol. X, p. 424; Sivos, 'Vite dei Dosi', f. 93v. For examples see E. Cornet, 'Paolo V e la Repubblica Veneta: Nuova serie di documenti', *Archivio veneto*, ser. I, vol. V (1873), 27–96, 222–318; vol. VI (1873), 68–131, documents nos. 63, 71–2, 81, 84–7, 106–10, 154 (the case of Francesco Torres de Mendoza), Grendler, *Roman Inquisition*, pp. 188–9, and below, p. 136.

Chapter 3. Sarpi's place in Europe

1 P. Sarpi, *Trattato delle materie beneficiarie* (1st edn, 1675; edn cit. G. and L. Cozzi, eds., *Opere*, pp. 331–457; there is an English translation in Burke, ed., *History of Benefices*).

2 'Cosi le mutazioni degl'interessi portano seco mutazione e contrarietà di dottrina' (ibid., p. 434).

3 P. Prodi, 'The structure and organisation of the Church in Renaissance Venice: suggestions for research,' in Hale, ed., *Renaissance Venice*, pp. 409–30; pp. 419–20.

4 Micanzio attributed to Sarpi 'la pietà e religione cristiana nuda come nella sua origine, prima che gl'interessi umani la transformassero in tante alterazioni' (quoted by G. and L. Cozzi, eds., *Opere*, p. 34 from MS notes for the *Vita*). But Micanzio is not always to be trusted: see pp. 120, 136–45, 169 (n. 109).

5 The most useful life of du Perron is P. Feret, *Le Cardinal du Perron: orateur, controversiste, écrivain* (Paris, 1877).

6 This is evident if one compares du Perron's letters to Villeroi with those to Sully in his *Ambassades et negotiations*. It was to Sully that du Perron owed his appointments, and it was to counterbalance the *dévot* foreign policy at first of d'Ossat and then of Villeroi's son d'Alincourt that he was sent to Rome.

7 'Oraison funebre sur la mort de Monsieur de Ronsard' (1586), in *Les diverses oeuvres de l'Illustrissime et Reverendissime Cardinal du Perron* (3rd rev. ed, Paris 1633), pp. 649–676; p. 656.

8 J. D. du Perron, *Traitté du Sainct Sacrement de l'Eucharistie* (Paris, 1622).

9 Feret, *Du Perron*, p. 138.

10 [T. A. d'Aubigné], *Confession Catholique du Sieur de Sancy* (1st [posthumous] edn, 1660; edn cit. in *Recueil de diverses pièces servans à l'histoire de Henri III* (Cologne, 1662, pp. 315–464)), pp. 317–18.

11 *Perroniana sive excerpta ex ore Cardinalis Peronii*, ed. J. and P. Dupuy (Geneva, 1667), arts. *Baronius, Bellarmine, Suarez*. In general the *Perroniana* seem to give succinct expression to views which du Perron certainly held.

12 Feret, *Du Perron*, p. 364.

13 J. D. du Perron, *An Oration made on the part of the Lordes Spirituall, in the Chamber of the Third Estate (or Communalty) of France, upon the Oath (pretended of Allegiance) exhibited in the late Generall Assembly of the Three Estates of the Kingdome* (1st [French] edn, 1615; edn cit. St Omer, 1616), p. 9.

14 J. and P. Dupuy, eds., *Perroniana*, art. *Hérésie* (edn cit. pp. 168–70).

15 ibid., arts. *Eglise* (pp. 119–23; 128–30); *Sermon faict en l'Eglise de Nostre Dame, le jour de la Pentecoste* (n.d.), du Perron, *Oeuvres diverses*, pp. 681–704.
16 J. and P. Dupuy, eds., *Perroniana*, art. *Ecriture* (edn cit. pp. 136–40).
17 *Examen pacifique de la doctrine des Huguenots* (Paris (in fact London), 1589), a work traditionally ascribed to du Perron, but see D. Rogers, '*The Catholic Moderator*, a French reply to Bellarmine and its English author, Henry Constable', *Recusant History*, V (1960), 224–35. On Constable see G. Wickes, 'Henry Constable', *Biographical Studies*, II (1954), 272–300. Constable wrote the *Examen pacifique* when employed as a secret agent for the English government. It was not until 1591 that he declared himself a Catholic, although he himself dated his conversion from 1589. The *Examen pacifique* can be read equally well as propaganda for an Anglican settlement or as the work of 'a politique papist' concerned to bring about 'a reconciliation between the two religions' (the Earl of Shrewsbury, quoted in Wickes, 'Henry Constable', p. 275). Constable's uncompromising commitment to royal authority led him to write an attack on the democratic theories of the Jesuit, Robert Parsons (*A Discoverye of a Counterfecte Conference* (n. l., 1600)). Both works suggest that he was concerned to reduce not only the role of religion in politics, but also the Church's responsibility for the maintenance of social order (cf. J. Bossy, 'The Character of Elizabethan Catholicism' (1962), in T. Aston, ed., *Crisis in Europe 1560–1660* (London, 1965), pp. 223–47; p. 244). I. Gentillet had earlier argued that, implicitly, all Catholics accepted Protestant doctrine regarding, for instance, transsubstantiation: *Anti-Machiavel* (1576), ed. C. E. Rathé (Geneva, 1968), p. 171.
18 *Sermon faict en l'Eglise de Nostre Dame*, du Perron, *Oeuvres diverses*, p. 691.
19 Savio, ed., 'Per l'epistolario', *Aevum*, XIV, 83–4.
20 du Perron, *Ambassades*, letter of 12 Jan. 1605; Mousnier, *Assassination*, pp. 122–3.
21 du Perron, *Ambassades*, letter of 25 Jan. 1605.
22 ibid., letter of 23 Jan. 1606 (the main exception being the English Jesuits). The Spanish were consequently willing to see the Jesuits remain excluded from Venice in 1607. Henri had expressed his policy towards the Jesuits forcibly in a letter to the Parlement of 20 Sept. 1603 (*Lettres missives de Henri IV*, vol. VI): 'L'on dit que le roi d'Espagne s'en sert; je dis aussy que je veux m'en servir, et que la France ne doibt estre de pire condition que l'Espagne, puisque tout le monde les juge utiles.' Sarpi, however, insisted on regarding the Jesuits as part of the infamous alliance between Spain and Rome which he referred to as *diacatholicon* (e.g. Ulianich, ed., *Lettere ai Gallicani*, pp. 191, 200; Savio, ed., 'Per l'epistolario', *Aevum*, XIV, 24, 38, 62).
23 du Perron, *Ambassades*, letter of de Joyeuse, n.d., pp. 313–43.
24 ibid., letter of 19 May 1605. The Spanish were, however, later to make the same claim: see Taucci, *Intorno alle lettere*, pp. 250–1.
25 du Perron, *Ambassades*, letter of 4 Oct. 1605.
26 ibid., 30 July 1606.
27 'Relazione di Francia di Pietro Priuli', in Barozzi and Berchet, eds., *Relazioni* ser. II, *Francia*, vol. I, pp. 174–287; pp. 265–6.
28 ibid., pp. 264–5.
29 du Perron, *Ambassades*, letter of 14 Dec 1605.
30 ibid., letter to Canaye de Fresnes, 5 Aug. 1606; letters of 1 Sept. 1606, 9 and 22 Jan. 1607; letter from Canaye de Fresnes, 17 Feb. 1607.
31 C. P. de Magistris, ed., *Carlo Emmanuele I e la contesa fra la Repubblica Veneta e Paolo V* (Venice, 1906).

32 P. Sarpi, *Istoria dell'Interdetto e altri scritti editi e inediti*, ed. M. D. Busnelli and G. Gambarin (3 vols., Bari, 1940), vol. I, p. 119.

33 du Perron, *Ambassades*, letter of 2 Dec. 1606.

34 ibid., letter of 29 June 1607.

35 ibid., letter from de Brèves of 21 Aug. 1608.

36 ibid., letter of 20 March 1607; letter of 5 April 1607 in du Perron, *Oeuvres diverses*, pp. 872–81.

37 du Perron, *Ambassades*, letter of 1 May 1607.

38 On Taucci's book, and in particular on the argument of chapter 2, see G. Cozzi, 'Paolo Sarpi: il suo problema storico, religioso e giuridico nella recente letteratura', *Il diritto ecclesiastico*, LXIII (1952), 52–88, pp. 54–70.

39 e.g. Secchi, *Foscarini*, pp. 34–50.

40 Mousnier, *Assassination*, pp. 274–9; J. M. Hayden, *France and the Estates General of 1614* (Cambridge, 1974) ch. 8: 'The first article of the Third Estate' (pp. 131–48).

41 du Perron, *An Oration*, pp. 110–11.

42 *Response à la Harangue faite par l'Illustrissime Cardinal du Perron, à Paris l'an 1615...par MVDCCD* (n. l. (1615), edn cit. of 65 pp.), p. 56. Du Tillet's work was written in 1551, but first published posthumously in 1594.

43 ibid., p. 60.

44 ibid., p. 30.

45 J. and P. Dupuy, eds., *Perroniana*, art. *Religion* (edn cit. p. 278).

46 Martin, *Gallicanisme*, pp. 364–91, esp. pp. 374, 383. Du Perron's role is acknowledged in the papal brief of 8 August 1615 (in du Perron, *Ambassades*).

47 Cozzi, 'Sarpi...Canaye...Casaubon', p. 17.

48 ibid., pp. 107–13.

49 ibid., p. 110.

50 ibid., pp. 111–12.

51 ibid., pp. 113, 126.

52 ibid., pp. 113–14, 120, 124–5.

53 *A letter written from Paris by the Lord Cardinall of Peron to Monsieur Casaubon in England* (n. l., 1612); *The Answer of Master Isaac Casaubon to the Epistle of the Most Illustrious and Most Reverend Cardinal du Perron* (London, 1612).

54 Cozzi, 'Sarpi...Canaye...Casaubon', pp. 96, 107.

55 I. Casaubon, *de Libertate Ecclesiastica Liber Singularis* (1607), edn cit. English translation by H. Bedford in G. Hickes, *Two Treatises* (2 vols.; 3rd enlarged edn, London, 1711), vol. II, pp. cxv–ccxciii; p. cxix.

56 Letter of 3 Aug. 1610, in Sarpi's *Lettere ai Protestanti*, ed. Busnelli, vol. II, p. 96. See also Sarpi's letter to Hotman of 23 June 1609, Ulianich, ed., *Lettere ai Gallicani*, pp. 185–6.

57 I follow Cozzi in presuming that Sarpi had already heard of Casaubon's plan to come to Venice ('Sarpi...Canaye...Casaubon', p. 120.) when he wrote his letter of 22 June 1610. As early as May 1609 he was aware of the rumours of Casaubon's conversion (Savio, ed., 'Per l'epistolario', *Aevum*, XIII, 580).

58 The original Latin text of the letters to Casaubon of 22 June 1610 and 17 August 1610 is to be found in the appendix to the first edition of 'Sarpi...Canaye... Casaubon' (*Bollettino dell'Istituto di storia della società e dello stato veneziano*, I (1959), pp. 148–54). An Italian translation of this letter (22 June) is in G. and L. Cozzi, eds., *Opere*, pp. 287–8.

59 Letter of 17 Aug. 1610; ibid., pp. 289–90.

60 27 May; ibid., p. 256 (Italian translation).

61 ibid., p. 271 (Italian translation). On this theme in Sarpi's work see the excellent review by M. Pozzi of G. and L. Cozzi, eds., *Opere* and da Pozzo, ed., *Scritti scelti*, in *Giornale storico della letteratura italiana*, CXLIII (1971), 384–97, pp. 389–92.
62 See G. and L. Cozzi's introduction to the *Scrittura su Vorstio*, ibid., pp. 701–13.
63 *Scrittura su Vorstio*, ibid., pp. 713–19; p. 714.
64 A complete halt to all theological debate had been recommended by the Dutchman Dirck Coornhert. Sarpi and Coornhert shared a similar view of the church as a purely spiritual community (Lecler, *Toleration*, vol. II, pp. 273–86).
65 G. and L. Cozzi, eds., *Opere*, pp. 714–17.
66 ibid., pp. 718–19.
67 On Wotton see L. P. Smith, *Life and Letters of Sir Henry Wotton* (2 vols., Oxford, 1907). For the Huguenot reaction to James' work see Du Plessis-Mornay, *Mémoires et correspondance*, vol. X, letter of 13 Aug. 1609.
68 Letter to Leschassier of 22 Dec. 1609 (Italian translation, da Pozzo, ed., *Scritti scelti*, p. 626).
69 Letters from Diodati to Du Plessis-Mornay, 22 April 1605 (sic) and 1 June 1605 (sic) in Du Plessis-Mornay, *Correspondance*, vol. X, pp. 80–4; 92–3.
70 B. Ulianich, 'Il principe Christian von Anhalt e Paolo Sarpi: dalla missione veneziana del Dohna alla relazione Diodati (1608)', *Annuarium Historiae Conciliorum*, VIII (1976), 429–506; pp. 430, 443–9.
71 Bedell, *Letters*, p. 76.
72 Pastor, although cautious, inclines to the first position, under the influence of G. Rein's *Paolo Sarpi und die Protestanten* (Helsingfors, 1904): *History of the Popes*, vol. XXV (edn cit., London, 1937), pp. 131–3; 196–211. F. Chabod, under the influence of Taucci's *Intorno alle lettere*, adopts the second: *La politica di Paolo Sarpi* (lectures delivered 1950–1; pub. Venice, 1962); now reprinted in his *Scritti sul Rinascimento* (Turin, 1974), pp. 459–588.
73 Ulianich, 'Christian von Anhalt', pp. 481–4, 486.
74 Bedell, *Letters*, pp. 69–75.
75 cf. von Dohna's notes on his visit to Venice, published by Ulianich in appendix to 'Christian von Anhalt', pp. 488–506; p. 501.
76 ibid., pp. 483–4; Vivanti, ed., *Istoria del Concilio Tridentino*, vol. I, pp. 397–9.
77 Ulianich, 'Christian von Anhalt', p. 483.
78 ibid., *Appendix*, p. 492.
79 ibid., *Appendix*, pp. 491–2.
80 Bedell, *Letters*, pp. 67–8. See G. Cozzi, 'Sir Edwin Sandys e la *Relazione dello stato della religione*', *Rivista storica italiana*, LXXIX (1967), 1096–121.
81 Ulianich, 'Christian von Anhalt', *Appendix*, pp. 493–501.
82 *Relazione dello stato della religione*, in G. and L. Cozzi, eds., *Opere*, pp. 295–330.
83 Bedell, *Letters*, p. 74.
84 ibid., pp. 45–57.
85 Ulianich, 'Christian von Anhalt', *Appendix*, pp. 490–1.
86 Bedell, *Letters*, p. 25.
87 Ulianich, 'Christian von Anhalt', p. 469; Taucci, *Intorno alle lettere*, p. 202. See also the report of Sarpi's statement that 'Sei mese sono c'erano occasioni di venire a qualche dichiarazione col papa: il quale da un bel pezzo in qua non dice nulla', 'Christian von Anhalt', *Appendix*, p. 499.
88 On the illegality of contacts between those with a knowledge of political affairs and the agents of foreign powers, where prior permission had not been obtained, see, in general, L. von Ranke, *Venezia nel Cinquecento* (1st [German] edn 1878; edn

cit. Rome, 1974), ch. 4: 'Gli inquisitori di stato' (pp. 179–210). It should be noted, however, that Badoer was charged with communicating with the nuncio as early as 1607, while Foscarini was not merely 'covered with ignominy by the Council of Ten', but also strung up (above, p. 65). Ranke maintains that the law prohibiting contact with the representatives of foreign powers came into force in 1612. Certainly after 1612 Sarpi required official permission for such contacts (Siri, *Memorie recondite*, vol. I, p. 437; G. and L. Cozzi, eds., *Opere*, p. 1281), while Micanzio's correspondence with Protestants seems to have been subject to some form of official supervision (see F. Micanzio, 'Letters to William Cavendish', British Library Add. MS 11309, p. 124). But 1612 saw merely a new vigor in the enforcement of an existing law (*Opere*, p. 638). Contacts with Protestants were already highly dangerous before then: cf. Ulianich, 'Christian von Anhalt', *Appendix*, p. 493; Smith, *Sir Henry Wotton*, vol. I, pp. 87, 95. The Venetian government, however, was willing to protect Sarpi, and others who had dealings with Wotton, from the rigor of the law (ibid., vol. I, pp. 95–6; Savio, ed., 'Per l'epistolario', *Aevum*, XIV, 51–4).

89 Savio, ed., 'Per l'epistolario', *Aevum*, XI, 314; P. Sarpi, *La Repubblica di Venezia, la casa d'Austria e gli Uscocchi*, ed. G. and L. Cozzi (Bari, 1965), p. 428.

90 According to the nuncio in France in June 1609, the Venetians 'pensano senz'alcun pericolo temporale introdurre nel loro stato la libertà di coscienza, la quale, come dice l'ambasciatore Foscarini, per nuova massima politica, è molto più utile per la conservatione e propagatione d'uno stato' (Savio, ed., 'Per l'epistolario', *Aevum*, X, 66). See also *Aevum*, XI, 305–7; *Aevum*, XVI, 137.

91 Taucci, *Intorno alle lettere*, p. 206. Savio, ed., 'Per l'epistolario', *Aevum*, X, 22, 67.

92 *Aevum*, XI, 26–7; XVI, 9, 31–5.

93 *Aevum*, X, 65–6; XVI, 114.

94 Taucci, *Intorno alle lettere*, pp. 34–5, 42.

95 Savio, ed., 'Per l'epistolario', *Aevum*, XVI, 16; Ulianich, 'Christian von Anhalt', pp. 433, 451–2.

96 ibid., *Appendix*, pp. 494, 501.

97 ibid., *Appendix*, p. 494.

98 ibid., *Appendix*, pp. 493, 497.

99 Du Plessis-Mornay, *Correspondance*, vol. X, p. 81.

100 Ulianich, 'Christian von Anhalt', pp. 436–7, 452. Letters to Groslot de l'Isle of 4 Sept. 1607 (G. da Pozzo, ed., *Scritti scelti* (Turin, 1968), pp. 555–8), 1 April 1608 (ibid., pp. 559–63); Savio, ed., 'Per l'epistolario', *Aevum*, XI, 18, 33, 38.

101 Ulianich, 'Christian von Anhalt', *Appendix*, p. 502. Sarpi had presumably read du Perron's despatch of 5 April 1607 which was widely disseminated.

102 da Pozzo, ed., *Scritti scelti*, p. 561. See also Ulianich, 'Christian von Anhalt', *Appendix*, p. 501: 'Come egli [Rome in alliance with Spain] ci combatte per la navigazione e Religione, cosi noi lo ribattiamo con le medesime armi.'

103 ibid., *Appendix*, 500–1.

104 Letter of 22 July 1608, in Busnelli, ed., *Lettere ai Protestanti*, vol. I, p. 23. By this point Sarpi was almost ready to disown Diodati's visit (Ulianich, 'Christian von Anhalt', *Appendix*, p. 493). For the most part Venetian politicians had probably sought to establish a Protestant connection as a precaution against Spanish attack. But some, like Sarpi, must have hoped to provoke a war between Venice and Rome. Sarpi implies that even after the abandonment of a 'Protestant' policy efforts to create an *opportunità* for war continued, and involved the doge and the Venetian

ambassador in Rome, at least in their official capacities (ibid., *Appendix*, p. 499). It must be doubted, however, whether Donà, who had led the peace party in 1607, would have personally wanted to provoke a war in 1608. The nuncio was certainly aware that Donà was less desirous of war than the more uncompromising anti-clericals in the post-Interdict period (Savio, ed., 'Per l'epistolario', *Aevum*, X, 48; XIV, 17; XVI, 137).

105 Taucci, *Intorno alle lettere*, pp. 17–18; Du Plessis-Mornay, *Correspondance*, vols. X and XI.

106 e.g. letter to Groslot de l'Isle of 27 April 1610, in da Pozzo, ed., *Scritti scelti*, p. 630.

107 Ulianich, 'Christian von Anhalt', p. 483, quoting Diodati.

108 See, for example, letters to Groslot de l'Isle of 8 July 1608 (Busnelli, ed., *Lettere ai Protestanti*, vol. I, p. 19) and 7 July 1609 (ibid., p. 86; da Pozzo, ed., *Scritti scelti*, p. 594).

109 Bedell, *Letters*, p. 17; for Diodati's view see Ulianich, 'Christian von Anhalt', p. 484 and Du Plessis-Mornay, *Correspondance*, vol. X, p. 273; see also von Dohna's view, reported by Ulianich, ibid., pp. 468, 477; and Sarpi's own affirmation that 'Fulgenzio qui [è il] solo [chi è] della Relig[ione]' (ibid., *Appendix*, p. 493). But although Micanzio gave perhaps greater apearance of religious fervour than Sarpi, one cannot exclude the possibility that his views were substantially identical to Sarpi's, for he not only failed to go into exile, even when urged to do so after Sarpi's death (see G. Cozzi, 'Sulla morte di fra Paolo Sarpi', p. 396), but his letters to Cavendish, which have been interpreted as evidence of his commitment to Protestantism, contain passages which seem to imply a marked religious scepticism. See V. Gabrielli, 'Bacone, la Riforma e Roma nella versione Hobbesiana d'un carteggio di Fulgenzio Micanzio', *English Miscellany* VIII (1957), 195–250, and the letters themselves, e.g. p. 57, where Micanzio is attacking James' plans for a Spanish marriage: 'I am sure of one thing: that to be Spaniard is not only to a degree to be Roman, but that they are things inseparable, being nothing else but faction. For anything else, its alike to have one belief, or another, or none at all.' One can scarcely doubt that Hobbes enjoyed translating some of these letters. In the margin of one, for example, there is the succinct summary: 'The pope doting. Religion not built upon men's brains' (p. 112). It is interesting too that Micanzio was evidently struck by Bacon's essay 'Of Superstition', which presents a more favourable account of moral atheism than any work prior to Bayle's *Pensées diverses* (see the passage quoted by Gabrielli, 'Bacone, la Riforma e Roma', pp. 219–20).

110 Bedell, *Letters*, p. 76; letter to Groslot de l'Isle of 28 April 1609 (da Pozzo, ed., *Scritti scelti*, p. 587).

111 Sarpi told Diodati that Venice had imprisoned more clergy since the settlement of the Interdict than in the previous twenty-five years: M. Ritter et al., eds., *Briefe und Akten zur Geschichte des 30 jährigen Krieges* (11 vols., Munich, 1870–1909), vol. II, p. 132.

112 Taucci, *Intorno alle lettere*, pp. 249–50. See also Savio, ed., 'Per l'epistolario', *Aevum*, XVI, 128.

113 As Sarpi had expressed it in a letter to Foscarini of 23 June 1609, Henri 'vuol far mercantia con Roma della libertà altrui': Savio, ed., 'Per l'epistolario', *Aevum*, XI, 278. Henri, in giving priority to establishing good relations with Rome, had ignored advice given him by Champigny in a letter of 18 Dec. 1607 (Ritter et al., eds., *Briefe und Akten*, vol. II, p. 355).

114 Du Plessis-Mornay, *Correspondance*, vol. X, pp. 425, 458; letter to Groslot de l'Isle

of 26 May 1609 (da Pozzo, ed., *Scritti scelti*, pp. 589–92); letter to Francesco Priuli of 6 Nov. 1609 (Sarpi, *Opere* (Helmstadt), vol. VI, pp. 129–31). In his letters to Priuli, who favoured closer relations between Venice, Spain and Rome (see his *Relazione di Spagna* and the nuncio's assessment of him (Savio, ed., 'Per l'epistolario', *Aevum*, X, 32)) Sarpi expresses a rather different attitude to the improvement in Veneto-papal relations from that which he expresses when writing to Protestants.

115 Letter to Groslot de l'Isle of 27 April 1610 (da Pozzo, ed., *Scritti scelti*, pp. 628–31).

116 F. Seneca, *La politica veneziana dopo l'interdetto* (Padua, 1957), pp. 144–5; Sarpi, letter to Groslot de l'Isle of 11 April 1617 (da Pozzo, ed., *Scritti scelti*, pp. 659–61).

117 Bedell, *Letters*, p. 17.

118 Taucci, *Intorno alle lettere*, pp. 217ff.

119 'Ragionamento col Prencipe di Condé', G. and L. Cozzi, eds., *Opere*, pp. 1281–6; p. 1283.

120 ibid., pp. 237–9.

121 The standard edition must now be Vivanti, ed., *Istoria del Concilio Tridentino*, although Vivanti's decision to base his text on that of the London edition of 1619, rather than on that of the MS (followed by previous modern editions) has been criticised by G. da Pozzo, 'Vicende editoriale e forza del testo (Un esempio Sarpiano)', *Belfagor*, XXXI (1976), 327–39; pp. 334–8. There is an English translation by N. Brent, first published in London, 1620. I have preferred, however, to make my own translation of quotations.

122 Burke, ed., *History of Benefices*, p. xxvii; Vivanti, ed., *Concilio Tridentino*, p. lxvii. Sarpi's originality is not, I think, sufficiently stressed in E. Cochrane, *Historians and Historiography in the Italian Renaissance* (Chicago, 1981), pp. 472–8.

123 *History of Benefices*, pp. xxix–xxx; *Concilio Tridentino*, vol. I, p. 5.

124 *Concilio Tridentino*, vol. I, p. 6.

125 See for example A. Momigliano, 'Lo stile del Sarpi' (1936), in his collection of essays *Studi di poesia* (rev. edn, Florence, 1960), pp. 101–5; G. Getto, *Paolo Sarpi* (1941; rev. edn, Florence, 1967), ch. 7: 'Lingua e pensiero' (pp. 333–54).

126 H. Jedin, 'Sarpi storico del concilio di Trento', *Humanitas*, VII (1952), 495–504; id., *A History of the Council of Trent* (2 vols., London, 1957–61), vol. II, pp. 518–21.

127 S. Pallavicino, *Istoria del Concilio di Trento...ove insieme rifiutasi...un istoria falsa divolgata...sotto nome di Pietro Soave Polano* (2 pts, Rome, 1656–7).

128 Vivanti, ed., *Concilio Tridentino*, pp. lxxii–lxxxii; id., 'Una fonte del *Istoria del Concilio Tridentino* di Paolo Sarpi', *Rivista storica italiana*, LXXXIII (1971), 608–32.

129 The conflicts between Donà and the senate were stressed by contemporaries: above, ch. 2, no. 62. On the *Trattato* see G. and L. Cozzi, eds., *Opere*, pp. 1023–7.

130 Burke, ed., *History of Benefices*, pp. xix–xx, xxv–xxvii. On the *History of the Interdict* see Ulianich's introduction to *Lettere ai Gallicani*, pp. ciii–cvii. Pietro Priuli, on return from his embassy to France, had announced to the senate de Thou's desire to include an account of the Interdict in his *History* ('Relazione di Francia', in Barozzi and Berchet, eds., *Relazioni*, ser. II, vol. I, p. 286).

131 Cicogna, *Inscrizioni Veneziane*, vol. IV, pp. 359–60; 365–8.

132 Savio, ed., 'Per l'epistolario', *Aevum*, XI, 25.

133 On Sarpi's distrust of episcopal authority as a potential threat to secular authority see M. Simon, 'Isaac Casaubon, Fra Paolo Sarpi et l'Eglise d'Angleterre', in *Aspects de l'Anglicanisme: Colloque de Strasbourg, 14–16 juin, 1972* (Paris, 1974), pp. 39–66; pp. 57–8.

134 Yates, 'Sarpi's History', esp. p. 142. Compatible with this view is the claim, often

made, that the heart of the work is its appeal to the doctrines and values of the early Church – e.g. L. Salvatorelli, 'L'opera storica di Paolo Sarpi' (c. 1935), in his collection of essays *La Chiesa e il mondo* (Rome, 1948), pp. 81–6; p. 86, and G. da Pozzo, ed., *Scritti scelti*, introduction (pp. 1–85), p. 65.

135 G. Cozzi, 'Fra Paolo Sarpi, l'anglicanesimo e la *Historia del Concilio Tridentino*', *Rivista storica italiana*, LXIII (1956), 559–619. Yates, it must be said, was aware that there was a difference in tone between de Dominis' dedication and Sarpi's *History* (art. cit., pp. 129, 131) and was even aware of the true story of the MS's journey to England (ibid., p. 130). She was convinced however that de Dominis and Sarpi shared the same values (ibid., p. 134), and was able to show that the *History* was taken by later generations in England and France to be an eirenicist work.

136 G. and L. Cozzi, eds., *Opere*, p. 735.

137 Vivanti, ed., *Concilio Tridentino*, vol. I, p. 354.

138 ibid., vol. I, pp. 5–6.

139 B. Ulianich, 'Sarpiana: la lettera del Sarpi allo Heinsius', *Rivista storica italiana*, LXIII (1956), 425–46; G. Cozzi, 'Paolo Sarpi e Jan van Meurs', *Bollettino dell'Istituto di storia della società e dello stato veneziano*, I (1959), 179–86.

140 'Scrittura de Auxiliis' (1609), in Amerio, ed., *Scritti filosofici*, pp. 145–54. On the date of this work, see G. and L. Cozzi, eds., *Opere*, p. 141.

141 Letter to Jean Hotman de Villiers, 28 April 1609 (da Pozzo, ed., *Scritti scelti*, pp. 584–5). See also, for example, Busnelli, ed., *Lettere ai Protestanti*, vol. I, p. 80; vol. II, p. 148.

142 G. and L. Cozzi, eds., *Opere*, pp. 293; 107.

143 For Sarpi's hostility to clerical influence, see, for example, da Pozzo, ed., *Scritti scelti*, p. 587. For an example of continuity with the attitude to God recommended in the *Pensieri* see the letter to Hotman cited above, n. 20: 'le forze umane non sono mai tanto abassate quanto meritano, nè la grazia divina così esaltata come è debito'. For Sarpi's denial of free-will, see 'Arte di ben pensare', Amerio, ed., *Scritti filosofici*, pp. 121–44; p. 141.

144 Letter to Groslot de l'Isle, 14 Sept. 1610 (da Pozzo, ed., *Scritti scelti*, p. 644); on the secular and stoic connotations of Sarpi's references to providence see Getto, *Sarpi*, pp. 169–71, 193–4; Burke, 'The Great Unmasker', p. 430.

145 Vivanti, ed., *Concilio Tridentino*, vol. II, p. 790.

146 M. P. Gilmore, *Humanists and Jurists: Six Studies in the Renaissance* (Cambridge, Mass., 1963), pp. 51–3.

147 Burke, ed., *History of Benefices*, pp. xxxi–xxxii.

148 Vivanti, ed., *Concilio Tridentino*, vol. I, pp. 35–55.

149 ibid., vol. I, p. 144, n. 41. A number of Sarpi's sources are identified by G. and L. Cozzi in their notes to this section of the *History*: *Opere*, pp. 770–87.

150 J. Sleidan, *The General History of the Reformation* (1st [Latin] edn, 1556; edn cit. London, 1689), p. 60.

151 F. Guicciardini, *Istoria d'Italia*, edn cit. in *Opere* (9 vols., Bari, 1929–36, vols. I–V), vol. IV, pp. 145–6, 170–1, 195.

152 [O. Panvinio], *La historia di Battista Plantina delle vite de' Pontefici...con le vite de gli altri Pontefici...scritti dal P. F. Honofrio Panvinio...*(1st [Latin] edn, 1557; edn cit. Venice, 1563), ff. 329r–330v; P. Giovio, *Le vite di Leon Decimo et d'Adriano sesto...*(1st [Latin] edn, 1548; edn cit. Florence, 1549), pp. 442–3, 447–53. On Giovio, see F. Chabod, 'Paolo Giovio' (1954), in his *Scritti sul Rinascimento*, pp. 241–67.

153 [G. Ranchin], *A Review of the Counsell of Trent* (1st [French] edn, 1600; edn cit. Oxford, 1638), p. 1. For Sarpi's knowledge of this work, see G. and L. Cozzi, eds., *Opere*, p. 722.

154 D. R. Kelley, '*Fides Historiae*: Charles Dumoulin and the Gallican view of history', *Traditio*, XXII (1966), 347–402; p. 376.

155 Burke, 'The Great Unmasker'; Burke, ed., *History of Benefices*, p. xxxiv.

156 Letter to Groslot de l'Isle, 26 May 1609 (da Pozzo, ed., *Scritti scelti*, p. 591).

157 G. and L. Cozzi, eds., *Opere*, p. 298.

158 Letter of 28 April 1609 (ibid., p. 584). See also Sarpi's letter to Gillot of 2 March 1610: 'Nominibus nulla cura habenda esset, nisi abusu significationum' (Ulianich, ed., *Lettere ai Gallicani*, p. 143). In Sarpi's view the theological differences between Protestants were merely verbal and would disappear with the abolition of papal authority (letter to Groslot de l'Isle of 6 Dec. 1611, Busnelli, ed., *Lettere ai Protestanti*, vol. I, p. 207; see also the letter to Leschassier of 7 Dec. 1610, *Lettere ai Gallicani*, p. 98).

159 Burke, ed., *History of Benefices*, p. xxxiv. On the page before, however, Burke quotes a passage from the *History* on the death of Luther which makes clear that Sarpi gave only a limited weight to personal factors: 'The fathers in Trent and the Curia in Rome became extremely hopeful when they saw dead . . . the principal and almost sole cause of the divisions . . . but the events that followed, up to our own time, have made it clear that Martin was only one of the instruments, and that the causes were different, more powerful and more hidden' (Vivanti, ed., *Concilio Tridentino*, vol. I, pp. 254–5; Burke's translation).

160 Similarly in 1612 Sarpi expressed approval that the Parlement of Paris had attacked the doctrines of the Jesuit order, not the views of individual Jesuits: 'Doctrina communis est omnium, virtutes et vitia personas distingunt' (Letter to Leschassier of 14 Feb. 1612, Ulianich, ed. *Lettere ai Gallicani*, p. 102).

161 For one discussion of the differences between *The Prince* and *The Discourses*, see J. G. A. Pocock, *The Machiavellian Moment* (Princeton, 1975), chs. 6 and 7.

162 Meinecke, *Machiavellism*, p. 72.

163 Commentary on Sandys' *Relazione dello stato della religione*, in G. and L. Cozzi, eds., *Opere*, p. 298; letter to Jacques Gillot of 15 Sept. 1609 (ibid., p. 275).

164 Letter to Achatius von Dohna, 19 Oct. 1612, in Busnelli, ed., *Lettere ai Protestanti*, vol. I, p. 197.

165 e.g. da Pozzo, ed., *Scritti scelti*, pp. 649–51 (letters to Groslot de l'Isle of 22 July 1611 and 22 May 1612). This second letter, with its suggestion that conflict with the papacy is good for the Republic, is reminiscent of the *Pensieri* (above, p. 20).

166 See for example Sarpi's letter to Castrino of 28 Sept. 1610: 'li preti, se bene [non] hanno il medesimo desiderio che li primi [the Spanish], nondimeno, havendo l'istessi interessi con loro, faranno l'istessa risolutione' (Savio, ed., 'Per l'epistolario', *Aevum*, XIV, 62).

167 H. R. Trevor-Roper, 'The historical philosophy of the Enlightenment', *Studies on Voltaire and the Eighteenth Century*, ed. T. Besterman, vol. XXVII (1963), pp. 1667–87; p. 1671.

168 Trevor-Roper, 'Religious origins', pp. 200–2, 227–8.

169 Trevor-Roper, 'Historical philosophy', p. 1676.

170 On Sarpi's conception of *opportunità* see Getto, *Sarpi*, pp. 158–61; C. Vivanti, 'In margine a studi recenti su Paolo Sarpi', *Rivista storica italiana*, LXXIX (1967), 1075–95; pp. 1089–95; above p. 101. Sarpi's pessimism is Getto's main justification for regarding him as a pure intellectual, seeking to understand the world, not change it.

171 Above, p. 3.

172 *Aggionta*, in G. and L. Cozzi, eds., *La repubblica di Venezia*, pp. 7–70; p. 13: 'Ho giudicato dover trapassare li termini dell'istorico e più tosto allargarmia far l'ufficio di chi informa in controversia giudicale, a fine che sia prononciata sincera e giusta sentenza.'

173 de Mas, *Sovranità politica*, pp. 229–30 (letter to William Cavendish of 1 March 1624).

174 Micanzio is particularly incisive in his insistence on the hopelessness of Marc Antonio de Dominis' mission to Rome to convert the pope to apostolic values: employing arguments possibly derived from Sarpi's account of the pontificate of Adrian VI, he insists that the policies of the papacy are based not upon the pope's perception of Christian values, but upon the material interests of 'la Corte di Roma' (de Mas, *Sovranità politica*, pp. 226–8). Hobbes does not seek to analyse power in concrete terms even in his *Behemoth* (1st edn, London, 1679), a history of the Civil War.

Chapter 4. The man and his masks

1 Ulianich, ed., *Lettere ai Gallicani*, p. 133.

2 Yates, 'Sarpi's *History*', pp. 136–8.

3 ibid., pp. 137–8.

4 Jedin, 'Sarpi storico', p. 495.

5 Vivanti, ed., *Concilio Tridentino*, vol. I, p. 445.

6 Cozzi, 'Sulla morte di fra Paolo Sarpi'. There is a certain irony in the subject matter of A. Niero, 'Miracoli post-mortem di fra Paolo Sarpi?', *Studi veneziani*, X (1968), 599–620.

7 Taucci, *Intorno alle lettere*; the influence of Taucci's work is to be seen particularly in L. Salvatorelli, 'Le idee religiose di fra Paolo Sarpi', *Atti dell'Accademia Nazionale dei Lincei–Memorie*, ser. VIII, vol. V (1954), 311–60, and in Chabod, *La politica di Paolo Sarpi*.

8 Da Pozzo, ed., *Scritti scelti*, p. 65; Yates 'Sarpi's History'; H. R. F. Brown, 'Paolo Sarpi, the man', in his *Studies in the History of Venice* (2 vols., London, 1907), vol. II, pp. 208–44.

9 G. and L. Cozzi, eds., *Opere*, pp. 723–5.

10 B. Ulianich, 'Considerazioni e documenti per una ecclesiologia di Paolo Sarpi', in *Festgabe J. Lortz* (2 vols., Baden-Baden, 1958), vol. II, pp. 363–444; p. 434.

11 Pastor, *History of the Popes*, edn cit., vol. XXV, chs. 4, 5 (pp. 111–216). Ulianich, 'Sarpiana'; Cozzi, 'Paolo Sarpi, l'anglicanesimo'.

12 See, for example, 'Sopra un decreto della Congregazione in Roma' (1616); G. and L. Cozzi, eds., *Opere*, pp. 603–5; p. 603.

13 Above, p. 95.

14 W. J. Bouwsma, 'Paolo Sarpi and the Renaissance tradition' (1st [Italian] edn, 1962), in E. Cochrane, ed., *The Late Italian Renaissance* (New York, 1970), pp. 353–69. Above, p. 120.

15 Ulianich, 'Considerazioni...per una ecclesiologia'.

16 Above, pp. 91–3.

17 Chabod, *La politica di Paolo Sarpi*; Bouwsma, *Republican Liberty*. Ulianich, 'Considerazioni...per una ecclesiologia', argues that Sarpi's preoccupations were primarily political.

18 Above, p. 88.

19 e.g. G. and L. Cozzi, eds., *Opere*, pp. 237–9.
20 P. Sarpi, *Scritti giurisdizionalistici*, ed. G. Gambarin (Bari, 1958), pp. 312–14. The text is on pp. 119–212.
21 ibid., pp. 133, 138, 176.
22 ibid., pp. 153–4.
23 ibid., p. 188.
24 ibid., p. 204. On this passage see Bouwsma, *Republican Liberty*, p. 538.
25 Letter to Leschassier, 14 Sept. 1610, in G. and L. Cozzi, eds., *Opere*, pp. 267–72; p. 267.
26 Above, note 10. See also *Lettere ai Protestanti*, vol. II, p. 123.
27 Sarpi, it is true, warned Gillot against Coton on the grounds that Coton was an atheist (4 July 1617; Ulianich, ed., *Lettere ai Gallicani*, p. 163). But he recommended Badoer to his friends, knowing him to be an atheist: below, p. 129.
28 See for example above, note 21.
29 G. and L. Cozzi, eds., *Opere*, p. 92.
30 ibid., pp. 246, 281–4.
31 Ulianich, ed., *Lettere ai Gallicani*, introduction, pp. cx–cxiii.
32 ibid., pp. cxi, cxiii, 163.
33 *Journal de l'Estoile pour le règne de Henri IV (t. III) et le début du règne de Louis XIII*, ed. A. Martin (Paris, 1960), pp. 10, 13–14.
34 The text of this sentence may be corrupt: 'Son così solitario che temo vivendo più al longo farmi melancholico, e pertanto un altro, et entro nelli discorsi di Socrate che sii una gran ventura lasciar la vita in tempo.'
35 Ulianich, ed., *Lettere ai Gallicani*, p. cxi.
36 Yates, 'Sarpi's *History*', p. 138.
37 The same was not true of some of Venice's other theologians, on whom see G. Benzoni, 'I "teologi" minori dell'Interdetto', *Archivio veneto*, ser. V, vol. XCI (1970), 31–108. Nor is the picture we get from Micanzio's biography and from Sarpi's own writings necessarily a correct one: see below, pp. 136–45.
38 Brown, 'Sarpi, the man', p. 209.
39 *Pensieri filosofici*, no. 471.
40 ibid., nos. 525–8.
41 P. Bayle, *Pensées diverses sur la comète*, ed. A. Prat (2 vols., Paris, 1939), ch. 178.
42 P. L. Joly, *Remarques critiques sur le dictionnaire de Bayle* (Dijon, 1752), art. *Crémonin*.
43 See J. Milton, *Complete Prose Works*, ed. D. M. Wolfe (5 vols. in 7, New Haven, 1953–71), vol. II (ed. E. Sirluck), p. 492.
44 Quoted from the MS in J. Dunn, *The Political Thought of John Locke* (Cambridge, 1969), p. 1.

Appendix

1 Micanzio, *Vita*, pp. 1361–5. Part of Giovanni Francesco's account is quoted in A. G. Campbell, *The Life of Fra Paolo Sarpi* (London, 1869), pp. 184–6. The assassination plot is reported by Sarpi in a letter to Groslot de l'Isle of 30 March 1609 (Busnelli, ed., *Lettere ai Protestanti*, vol. I, pp. 73–5).
2 Consiglio dei dieci – Criminal Reg. 26. 16 March 1609: Giovanni Francesco offered choice between drowning and imprisonment (ff. 59r–6or). 20 March: Giovanni Francesco accuses Antonio, who is arrested (6orv). 27 March: the decision is taken not to torture Antonio, but to remit Giovanni Francesco's death sentence (61r). 4 May: finally, after much dispute, Antonio is sentenced in secret to two years' banishment (66v; 71rv). (I owe these references to Lina Frizziero.)

3 See for example Ottaviano Bon (quoted in Cozzi, *Contarini*, p. 231); Possevino (quoted in Sivos, 'Vite dei Dosi', f. 113rv; see also f. 185v); Bedmar, 'Una relazione sui Veneziani', pp. 17–18, 22–4; Boccalini (quoted in Cicogna, *Inscrizioni veneziane*, vol. IV, p. 565); Anon, 'Relatione dello stato', f. 6r. The Venetian legal system was also widely attacked, both because it was not Roman in inspiration, and because it was arbitrary. See Carleton, 'Particular notes': 'Whereas other governments are ruled by laws, the Venetian hath little other than reason of state to which they do resort in all occasions'; Pastor, *History of the Popes*, vol. XXV, p. 111; G. Cozzi, 'Politica e diritto in alcune controversie confinarie tra lo stato di Milano e la Repubblica di Venezia, 1564–1622', *Archivio storico lombardo*, LXXVIII–LXXIX (1951–2), 4–44. It is defended by Sarpi (G. and L. Cozzi, eds., *Opere*, p. 259).

4 On the 'Galanti huomini', see above, pp. 6, 67. A useful index of the anti-clericalism of the poorer and younger nobles is the popular support for anti-clerical candidates in ducal elections: see Sivos, 'Vite dei Dosi', ff. 82v *et seqq.*, 185v, for the elections of Donà and Memmo.

5 The issue was at the heart of political debate during the Interdict crisis. See for example Cornet, ed., 'Nuova serie de documenti', nos. 77–80, and Antonio Querini's 'Historia della scomunica', Biblioteca Marciana, MS it. VII 536 (8495), the conclusions of which are in Cornet, ed., *Paolo V e la Repubblica Veneta*, appendix 20.

6 B. Ulianich, 'Paolo Sarpi, il generale Ferrari e l'Ordine dei Serviti durante le controversie veneto-pontificie', in *Studi in Onore di Alberto Pincherle* (2 vols., Rome, 1967), vol. II, pp. 582–645; pp. 588–9.

7 See Micanzio, *Vita*, p. 1285. Above, pp. 128–31.

8 The motives attributed to Sarpi by Giovanni Francesco may be compared with those attributed to Etienne Dolet by Lucien Febvre in his essay 'Un cas désespéré: Dolet propagateur de l'Evangile' (1945), *Au coeur religieux*, pp. 172–224.

9 Neither Campbell, *Paolo Sarpi*, nor Ulianich, 'Paolo Sarpi, il generale Ferrari, e l'ordine dei Serviti' recognises the conflict between the testimony of Micanzio and Giovanni Francesco. Sarpi's correspondence, particularly his letters to Groslot de L'Isle of 8 June 1609 and Castrino of 12 May 1609 (Busnelli, ed., *Lettere ai Protestanti*, vol. I, pp. 83–4; vol. II, pp. 33–6), certainly suggests that the case was not as straightforward as Micanzio claims.

10 Campbell, who stands at the summit of the hagiographical tradition of Sarpi scholarship, provides a good example of the way in which the evidence of Sarpi's moral atheism has been brushed aside when, probably with Acton in mind, she writes: 'Prejudice against him ought not to exist, either as to disbelief in the immortality of the soul, or as to his being an atheist... The fact alone that atheism has generally been professed by persons of shallow understanding might have shielded Sarpi from such an aspersion' (*Paolo Sarpi*, p. 83). Micanzio's *Vita*, the main source for Campbell and other biographers of Sarpi is, however, in reality a partisan effort to defend Sarpi – and Micanzio himself – against charges of the sort made by Giovanni Francesco: see pp. 1366–7, 1412–13.

11 On Marlowe and Raleigh see G. T. Buckley, *Atheism in the English Renaissance* (Chicago, 1932), pp. 121–52; Strathman, *Ralegh*, pp. 17–60; P. Lefranc, *Sir Walter Ralegh, écrivain: L'oeuvre et les idées* (Paris, 1968), pp. 335–410. On Aikenhead see T. B. Howell, ed., *A Complete Collection of State Trials* (33 vols., London, 1809–26), vol. XIII, cols. 917–40.

12 See for example F. E. Manuel, *The Eighteenth Century Confronts the Gods* (Cambridge, Mass., 1959).

13 On *de Tribus Impostoribus* see P. Bayle, *Dictionnaire historique et critique* (16 vols., Paris, 1820), art. Arétin, Léonard. Most modern scholars have followed Bayle in denying that there ever existed an authentic sixteenth-century text of this work: e.g. D. C. Allen, *Doubt's Boundless Sea: Skepticism and Faith in the Renaissance* (Baltimore, 1964), pp. 224–43. In defence of its existence see H. Busson, 'Les noms des incrédules au seizième siècle', *Bibliothèque d'Humanisme et Renaissance*, XVI (1954), 273–80, p. 280, and J. J. Denonain, 'Le livre des trois imposteurs', in *Aspects du libertinisme au XVIe siècle* (Paris, 1974), pp. 215–26.

14 See above, ch. 1, notes 16, 25, 30. On Garimberto (1506–75), see I. Affò and A. Pezzana, *Memorie degli scrittori e letterati Parmigiani* (7 vols., Parma, 1789–1833), vol. IV, pp. 135–44; vol. VI, pp. 542, 970.

15 *Pensieri filosofici*, no. 550.

16 Sarpi owned no less than three texts of the *Timaeus*: in Greek, Latin and Italian (Masetti Zannini, 'Libri di fra Paolo', appendix, nos. 84, 192, 200).

17 On chronology see Sarpi's letter to Hotman of 22 July 1608 (G. and L. Cozzi, eds., *Opere*, pp. 272–5). Sarpi owned several orthodox works of chronology, e.g. J. Lucidus, *de Emendationibus Temporum* (Venice, 1537: Masetti Zannini, 'Libri di fra Paolo', appendix, no. 69).

18 ibid., no. 193. For other difficulties which concerned contemporaries with regard to the Biblical account of the Flood, see D. C. Allen, *The Legend of Noah: Renaissance rationalism in art, science, and letters*, (Urbana, 1949), pp. 66–92. The geological theories of this period are briefly discussed in F. C. Haber, *The Age of the World: Moses to Darwin* (Baltimore, 1959), pp. 38–50.

   There is a need for further research amongst the books owned by Sarpi. Nevertheless the catalogue of his library has two major limitations as a guide to his reading. In the first place he depended very largely on borrowed books, and had a photographic memory for everything he read; in the second the catalogue published by Masetti Zannini was drawn up as part of a general enquiry to locate forbidden books: we cannot tell whether Sarpi owned books which he successfully concealed.

19 'Ego vero saepius recusavi: cum mihi opus hoc difficillimum videretur. Deum namque testor cum frequenter id aggredi temptassem: id mihi contingisse quod in proverbio dici solet: qui magis manu anguillam stringit: minus retinent: quoniam aptius labitur.' P. Pomponazzi, *Tractatus utilissimus in quo disputatur penes quid intensio et remissio formarum attendantur* (Bologna, 1514), f. 3r.

Bibliography

I. Manuscript sources

(i) *Archivio di Stato, Venice*

Consiglio dei dieci – Criminal Reg. 26

Vicenzo Gussoni, M. 'Relazione nel ritorno di Podestà di Vicenza,' 15 May 1607

(ii) *Biblioteca Correr, Venice*

Anon. 'Relatione dello stato, costumi, disordini et rimedii di Venetia', MSS 2989–90.

(iii) *Biblioteca Nazionale Marciana, Venice*

'Discorsi fatti dal Nob. Ho. B.M....l'anno 1606', MS It. VII 155 (8159)

Querini, A. 'Historia della scomunica', MS It. VII 536 (8495)

Sivos, G. C. 'Delle vite dei Dosi di Venetia, Libero Terzo', MS 1818 (9436)

(iv) *Bodleian Library, Oxford*

Anon. 'Cause per le quali la Republica Venetia non deve aspettare la scommunica', Bodleian Library, Italian MSS c5/n

Anon. 'Ravedimento, o sia protesto di un clarissimo senatore veneto', Rawlinson MSS D. 625/31

(v) *British Library, London*

Anon. 'Origine e cause della scommunica fulminata da Papa Paolo V', Add. MSS 10786

Graziani, G. F. 'Ragguaglio del caso occorso intorno alla mia persona in Venetia', Add. MSS 6877

Malatesta, G. 'Relatione historica e politica delle differenze nate tra Paolo V et i Venetiani', Add. MSS 8589

Micanzio, F. 'Letters to William Cavendish', Add. MSS 11309

(vi) *Public Record Office, London*

Carleton, D. 'Particular Notes of the Government and State of Venice', State Papers 99, file 8, ff. 340–4

Bibliography

II. Printed sources

Ammirato, S. *Discorsi sopra Cornelio Tacito* (Florence, 1594)

Anon. *De la concorde de l'estat par l'observation des edicts de pacification* (n.l., 1599)

Anon. 'Discorso sopra la fragilità di Venetia', in L. Amabile, *Fra Tommaso Campanella nei castelli di Napoli, in Roma ed in Parigi* (2 vols., Naples, 1887), vol. II, no. 198

Anon. *Squitinio della libertà Venetiana* (Mirandola, 1612)

Anon. *De la vraye et legitime constitution de l'estat* (n.l., 1591)

d'Aubigné, T. A. *Confession Catholique du Sieur de Sancy*, in *Receuil de diverses pièces servans à l'histoire de Henry III* (Cologne, 1662), pp. 315–464

Averroes, *Aristotelis Opera cum Averrois Commentariis* (12 vols., Venice, 1562–74)

   On Plato's Republic, ed. R. Lerner (Ithaca, 1974)

   On the Harmony of Religion and Philosophy, ed. G. F. Hourani (London, 1961)

   Tahāfut al-tahāfut, ed. S. van den Bergh (2 vols., London, 1954)

Bacon, F. *Essays* (London, 1625)

Barozzi, N. and Berchet, G., eds. *Relazioni degli stati europei lette al senato dagli ambasciatori veneti nel secolo decimosettimo* (10 vols. in 11, Venice, 1856–78)

Bayle, P. *Pensées diverses sur la comète*, ed. A. Prat (2 vols., Paris, 1939)

Bedell, W. *Some Original Letters*, ed. E. Hudson (Dublin, 1742)

Bedmar, Marquis de. 'Una relazione...sui Veneziani', ed. I. Raulich, *Nuovo archivio veneto*, XVI (1898), 5–32

Bellarmine, R. *Responsio ad Praecipua Capita Apologiae quae Falso Catholica Inscribitur* (Fani, 1591)

   Risposta al trattato dei sette theologi di Venetia, with Bellarmine, *Risposta alle oppositioni di fra Paolo Sarpi* (Rome, 1607)

   Scritti politici, ed. C. Giacon (Bologna, 1950)

de Belloy, P. *Apologie Catholique...par E.D.L.I.C.* (n.l., 1585)

Boccalini, T. *La bilancia politica di tutte le opere*, ed. L. du May (2 vols., Castellana, 1678)

   Ragguagli di Parnaso e scritti minori, ed. L. Firpo (3 vols., Bari, 1948)

Bodin, J. *Colloquium of the Seven about Secrets of the Sublime*, ed. M. L. D. Kuntz (Princeton, 1975)

Botero, G. *Della ragion di stato*, ed. F. Chabod (Turin, 1948)

Campanella, T. *Antiveneti*, ed. L. Firpo (Florence, 1945)

Canaye de Fresnes, P. *Lettres et ambassades* (3 vols., Paris, 1635–6)

Cassirer, E., Kristeller, P. O. and Randall, J. H., eds. *The Renaissance Philosophy of Man* (Chicago, 1948)

Casaubon, I. *The Answer...to the Epistle...of Cardinal du Perron* (London, 1612)

   de Libertate Ecclesiastica Liber Singularis, in G. Hickes, *Two Treatises* (2 vols., London, 1711), vol. II, pp. cxv–ccxciii

Charron, P. *De la sagesse* (4 vols., Dijon, 1801)

   Les trois veritez (Bordeaux, 1593)

Cicero. *de Finibus Bonorum et Malorum*, ed. H. Rackham (London, 1914)

Constable, H. *Examen pacifique de la doctrine des Huguenots* (Paris, 1589)

Contarini, G. *de Magistratibus et Republica Venetorum Libri Quinque* (Paris, 1543)

Cornet, E., ed. *Paolo V e la Repubblica Veneta: giornale dal 22 Ottobre 1605–9 Giugno 1607* (Vienna, 1859)

   'Paolo V e la Repubblica Veneta: Nuova serie di documenti', *Archivio veneto*, ser. I, vol. V (1873), 27–96, 222–318; vol. VI (1873), 68–131

Croce, B. and Caramella, S., eds. *Politici e moralisti del seicento* (Bari, 1930)

Bibliography

Darwin, C. R. *Autobiography*, ed. N. Barlow (London, 1958)

Donà, L. *La corripondenza da Madrid, 1570–3*, ed. M. Brunetti and E. Vitale (2 vols., Venice, 1963)

Dumoulin, C. *Concile sur le faict du Concile de Trente* (Lyons, 1564)

Du Plessis-Mornay, P. *Mémoires et correspondance* (12 vols., Paris, 1824–5)

Dupuy, J. and P., eds. *Perroniana sive excerpta ex ore Cardinalis Peronii* (Geneva, 1667)

Erasmus, D. *Enchiridion Militis Christianae* (Antwerp, 1504)

d'Espesse, J. F. *Advertissement sur la réception et publication du Concile de Trente*, in E. Mignot, *Histoire de la réception du Concile de Trente* (2 vols., Amsterdam, 1576), vol. II, pp. 104–42

de l'Estoile, P. *Journal...pour le règne de Henri IV (t. III) et le début du règne de Louis XIII*, ed. A. Martin (Paris, 1960)

Fabri, F. *Adversus Impios Atheos* (Venice, 1627)

Faenzi, V. *Dialogus de montium origine* (Venice, 1561)

Firpo, L., ed. *Il pensiero politico del rinascimento e della controriforma* (Milan, 1966)

de Franceschi, O. *Ducento e più calonnie opposte da G. Marsilio all'Illustrissima Cardinale Bellarmino confutate* (Macerata, 1607)

Garimberto, H. *Problemi naturali e morali* (Venice, 1549)

Gentillet, I. *Anti-Machiavel*, ed. C. E. Rathé (Geneva, 1968)

Giovio, P. *Le vite di Leon Decimo et d'Adriano sesto* (Florence, 1549)

Guicciardini, F. *Istoria d'Italia*, in Guicciardini, *Opere* (9 vols., Bari, 1929–36), vols. 1–5

Henri IV. *Receuil des lettres missives*, ed. M. Berger de Xivrey and J. Guadet (9 vols., Paris, 1843–76)

Herbert, E. *de Veritate*, ed. M. H. Carré (Bristol, 1937)

Hobbes, T. *Behemoth*, ed. W. Molesworth (New York, 1963)

Hoffman, W. *Avvertimento et ammonitione Catolica al Padre A. Possevino* (n.l., 1607)

Howell, T. B., ed. *A Complete Collection of State Trials* (33 vols., London, 1809–26)

L.B. *Opinions et raisons d'Estat proposées en un discours tenu au Grand Conseil de Venise* (n.l., 1606)

Lipsius, J. *Six Bookes of Politickes or Civil Doctrine* (New York, 1970)
  Two Bookes of Constancie, ed. R. Kirk (New Brunswick, 1939)

Lollino, L. *Vita del cavalier Ottaviano Bon* (Venice, 1854)

Lucidus, J. *de Emendationibus Temporum* (Venice, 1537)

Lucretius. *On the Nature of Things*, trans. C. Bailey (Oxford, 1910)

M.V.D.C.C.D. *Response à la Harangue faite par l'Illustrissime Cardinal du Perron* (n.l., 1615)

de Magistris, C. P., ed. *Carlo Emmanuele I e la contesa fra la Repubblica veneta e Paolo V* (Venice, 1906)

Mersenne, M. *De l'impiété des déistes, athées et libertins de ce temps* (2 vols., Paris, 1624)
  La vérité des sciences, contre les septiques ou Pyrrhoniens (Paris, 1625)

Micanzio, F. *Vita del Padre Paolo*, in P. Sarpi, *Istoria del Concilio Tridentino*, ed. C. Vivanti (2 vols., Turin, 1974), vol. II, pp. 1273–413

Milton, J. *Complete Prose Works*, ed. D. M. Wolfe (5 vols. in 4, New Haven, 1953–71)

de Montaigne, M. *Essais*, ed. M. Rat (3 vols., Paris, 1941–2)

Nardi, B. *Apologia...con due discorsi politici* (Naples, 1607)

Ockham, William of. *Philosophical Writings*, ed. P. Boehmer (Edinburgh, 1957)

Pallavicino, S. *Istoria del Concilio di Trento* (2 pts., Rome, 1656–7)

Panvinio, O. *La historia di Battista Plantina delle vite de'Pontefici* (Venice, 1563)

Parsons, R. *A Discoverye of a Counterfecte Conference* (n. l., 1600)

Bibliography

Paruta, P. *Della perfettione della vita politica* (Venice, 1579)
de Peiresc, N. C. F. *Lettres aux frères Dupuy*, ed. P. T. de Larroque (7 vols., Paris, 1888–98)
Pellegrini, A. *I segni de la natura ne l'huomo* (Venice, 1546)
du Perron, J. D. *Les ambassades et negotiations* (Paris, 1629)
   Les diverses oeuvres (Paris, 1633)
   A letter written from Paris…to Monsieur Casaubon (n.l., 1612)
   An Oration made on the part of the Lordes Spirituall, in the Chamber of the Third Estate (St Omer, 1616)
   Traitté du Sainct Sacrement de l'Eucharistie (Paris, 1622)
Pithou, D. *Les libertez de l'Eglise Gallicane* (Paris, 1594)
Plato, *The Timaeus*, ed. F. M. Cornford (London, 1937)
Pomponazzi, P. *Tractatus de Immortalitate Animae*, ed. G. Morra (Bologna, 1954)
   Tractatus utilissimus in quo disputatur penes quid intensio et remissio formarum attendantur (Bologna, 1514)
Possevino, A. *Risposta di Teodoro Eugenio di Famagosta all'aviso mandato fuori dal signore A. Quirino* (Bologna, 1606)
Pufendorf, S. *de Iure Naturae et Gentium Libri Octo*, trans, C. H. and W. A. Oldfather (2 vols., Oxford, 1934)
Querini, A. *Aviso dalle ragioni della serenissima republica di Venetia* (Venice, 1606)
Ranchin, G. *A Review of the Counsell of Trent* (Oxford, 1638)
Richer, E. *A Treatise of Ecclesiasticall and Politicke Power* (London, 1612)
Ritter, M., et al, eds. *Briefe und Akten zur Geschichte des 30 jährigen Krieges* (11 vols., Munich, 1870–1909)
Sarpi, P. *Apologia per le oppositioni fatte dall'…Cardinale Bellarmino* (Venice, 1606)
   'History of Benefices' and selections from 'History of the Council of Trent', ed. P. Burke (New York, 1967)
   Istoria del Concilio Tridentino, ed. C. Vivanti (2 vols., Turin, 1974)
   Istoria dell'Interdetto e altri scritti editi e inediti, ed. M. D. Busnelli and G. Gambarin (3 vols., Bari, 1940)
   Lettere ai Gallicani, ed. B. Ulianich (Wiesbaden, 1961)
   Lettere ai Protestanti, ed. M. D. Busnelli (2 vols., Bari 1931)
   (attrib.) *The Maxims of the Government of Venice* (London, 1707)
   Opere (8 vols., Helmstadt–Verona, 1761–8)
   Opere, ed. G. and L. Cozzi (Milan, 1969)
   Pensieri, ed. G. and L. Cozzi (Turin, 1976)
   La Repubblica di Venezia, la casa d'Austria e gli Uscocchi, ed. G. and L. Cozzi (Bari, 1965)
   Scritti filosofici e teologici editi e inediti, ed. R. Amerio (Bari, 1951)
   Scritti giurisdizionalistici, ed. G. Gambarin (Bari, 1958)
   Scritti scelti, ed. G. da Pozzo (Turin, 1968)
Savio, P., ed. 'Per l'epistolario di Paolo Sarpi', *Aevum*, X (1936), 1–104; XI (1937), 13–74, 275–322; XIII (1939), 558–622; XIV (1940), 3–84; XVI (1942), 105–38
Sextus Empiricus. *Outlines of Pyrrhonism*, ed. R. G. Bury (4 vols., London, 1933–49)
Siri, V. *Memorie recondite dell'anno 1601 all'anno 1641* (8 vols., Ronco, 1677–9)
Sleidan, J. *The General History of the Reformation* (London, 1689)
du Vair, G. *The Moral Philosophie of the Stoicks*, ed. R. Kirk (New Brunswick, 1951)
Valla, L. *On Pleasure*, ed. M. P. de Lorch (New York, 1977)

III. Secondary literature

Acton, Lord. 'Fra Paolo Sarpi', in Acton, *Essays on Church and State* (London, 1952), pp. 251–60

Affò, I. and Pezzana, A. *Memorie degli scrittori e letterati Parmigiani* (7 vols., Parma, 1789–1833)

Alberigo, G. 'Carlo Borromeo come modello di vescovo nella chiesa post-tridentina', *Rivista storica italiana*, LXXIX (1967), 1031–52

Allen, D. C. *Doubt's Boundless Sea: skepticism and faith in the Renaissance* (Baltimore, 1964)

    The Legend of Noah: Renaissance rationalism in art, science, and letters (Urbana, 1949)

Amerio, R. *Il Sarpi dei Pensieri filosofici inediti* (Turin, 1950)

Anderson, P. *Lineages of the Absolutist State* (London, 1974)

Baxter, C. R. 'Jean Bodin's daemon and his conversion to Judaism', in *Jean Bodin: Verhandlungen der internationalen Bodin Tagung in München* (Munich, 1973), pp. 1–21.

Bayle, P. *Dictionnaire historique et critique* (16 vols., Paris, 1820)

Benzoni, G. 'I "teologi" minori dell'Interdetto', *Archivio veneto*, ser. V, vol. XCI (1970), 31–108

Bertone, C. 'Fra Paolo Sarpi nelle scienze esatte e naturali', in *Paolo Sarpi e i suoi tempi* (Città di Castello, 1923), pp. 87–98

Bianchi-Giovini, G. *Biografia di fra Paolo Sarpi* (2 vols., Brussels, 1836)

Bossy, J. 'The character of Elizabethan Catholicism', in T. Aston, ed., *Crisis in Europe 1560–1660* (London, 1965), pp. 223–47

    'The social history of the confessional', *Transactions of the Royal Historical Society*, ser. V, vol. XXV (1975), 21–38

Bouwsma, W. J. 'Paolo Sarpi and the Renaissance tradition', in E. Cochrane, ed., *The Late Italian Renaissance* (New York, 1970), pp. 353–69

    'The Venetian Interdict and the problem of order', *Archiwum Historii Filozofii i Mysli Spolecznej*, XII (1966), 127–40

    Venice and the Defence of Republican Liberty: Renaissance values in the age of Counter-Reformation (Berkeley, 1968)

    'Venice and the political education of Europe', in J. R. Hale, ed., *Renaissance Venice*, (London, 1973), pp. 445–66

Brodrick, J. *The Life and Work of Blessed Robert Francis Cardinal Bellarmine, S.J., 1542–1621* (2 vols., London, 1928)

Brown, H. R. F. 'Paolo Sarpi, the man', in Brown, *Studies in the History of Venice* (2 vols., London, 1907), vol. II, pp. 208–44

Buckley, G. T. *Atheism in the English Renaissance* (Chicago, 1932)

Burke, P. 'The Great Unmasker: Paolo Sarpi, 1552–1623', *History Today*, XV (1965), 426–32

    'Tacitism', in T. A. Dorey, ed., *Tacitus* (London, 1969), pp. 149–71

    Venice and Amsterdam: A study of Seventeenth-Century elites (London, 1974)

Busson, H. *Le rationalisme dans la littérature française de la Renaissance, 1533–1601* (Paris, 1957)

    'Les noms des incrédules au seizième siècle', *Bibliothèque d'Humanisme et Renaissance*, XVI (1954), 273–80

Campbell, A. G. *The Life of Fra Paolo Sarpi* (London, 1869)

Chabod, F. 'Paolo Giovio', in Chabod, *Scritti sul Rinascimento* (Turin, 1974), pp. 241–67

    'La politica di Paolo Sarpi', in Chabod, *Scritti sul Rinascimento* (Turin, 1974), pp. 459–588

Chayanov, A. V. *The Theory of Peasant Economy* (Homewood, 1966)

Cicogna, E. A. *Delle inscrizioni veneziane* (6 vols., Venice, 1824–53)

Cochrane, E. *Historians and Historiography in the Italian Renaissance* (Chicago, 1981)

Cozzi, G. *Il doge Nicolò Contarini : richerche sul patriziato Veneziano agli inizi del seicento* (Venice, 1958)

'Sir Edwin Sandys e la *Relazione dello stato della religione*', *Rivista storica italiana*, LXXIX (1967), 1096–121

'Galileo Galilei, Paolo Sarpi e la società veneziana', in Cozzi, *Paolo Sarpi tra Venezia e l'Europa* (Turin, 1979), pp. 135–234

'Sulla morte di fra Paolo Sarpi', in *Miscellanea in onore di Roberto Cessi* (2 vols., Rome, 1958), vol. II, pp. 387–96

'Fra Paolo Sarpi, l'anglicanesimo e la *Historia del Concilio Tridentino*', *Rivista storica italiana*, LXIII (1956), 559–619

'Paolo Sarpi tra il cattolico Philippe Canaye de Fresnes e il calvinista Isaac Casaubon', in Cozzi, *Paolo Sarpi tra Venezia e l'Europa* (Turin, 1979), pp. 3–133

'Paolo Sarpi e Jan van Meurs', *Bollettino dell'Istituto di storia della società e dello stato veneziano*, I (1959), 179–86

'Paolo Sarpi: il suo problema storico, religioso e giuridico nella recente letteratura', *Il diritto ecclesiastico*, LXIII (1952), 52–88

'Politica e diritto in alcune controversie confinarie tra lo stato di Milano e la Repubblica di Venezia, 1564–1622', *Archivio storico lombardo*, LXXVII–LXXIX (1951–2), 4–44

'Traiano Boccalini, il Cardinal Borghese e la Spagna, secondo le riferte di un confidente degli inquisitori di stato', *Rivista storica italiana*, LXIII (1956), 230–44

'Una vicenda della Venezia barocca: Marco Trevisan e la sua "eroica amicizia"', *Bollettino dell'Istituto di storia della società e dello stato veneziano*, II (1960), 61–154

Cozzi, L. 'La tradizione settecentesca dei *Pensieri* Sarpiani', *Studi veneziani*, XIII (1971), 393–448

Denonain, J. J. 'Le livre des trois imposteurs', in *Aspects du libertinisme au XVIe siècle* (Paris, 1974), pp. 215–26

Dunn, J. *The Political Thought of John Locke* (Cambridge, 1969)

Emery, L. 'Religione e politica nella mente di Paolo Sarpi', *Nuova rivista storica*, VIII (1924), 304–29, 443–75

Evans-Pritchard, E. E. *Witchcraft, Oracles and Magic among the Azande* (Oxford, 1937)

Evenett, H. O. *The Spirit of the Counter-Reformation*, ed. J. Bossy (Cambridge, 1968)

Favaro, A., review of L. Mabileau, *Etude historique sur la philosophie de la Renaissance en Italie (Cesare Cremonini)*, *Archivio veneto*, XXV (1883), 430–50

Febvre, L. 'The origins of the French Reformation: a badly-put question?', in Febvre, *A New Kind of History*, ed. P. Burke (London, 1973), pp. 44–107

La religion de Rabelais: le problème de l'incroyance au seizième siècle (Paris, 1942)

'De l'à peu près à la précision en passant par ouï-dire', in Febvre, *Au coeur religieux du XVIe siècle* (Paris, 1957), pp. 293–300

'Un cas désespéré: Dolet propagateur de l'Évangile', in Febvre, *Au coeur religieux du XVIe siècle* (Paris, 1957), pp. 172–224

'Sorcellerie, sottise ou révolution mentale?', in Febvre, *Au coeur religieux du XVIe siècle* (Paris, 1957), pp. 301–9

Fenlon, D. B. '*Encore une question*: Lucien Febvre, the Reformation and the School of Annales', *Historical Studies*, IX (Belfast, 1974), pp. 65–81

Feret, P. *Le Cardinal du Perron: orateur, controversiste, écrivain* (Paris, 1877)

Figgis, J. N. 'Political thought in the sixteenth century', *The Cambridge Modern History of Europe*, vol. III (Cambridge, 1904), pp. 736–69

Firpo, L. 'Appunti Campanelliani XXV: storia di un furto', *Giornale critico della filosofia italiano*, XXXV (1956), 541–9

Fontanini, G. *Storia arcana della vita di Fra Paolo Sarpi Servita* (Venice, 1807)

Forster, L. 'Lipsius and Renaissance neo-Stoicism', in *Festschrift for Ralph Farrell* (Bern, 1977), pp. 201–20

Gabrielli, V. 'Bacone, la Riforma e Roma nella versione Hobbesiana d'un carteggio di Fulgenzio Micanzio', *English Miscellany*, VIII (1957), 195–250

Gaeta, F. 'Alcune considerazioni sul mito di Venezia', *Bibliothèque d'Humanisme et Renaissance*, XXIII (1961), 58–75

Garfunkel, A. 'Note sul problema dell'infinita nella *Cosmologia* di Tommaso Campanella', in *Tommaso Campanella (1568–1639): Miscellanea di studi nel 4° centenario della sua nascita* (Naples, 1969), pp. 385–91

Gaskin, J. C. A. 'Hume, atheism, and the "interested obligation of morality"', in *McGill Hume Studies*, ed. D. F. Norton and N. Capaldi (San Diego, 1979), pp. 147–60

Gauthier, L. *La théorie d'Ibn Rochd (Averroès) sur les rapports de la religion et la philosophie* (Paris, 1909)

Getto, G. *Paolo Sarpi* (Florence, 1967)

Gewirth, A. *Marsilius of Padua, the Defender of Peace* (2 vols., New York, 1951–6)

Gilbert, F. 'Venice in the crisis of the League of Cambrai', in J. R. Hale, ed., *Renaissance Venice* (London, 1973), pp. 274–92

Gilmore, M. P. *Humanists and Jurists: Six studies in the Renaissance* (Cambridge, Mass., 1963)

 'Myth and reality in Venetian political theory', in J. R. Hale, ed., *Renaissance Venice* (London, 1973), pp. 431–44

Ginzburg, C. *Il formaggio e i vermi: il cosmo di un mugnaio del '500* (Turin, 1976)

Grendler, P. F. *The Roman Inquisition and the Venetian Press 1540–1605* (Princeton, 1977)

 'Books for Sarpi: the smuggling of prohibited books into Venice during the Interdict of 1606–7', in S. Bertelli and G. Ramckus, eds., *Essays Presented to Myron P. Gilmore* (2 vols., Florence, 1978), vol. I, pp. 105–14

Haber, F. C. *The Age of the World: Moses to Darwin* (Baltimore, 1959)

Hayden, J. M. *France and the Estates General of 1614* (Cambridge, 1974)

Hill, C. *Milton and the English Revolution* (London, 1977)

 Irreligion in the 'Puritan' Revolution (Barnett Shine Foundation Lecture, London, 1974)

 'Plebeian irreligion in seventeenth century England', in M. Kossok, ed., *Studien über die Revolution* (Berlin, 1971), pp. 46–61

Hunter, M. *Science and Society in Restoration England* (Cambridge, 1981)

Jedin, H. *A History of the Council of Trent* (2 vols., London, 1957–61)

 'Sarpi storico del concilio di Trento', *Humanitas*, VII (1952), 495–504

Joly, P. L. *Remarques critiques sur le dictionnaire de Bayle* (2 vols., Dijon, 1752)

Kelley, D. R. '*Fides Historiae*: Charles Dumoulin and the Gallican view of history', *Traditio*, XXII (1966), 347–402

Keohane, N. O. *Philosophy and the State in France, the Renaissance to the Enlightenment* (Princeton, 1980)

Kogel, R. *Pierre Charron* (Geneva, 1972)

Koyré, A. *From Closed Space to the Infinite Universe* (Baltimore, 1957)

 La révolution astronomique (Paris, 1961)

Kristeller, P. O. 'The myth of Renaissance atheism and the French tradition of free thought', *Journal of the History of Philosophy*, VI (1968), 233–43

Lecler, J. *Toleration and the Reformation* (2 vols., New York, 1960)

Bibliography

Leff, G. *William of Ockham: the Metamorphosis of Scholastic Discourse* (Manchester, 1975)

Lefranc, P. *Sir Walter Ralegh, écrivain: L'oeuvre et les idées* (Paris, 1968)

Livesay, J. L. *Venetian Phoenix: Paolo Sarpi and some of his English friends* (Lawrence, 1973)

Loemker, L. E. *Struggle for Synthesis: the seventeenth-century background of Leibniz's synthesis of order and freedom* (Harvard, 1972)

Logan, O. M. T. 'Studies in the religious life of Venice in the sixteenth and seventeenth centuries', (Ph.D. thesis, Cambridge, 1967)

Lowry, M. J. C. 'The reform of the Council of Ten, 1582–3: an unsettled problem', *Studi veneziani*, XIII (1973), 275–310

Manuel, F. E. *The Eighteenth Century Confronts the Gods* (Cambridge, Mass., 1959)

Martin, V. *Le Gallicanisme et la Réforme Catholique: essai historique sur l'introduction en France des décrets du Concile de Trente, 1563–1615* (Paris, 1919)

Marx, K. *Capital* (3 vols., New York, 1967)

de Mas, E. *Sovranità politica e unità cristiana nel seicento anglo-veneto* (Ravenna, 1975)

Masetti Zannini, G. L. 'Libri di fra Paolo Sarpi e notizie di altre biblioteche dei Servi (1599–1600)', *Studi storici dell'ordine dei servi di Maria*, XX (1970), 174–202

de Mattei, R. *Il pensiero politico di Scipione Ammirato* (Milan, 1963)

Mazzeo, J. A. *Renaissance and Revolution: the remaking of European thought* (London, 1967)

Meinecke, F. *Machiavellism: the doctrine of raison d'etat and its place in modern history*, ed. W. Stark (New Haven, 1957)

Momigliano, A. 'The first political commentary on Tacitus', in Momigliano, *Essays in Ancient and Modern Historiography* (Oxford, 1977), pp. 205–29

'Lo stile del Sarpi', in Momigliano, *Studi di poesia* (Florence, 1960), pp. 101–5

Mousnier, R. *The Assassination of Henry IV: the tyrranicide problem and the consolidation of the French absolute monarchy in the early seventeenth century* (London, 1973)

Nardi, B. 'Filosofia e religione', in Nardi, *Studi su Pietro Pomponazzi* (Florence, 1965), pp. 122–48

'Il preteso desiderio dell'immortalità', in Nardi, *Studi su Pietro Pomponazzi* (Florence, 1965), pp. 247–68

Needham, J. 'Human law and the laws of nature', in Needham, *The Grand Titration: science and society in East and West* (Toronto, 1969), pp. 299–330

Niero, A. 'Miracoli post-mortem di fra Paolo Sarpi?', *Studi veneziani*, X (1968), 599–620

Oakley, F. 'Christian theology and the Newtonian science: the rise of the concept of the laws of nature', *Church History*, XXX (1961), 433–57

Odorici, F. 'Paolo V e le città di Terraferma', *Archivio storico italiano*, new series XII (1859), 171–80

Ospovat, D. 'God and natural selection: the Darwinian idea of design', *Journal of the History of Biology*, XIII (1980), 169–94

Pastor, L. *History of the Popes* (40 vols., London, 1891–1953)

Pintard, R. *Le libertinage érudit dans la première moitié du XVIIe siècle* (2 vols., Paris, 1943)

Pirri, P. 'Come Paolo Sarpi non fu vescovo di Nona', *Civiltà Cattolica*, IV (1936), 196–206

Pocock, J. G. A. *The Machiavellian Moment* (Princeton, 1975)

Popkin, R. H. *The History of Scepticism from Erasmus to Descartes* (Assen, 1964)

Poppi, A. 'Un teologo di fronte alla cultura libertina del Rinascimento italiano: l'*Adversus Impios Atheos* di Filippo Fabri', *Quaderni per la storia dell'Università di Padova*, IV (1971), 103–18

Potterton, H. *Venetian Seventeenth Century Painting* (London, 1979)

Bibliography

Pou y Marti, J. M. 'La intervencion española en el conflicto entre Paulo V y Venesia (1605–7)', in *Miscellanea Pio Paschini* (2 vols., Rome, 1948–9), vol. II, pp. 359–81

Pozzi, M., review of G. and L. Cozzi, eds., *Opere* and da Pozzo, ed., *Scritti scelti, Giornale storico della letteratura italiana*, CXLIII (1971), 384–97

da Pozzo, G. 'Per il testo dei *Pensieri* del Sarpi', *Bollettino dell'Istituto di storia della società e dello stato veneziano*, III (1961), 139–76

'Vicende editoriale e forza del testo (Un esempio Sarpiano)', *Belfagor*, XXXI (1976), 327–39

Prodi, P. 'The structure and organisation of the Church in Renaissance Venice: suggestions for research', in J. R. Hale, ed., *Renaissance Venice* (London, 1973), pp. 409–30

Pullan, B. S. 'The occupations and investments of the Venetian nobility in the middle and late sixteenth century', in J. R. Hale, ed., *Renaissance Venice* (London, 1973), pp. 379–408

'Poverty, charity and the reason of state: some Venetian examples', *Bollettino dell'Istituto di storia della società e dello stato veneziano*, II (1960), 17–60

Rich and Poor in Renaissance Venice (Oxford, 1971)

'Service to the Venetian state: aspects of myth and reality in the early seventeenth century', *Studi secenteschi*, V (1964), 95–148

'Wage earners and the Venetian economy, 1550–1630', in Pullan, ed., *Crisis and Change in the Venetian Economy* (London, 1968), pp. 146–74

von Ranke, L. *Venezia nel Cinquecento* (Rome, 1974)

Rapp, R. T. *Industry and Economic Decline in Seventeenth Century Venice* (Cambridge, Mass., 1976)

Rein, G. *Paolo Sarpi und die Protestanten* (Helsingfors, 1904)

Rekers, B. *Benito Arias Montano, 1527–98* (London, 1972)

Renan, E. *Averroès et l'Averroïsme* (5th edn, Paris, n.d.)

Rogers, D. '*The Catholic Moderator*, a French reply to Bellarmine and its English author, Henry Constable', *Recusant History*, V (1960), 224–35

Salvatorelli, L. 'Le idee religiose di fra Paolo Sarpi', *Atti dell'Accademia Nazionale dei Lincei–Memorie*, ser. VIII, vol. V (1954), 311–60

'L'opera storica di Paolo Sarpi', in Salvatorelli, *La Chiesa e il mondo* (Rome, 1948), pp. 81–6

Savio, P. 'Il nuncio a Venezia dopo l'Interdetto', *Archivio veneto*, ser. V, vol. LVI–LVII (1955), 55–110

Schmitt, C. B. 'Filippo Fabri and scepticism: a forgotten defence of Scotus', in *Storia e cultura al Santo*, ed. A. Poppi (Vicenza, 1976), pp. 309–12

'Renaissance Averroism studied through the Venetian editions of Aristotle–Averroes', *Atti dei convegni Lincei*, XL (1979), 121–42

Secchi, S. *Antonio Foscarini: un patrizio veneziano del '600* (Florence, 1969)

Seneca, F. *La politica veneziana dopo l'interdetto* (Padua, 1957)

Simon, M. 'Isaac Casaubon, Fra Paolo Sarpi et l'Eglise d'Angleterre', in *Aspects de l'Anglicanisme: Colloque de Strasbourg, 14–16 juin, 1972* (Paris, 1974), pp. 39–66

Skinner, Q. *The Foundations of Modern Political Thought* (2 vols., Cambridge, 1978)

'Meaning and understanding in the History of Ideas', *History and Theory*, VIII (1969), 3–53

'"Social Meaning" and the interpretation of social action', in *Philosophy, Politics and Society*, ser. IV, ed. P. Laslett, W. G. Runciman, Q. Skinner (Oxford, 1972), pp. 136–57

Smith, L. P. *Life and Letters of Sir Henry Wotton* (2 vols., Oxford, 1907)

Sosio, L. 'I *Pensieri* di Paolo Sarpi sul moto', *Studi veneziani*, XIII (1971), pp. 315–92

Spini, G. 'The art of history in the Italian Counter-Reformation', in E. Cochrane, ed., *The Late Italian Renaissance* (London, 1970), pp. 91–133
Ricerca dei libertini (Rome, 1950)
Spink, J. S. *French Free-Thought from Gassendi to Voltaire* (London, 1960)
Stella, A. *Chiesa e stato nelle relazioni dei nunzi pontifici a Venezia: Ricerche sul giurisdizionalismo veneziano del XVI al XVIII secolo* (Vatican City, 1964)
Strathman, E. A. *Sir Walter Ralegh: a study in Elizabethan skepticism* (New York, 1951)
Taucci, P. R. *Intorno alle lettere di Fra Paolo ad Antonio Foscarini* (Florence, 1939)
Tenenti, A. 'Il *de Perfectione Rerum* di Nicolò Contarini', *Bollettino dell'Istituto di storia della società e dello stato veneziano*, I (1959), 155–66
Thuau, E. *Raison d'état et pensée politique à l'époque de Richelieu* (Paris, 1966)
Toffanin, G. *Machiavelli e il 'Tacitismo': la 'politica storica' al tempo della controriforma* (Padua, 1921)
del Torre, M. A. *Studi su Cesare Cremonini* (Padua, 1968)
Tramontin, S. 'La visita apostolica del 1581 a Venezia', *Studi veneziani*, IX (1967), 453–533
Trevor-Roper, H. R. 'The historical philosophy of the Enlightenment', *Studies on Voltaire and the Eighteenth Century*, ed. T. Besterman, vol. XXVII (1963), pp. 1667–87
'Religion, the Reformation and social change', in Trevor-Roper, *Religion, the Reformation and Social Change* (London, 1967), pp. 1–45
'The religious origins of the Enlightenment', in Trevor-Roper, *Religion, the Reformation and Social Change* (London, 1967), pp. 193–236
Troilo, L. 'La filosfia di fra Paolo Sarpi', in *Paolo Sarpi e i suoi tempi* (Città di Castello, 1923), pp. 17–85
Ulianich, B. 'Considerazioni e documenti per una ecclesiologia di Paolo Sarpi', in *Festgabe J. Lortz* (2 vols., Baden–Baden, 1958), vol. II, pp. 363–444
'Il principe Christian von Anhalt e Paolo Sarpi: dalla missione veneziana del Dohna alla relazione Diodati (1608)', *Annuarium Historiae Conciliorum*, VIII (1976), 429–506
'Paolo Sarpi, il generale Ferrari e l'ordine dei Serviti durante le controversie veneto-pontificie', in *Studi in onore di Alberto Pincherle* (2 vols., Rome, 1967), 582–645
'Sarpiana: la lettera del Sarpi allo Heinsius', *Rivista storica italiana*, LXIII (1956), 425–46
Vivanti, C. 'Una fonte del *Istoria del Concilio Tridentino* di Paolo Sarpi', *Rivista storica italiana*, LXXXIII (1971), 608–32
Lotta politica e pace religiosa in Francia tra cinque e seicento (Turin, 1963)
'In margine a studi recenti su Paolo Sarpi', *Rivista storica italiana*, LXXIX (1967), 1075–95
'L'opera che mancava su Paolo Sarpi', *Rivista storica italiana*, LXXXII (1970), 917–25
Walker, D. P. *The Ancient Theology: Studies in Christian Platonism from the fifteenth to the eighteenth century* (London, 1972)
Wickes, G. 'Henry Constable', *Biographical Studies*, II (1954), 272–300
Woolf, S. J. 'Venice and the Terraferma: problems of the change from commercial to landed activities', in B. S. Pullan, ed., *Crisis and Change in the Venetian Economy* (London, 1968), pp. 175–203
Wright, A. D. 'The Venetian view of Church and State: Catholic Erastianism?', *Studi secenteschi*, XIX (1978), 75–106
'Why the *Venetian* Interdict?', *English Historical Review*, LXXXIX (1974), 534–50

Yates, F. A. 'Paolo Sarpi's *History of the Council of Trent*', *The Journal of the Warburg and Courtauld Institutes*, VII (1944), 123-43
    The Rosicrucian Enlightenment (London, 1972)
Zilsel, E. 'The genesis of the concept of physical law', *Philosophical Review*, LI (1942), 245-79

Index

Schools of thought are indexed under the associated proper names (e.g. *Epicureanism* under *Epicurus*).

Index

Lucian, 149
Lucretius, 151, 154
Luther, Martin, 10, 35, 49, 110, 115, 120, 172

Machiavelli, Nicolò, 9, 30, 33, 42, 48, 61,
  69–71, 73, 112–14, 143
Malipiero, Alessandro, 161
Mandeville, Bernard, 3
Manfredi, Fulgenzio, 106
Marlowe, Christopher, 143
Marsilio, Giovanni, 144
Marsilio of Padua, 48, 153
materialism, 15, 17–19, 37, 41–2, 123, 129,
  149
Meietti, Roberto, 146
Mersenne, Marin, 154
Meurs, Jan van, 108–9
Micanzio, Fulgenzio, 2, 14, 94–5, 101–3, 106,
  109, 117, 120, 137–43, 164, 168, 174
Milton, John, 112, 134
Minucci, Minuccio, 11
Miron, Robert, 87
Mocenigo, Leonardo, 140–1
Montaigne, Michel de, 9, 25, 66, 82, 155
Montorsoli, Angelo, 9
Morosini, Andrea and Nicolò, 9
Moses, 139–40, 143–4

Nani, Agostino, 98
Nardi, Balthasar, 60–3, 67–8
natural law, 36, 71
nature, laws of, 16–17, 151
Naudé, Gabriel, 3, 16, 35, 73
Nicoletti, Andrea, 41
Nis, Gerhard, 9, 41, 66

Ockham, William of, 17, 133
Olivo, Camillo, 8
opportunità, 101, 115

Pallavicino, Sforza, 104
Panvinio, Onofrio, 111
Parsons, Robert, 165
Paruta, Paolo, 6
Paul, St, 58, 89, 91, 108–9, 129
Paul III, 104
Paul V, 74, 85–6, 98–9, 136
Peiresc, Nicolas-Claude Fabri de, 40, 42
Pellegrini, Antonio, 149
Perron, Jacques Davy du, 81–8, 168
Philip III, 49
Pintard, René, 3
Pithou, Pierre, 55, 57
Plato, 91, 144–5
politiques, 9, 13, 34–5, 38, 48–9, 55–6, 72, 81,
  83, 86–8

Pomponazzi, Pietro, 9, 20–6, 33, 39, 41, 48,
  126, 131, 133, 151–2
Possevino, Antonio, 40, 60–3
Pozzo, Giovanni da, 121
Preau, Gabriel du, 13
predestination, 26, 29, 107–10, 171
Priuli, Francesco, 66
Priuli, Pietro, 65, 88, 170
Protestant: contemporaries describe Sarpi as,
  35, 48–50, 146; his links with
  Protestantism, 4, 9, 11, 38, 43, 93–104,
  106–8, 120–5, 127–8, 141–2; his
  contemporaries and Protestantism, 32, 72,
  81–3, 87–8, 92, 162
providence as foundation of social order:
  defined, 5; rejected by Sarpi, 3, 20–3, 28,
  131–5; accepted by others, 1, 33–4, 57,
  61–3, 71–2, 82–3, 155; and, in public, by
  Sarpi, 125–8
Pufendorf, Samuel von, 1, 148

Quatrains du déiste, 24, 27–8, 33
Querini, Antonio, 63–4, 160

Rabelais, François, 82
Raleigh, Walter, 143
reason of state, 42, 69, 86, 162–3, 172–3, 175
religion as policy, 72, 86, 96–7, 109, 143–4,
  163
republicanism: problem of, 6, 45, 146; decline
  of, 66–8, 133; Boccalini and, 45, 74–6;
  Sarpi's supposed, 122; his view of, 76, 124,
  162; he is influenced by, 113–16
Revision du Concile de Trente, 111
Ribadeneyra, Pietro, 61
Richer, Edmund, 35, 55–7, 86
Robertson, William, 114
Romans, religion of the 61, 70–1
Ronsard, Pierre de, 82

Sagredo, Giovanni Francesco, 65
Sandys, Edwin, 96–7, 100, 112
Savoy, Emmanuel Filiberto I, Duke of, 84
scepticism, 18, 36, 73, 89–91, 123, 154,
  157
scholasticism, 4, 14–23
science, 1–3, 9, 14, 61, 65, 129, 151, 154
secular: defined, 5; Sarpi's arguments secular,
  1, 18, 30, 91–3, 100, 109–10, 127;
  Boccalini's, 82; Botero's, 61; secular and
  religious authority compared, 114–16;
  contrasted, 51–2; *see also* providence,
  church and state
Servites, 8–10, 136–7, 143
Severina, Cardinal St, 141–2
Sextus Empiricus, 156